Nicole

Keep *tight* *it* *now* !

J— P. Ch

VOICES of
DETERMINATION

VOICES *of* DETERMINATION

Children that Defy the Odds

Kevin P. Chavous

With a foreword by Geoffrey Canada

Transaction Publishers
New Brunswick (U.S.A.) and London (U.K.)

Library of Congress Catalog Number: 2011022463
ISBN: 978-1-4128-4267-9
Printed in the United States of America

Library of Congress Cataloging-in-Publication Data

Chavous, Kevin P.
    Voices of determination : children that defy the odds / Kevin P. Chavous; with a foreword by Geoffrey Canada.
    p. cm.
Includes index.
ISBN 978-1-4128-4267-9
    1. Children with social disabilities—Education—United States. 2. Minorities—Education—United States. 3. Educational equalization—United States—Case studies. 4. Education—Sociological aspects—United States—Case studies. 5. Motivation in education—United States—Case studies. 6. Academic achievement—United states—Case studies. I. Title.
    LC4065.C47 2012
    379.2'60973—dc23

                                                        2011022463

I dedicate this book to my sons, Kevin Bass Chavous and Eric Bass Chavous. I am more proud of them than they will ever know for being the human beings that they are and the men that they have become.

Contents

Foreword

In "Voices of Determination," Kevin Chavous presents the exceptions to the rule—inspiring stories where children beat incredible odds, often with the help of a teacher or another adult in their lives.

But if we are to celebrate the exceptions, we should also look at the status quo that has stacked the odds so high for so many children. If not for a few lucky breaks, I would not have made it out of high school, much less the Harvard School of Education where I earned my master's degree. I was raised by a poor single mother in the south Bronx in the 1960s amid a neighborhood where learning to fight was more important than learning to read. But the overwhelming majority of the kids with whom I grew up did not get out of the neighborhood. For many it was a descent into unemployment, substance abuse, incarceration, and often an early grave. Before I was even a teenager, I knew something was wrong, and I vowed that when I grew up I would come back to save other children from the trap of poverty.

Since my days at PS 99, the situation for poor children, particularly children of color, has grown worse. Crack cocaine has torn apart poor neighborhoods, ruined countless lives, and ushered in a huge escalation in violence so that it is not unusual for preteens to be carrying handguns. To make matters worse, the market for low-skills jobs has moved overseas or just disappeared.

Today, one in five children—some fourteen million—live in poverty in America. It is no coincidence that you can pretty much predict a child's future by just looking at their Zip Code. Children born in impoverished communities typically have the worst schools, the worst health care, the worst community facilities, and have a much higher chance of being a victim of violence—often in their own home.

The key to breaking the cycle of generational poverty—today more than ever—is education. Yet, the circumstances in poor children's lives make it enormously difficult for them to get a good education. They often have chaotic family lives, see few positive role models, and have inadequate health care. And the centerpiece of their educational lives—the neighborhood public school—is often a horror show. Public schools in poor communities routinely get the most inexperienced teachers, lack the resources to adequately address children's needs, and often just pass kids along until students give up completely and drop out. Once out of school, these young men and women quickly find out that they are completely unprepared for the job market. If they can get a job, it usually is a low-skills, low-pay one that they can barely survive on. Unfortunately, many young men in our inner cities drift into antisocial behavior and turn to gangs and drugs. Statistics show that 60 percent of black men who have dropped out spend some time in prison by the time they hit their midthirties. This is also bad news for our nation as a whole, since it is predicted that our economy will need to fill 123 million high-skills jobs by the year 2020, but will only have 50 million people qualified enough to fill them. One recent report found that 75 percent of American young men are unfit for military service because of inadequate education or obesity.

But the situation is not hopeless. The key is hinted at in each of the stories in this book: getting kids connected to a lifeline, whether it is a caring teacher, a surrogate parent, a mentor, or an excellent school. All my training and experience over thirty years has confirmed one fact: that all children can learn. What many people, including educators, do not understand is that the ultimate responsibility for making that learning happen is on the shoulders of the adults around each child. The "secret" is hard, detail-oriented work over a long period of time.

In order to rewrite the narrative for the lives of our fourteen million poor children, we need to make their education a top priority on an ongoing basis. There is no quick fix. We also need to redefine what we mean by "education." We need to radically improve our schools, but education reform must go even further. We have to act from the understanding that education begins at birth. We now know that the very architecture of the brain—the foundation for future learning—is largely formed in the first three years of life. We already are seeing huge vocabulary gaps at the age of three between the children of poor parents and professional parents, so we need to educate caregivers in the simple techniques of engaging young minds from the very start of their lives. We need to make sure that all children arrive at kinder-garten ready for school. But then we need to stay with the children throughout their lives. As any good parent knows, there is no time in a child's development when you can stop being vigilant. There are potential challenges at every stage of a child's development and the adults around them need to be close at hand and ready to act effectively. That means we need to strengthen families and to rebuild the surrounding community too.

"Education" must also extend beyond the walls of the school. If a teacher at my charter school, the Harlem Children's Zone Promise Academy, suspects that a student is struggling with a problem outside the classroom, there are staff people at hand that can address the issue, whether it is substance abuse in the home or a chronic health problem such as asthma. The school staff also works to keep parents engaged their child's education, whether it is a "Dinner with Dada" night or sending a staff member to the home if a child has been absent for a number of days.

So, yes, let us celebrate the incredible victories that the children in this book have won. But let us also use their inspiring stories to energize ourselves so we can transform hope into action—and not just level the playing field, but elevate it for all.

Geoffrey Canada
President & CEO, Harlem Children's Zone

Preface

America loves heroes. We love reading about heroes. We love writing about heroes. We sing songs about heroes. We make movies about heroes. We worship our heroes.

Often, the heroes we worship have obvious and predictable pedigree. The political leader. The military leader. The religious leader. The community leader. Many of these folks do amazing work and are deserving of the praise and adulation that they receive. All such heroes, however, are usually adults.

This book is about less obvious, less predictable heroes: our children. Every day in this country, scores of children persevere against incredibly negative odds. Their struggles are virtually unnoticed. Their accomplishments are unheralded. But they survive and many succeed. In this book, you will meet ten young people from vastly different backgrounds, each with a drive to excel fueled by their commitment to be educated, against all odds. Their stories of determination reflect that intangible quality that represents the essence of the human spirit: the will to be better.

As you will see, each story is markedly different. From chapter to chapter, you will meet a diverse group of young people forced to navigate around the practical realities of today's most relevant social issues. All just to get their education. Inner-city neighborhood challenges, the immigration experience, indigent health care, addiction struggles, and wanton child abuse are merely some of the obstacles highlighted in these stories. Through it all, these remarkable young people continued to persevere. Our children can be our heroes. As you will undoubtedly come to see, these ten determined voices are indeed heroic.

Acknowledgments

To say that this project has been a labor of love would, indeed, be an understatement. Each of these stories are true, though I changed the names, schools, cities, and states of those who I profile. In the process of meeting with and interviewing all who are featured, I was unprepared for the level of attachment which resulted from getting to know these young people. They are all remarkable and I am fortunate to count many of them as friends. Zina even asked me about cologne choices for her new boyfriend! I will forever treasure the relationships developed as I researched for this book. More than anything, I am humbled by how those profiled reacted to my handling of their stories. From Chardi thanking me "a million and one times" for telling her story; to Javier humbly expressing his appreciation to me for "honoring his father's memory"; to my old friend Ronnie avoiding me for days after reading my treatment of his story because "he knew he would break down when we talked"; to Patrick telling me that I did a "fantastic" job conveying all that he and his father endured; I feel honored and blessed to be able to share these wonderful true stories.

So how did this book happen?

First, since leaving political life in Washington, DC, several years ago, I have been intimately involved in the national education reform and parental school choice movement in this country. As a result, I have visited countless schools in nearly every state, met children attending those schools, and I remain amazed by the incredible examples of determination found in many of our children. The stories that I present in this book represent a small sampling of the acts of courage exhibited by thousands of children each day. These children are bound together by an innate desire to become educated, extend themselves beyond what they know, and to do the right thing. As is evident from many of these stories, it is we adults that do them a disservice oftentimes by the way we treat them.

In the last chapter of my first book, "Serving Our Children: Charter Schools and the Reform of American Public Education," I wrote these words:

> In spite of all of the problems found in the American public education system, hope does springs eternal for one primary reason: the resiliency of our children. I have run into countless examples of children who come from dysfunctional home settings and who have received limited, if any, nurturing along the way, and they still have an inner drive to excel and succeed. These children demonstrate daily an indomitable spirit that guides them through hardships. Often the determining factor about their eventual ability to succeed or fail is reduced to one or more positive influences in their life.

Those words still ring true today. In meeting many of these inspiring young people, I became convinced that their resiliency and determination warranted recognition. I just had to share their stories.

Second, as I began to consider how to convey these stories, I reflected on the obstacles my father faced in trying to get his education. Yes, he grew up in another time, during a different era. But writing about his difficult daily walks to that one-room schoolhouse allowed me to view the stories I ultimately chose for this book with greater clarity. Just as I heard my father's "voice" while writing his story, I began to hear the "voices" of each of the subjects of this book while writing theirs. I pray that I did justice to those voices in their respective profiles.

One by-product of protecting the identities of those involved, is that I cannot properly thank all the folks who helped me through this process. I am eternally grateful to the young people who opened up to me and let me into their lives. Their graciousness extended beyond what I ever expected. I truly honor them with this book.

I am forever indebted to Geoffrey Canada for writing the Foreword to my book. Geoffrey is the real deal—he only supports what is best for kids. His Harlem Children's Zone has changed thousands of lives. Thank you, Geoffrey.

In addition, I thank the following people for helping at various stages of the book's development: Karen Anderson, B. J. Barakas, Dr. Lonnie Barber, Robyn Barnett, Chris Barbic, James Benedict, Lynn Black, Jason Botel, Junelle Cavero, Beverly Bass Chavous, Maurita Coley, Alan Fedman, Lori Frank, Kenneth Friedman, David Hardy,

Kathy Hollinger, David Holmes, Teisha Johnson, Donald Kamentz, Susie Kay, Deborah Kenny, Andrew Smith Lewis, Shawn McCullough, Cathy Cawthorne Miller, Dr. Bethanne Moore, Anne Marie Murphy, Joe Proietta, Dan Quisenberry, Heather Ramos, Tony Recasner, Joe Robert, Stephanie Rudat, Ricardo Rudolph, Russ Simnick, Bruce Stewart, Heather Dawn Thompson, Sandra L. Thompson, and Sarah Wilson.

Thanks to Jeanne Allen, Tony Bennett, Cory Booker, Joel Klein, Ed Lewis, Jay Mathews, Rod Paige, Michelle Rhee, and Margaret Spellings for their endorsements of this book.

Special thanks to Anne Bohner, Dr. Irving Louis Horowitz, Mary Curtis, and all of the Transaction Publishers family.

A big thanks to my sons, Kevin and Eric, my family, friends, and SNR Denton law firm colleagues who for years have put up with my missionary rants about changing the world by changing education. Your collective tolerance, patience, and love is really appreciated.

Thank you to my BAEO family and Dr. Howard Fuller, the unquestionable moral leader of the education reform movement in America.

Thank you, Amber Lewis.

Finally, it is my profound hope that those who read this book will better appreciate the circumstances facing many of our children. Those featured were all determined to get their education, in spite of the seemingly insurmountable odds facing them. On that score, they succeeded. Our charge, however, is to do whatever it takes, by any means necessary to ensure that ALL children have equal access to a high-quality education, irrespective of their background. As we strive for that goal, however, we can also do something more basic. Quite simply, let us start treating our children better.

Introduction

HP was scared. As he hid in the woods thirty feet from Green Pond road, he watched the carload of men empty out of their car and run toward the woods. They were headed in his direction.

The men did not see nine-year-old HP hiding, crouching behind a tree. Rather, they had one purpose in mind: to unload some of the beer they had been drinking. They were all "drunk out of their minds" as Pa Bradley liked to say.

The men were loud, obscene, and white. It was "white" part that scared nine HP the most. He knew if they saw him, he would be taunted, beaten, or killed. Maybe even lynched! That is the way things were in Aiken, South Carolina, in 1940. South Carolina was part of the old confederacy that split from the union during the civil war. The southern plantation mindset was dead set on preserving the old ways of the south, which, by definition, meant keeping African Americans as second-class citizens. During the Civil War Reconstruction period, violence and intimidation were regularly used to "keep Blacks in their place." Angry over losing the war and the ending of slavery, many southern whites lashed out at the newly freed slaves with increasing hostility and venom. As the nation entered the twentieth century, lynching emerged as one of the primary weapons of intimidation. The practice of lynching was as heinous an act that any human being could perpetuate on another. In most cases, a drunken mob of whites would grab, kidnap, or confiscate an African American citizen, beat them savagely, and then tie them to a tree from their neck by a knotted rope. The process could also include the castration, burning, and shooting of the victim. Many times, the mob and their families would enjoy a picnic in the shadow of the brutalized bodies hanging nearby. From 1882 to 1968, over 8,000 people were lynched by mobs, primarily in the south. During that time period, hundreds of African Americans were lynched in South Carolina, often for little or no reason.

HP had heard lynching stories for his entire life. He also knew that many whites who were involved in lynchings did so when they were drunk. As a result, anytime HP saw a drunk white man, he got scared. In his young mind, he knew a drunk white man would do unthinkable things to Black people. That is also why HP's family, his mother, Emma, his Aunt Rose, and her father, Great Uncle Pa Bradley, drilled in him the need to be alert when walking to and from school. "If you ever see a car," his momma said, "just go in the woods and stay there until it is out of sight!"

HP liked school. He liked it a lot. A whole lot better than working in the field. In fact, once his mother realized how naturally bright HP was, how well he took to letters and numbers, she talked with Pa Bradley about HP getting formal schooling. They all lived on Pa Bradley's 300-acre farm. It had been expected that HP would grow up and work on the farm like everyone else in the family. But like Emma, Pa Bradley could tell that HP was special. He agreed that school would be good for the boy and that he could attend the one-room schoolhouse run by Mrs. Gray.

Both knew, however, that the schoolhouse was seven miles away on the old Culver farm property. HP would have to walk alone three hours each way everyday just to go to school.

When Emma talked with HP about going to school, he listened intently. All he knew was life on the Bradley farm. But he hated working in the field. He did not mind his chores, but he dragged his feet when Pa Bradley made him do "real" farm work. HP was a thinker. He had a naturally analytical mind. Field work was anything but analytical. HP detested pushing the plow for hours in the hot sun. Farm work was boring. HP's mind would wander and he always found himself thinking about other things around him. How those things worked. Why they were there. Once, he spent half the morning in the field studying an ant farm, trying to understand the ants system of work and organization. Pa Bradley was not pleased when he found HP on all fours staring at the ground in the middle of the field, with little, if any of the field work having been completed. Quite naturally, when Emma offered HP the choice of continuing the farm work or going to school, there was really no choice. The walk did not matter. He would walk to and from school twenty miles each way, if need be, to stay out of the field.

HP kept reflecting on field work as he knelt quietly behind that tree, in the dark, terrified that those drunk white men would hear his breath, find him, and kill him. Recognizing that he may be waiting to die, HP decided that he would still rather be hiding behind that tree than plowing some field. "I must be crazy," HP kept thinking to himself. These men may kill me because I stayed too long after school reading a book, but I still think that being here is better than doing field work. Finding that hard for even him to reconcile, HP twisted his face in a manner that looked like he was squinting.

Another practical thought, however, nagged at HP. He could not help but think that he had to find a way to keep better track of the time of day. HP did not have a watch. The only person HP knew with a watch was Pa Bradley, who only put his watch on for church on Sunday.

HP followed time by the sun. When it started to fade a little in the west, it was time to head home. Knowing that it took him about three hours to walk those seven miles, he always tried to leave when the sun was about two-thirds from the top of the sky heading west, roughly 4:00 p.m., to make sure he was home before it got dark. HP had gotten pretty good using this approach to tell time, but he recognized that he may need a more exact method. What could be better than a watch?

The problem was that he liked school and loved to read. He would always stay after school to read more books or work on math problems. His teacher, Mrs. Gray, really took to HP. Of the nine children attending the one-room schoolhouse, HP was one of the youngest, but by far the brightest. He was good in math, English, everything. "Smart as a whip," Mrs. Gray would say. He was so smart that the precocious nine-year-old was helping the older kids with their math and reading. Mrs. Gray would smile when watching HP, smallish in size, with dark brown skin and those funny green eyes, standing next to Ellis, who was sixteen years old, nearly six feet tall and thick. Ellis would sit in that tiny school room seat while HP stood next to him showing him how to multiply and divide numbers. It was a funny sight.

Mrs. Gray kept telling HP that he had to keep coming to school because God blessed him with brains and he "was going places."

At that very moment, however, crouching behind that tree, HP was mad at himself. He should have never started to read that new book Mrs. Gray showed him. He should have waited until the next school day. It had to be close to 6:00 p.m. when he finally left, because it was dark when he passed the family cemetery, a burial site for his relatives dating back almost 200 years. HP knew Aunt Rose would yell at him.

That was the role she played when HP messed up and she played it well. Pa Bradley would probably frown a little, in that way he frowned when he is annoyed. But more than likely, all he would do is say that HP still had his chores to do and he still had to wake up at four thirty in the morning.

Pa Bradley was big on "preparing HP to be a man," so he gave him a lot of latitude. "You make your bed and you lie in it," he would always say. "If you want to walk in the dark for three hours, that's your choice," Pa Bradley once told him when he came home from school late one night.

But now, HP was hoping that he would live long enough to be chastised by his relatives. One of the white men said he thought he heard something in the woods. He was looking in HP's direction. HP wanted to cry.

The white man kept trying to get the others to listen to him. Fortunately for HP, that man's friends were more preoccupied with getting back in the car to go see "those girls" waiting for them. The drunk white men started arguing. HP was trying to stay quiet and be still, but something was crawling up his leg. Whatever it was, it was moving fast, so fast that it traveled from his left shin up past his cut-off britches before he could act. He looked down and as slowly as he could, he brushed a big spider off of his knee. HP knew he could not be still for much longer. Spiders were one thing, but he would have to make more noise to fend off a snake. He glanced around his feet to make sure that no snakes were nearby.

The arguing grew more intense. The man who had been pointing in HP's direction was getting more and more animated. He wanted to prove his point so he began to walk closer to HP's hiding place. His friends, however, were growing weary of his antics. "Only a fool," one of them said, "would be out here in the woods in the middle of the night." HP's face frowned again when he heard that statement.

With that, all of the man's friends piled into the car. They were threatening to leave their friend. While his friends were talking, the man leaned forward and pointed at the big tree near where HP was squatting. The man then said, "I'm telling ya'll, I know somebody's in them woods," the man said. "I can smell 'em!'" In response, the driver of the car pressed the accelerator and the car lurched forward. Finally, the man near HP relented and joined his friends in the car. As the door was closing, HP could hear the man say, "If you all would give me two minutes, I would flush that nigger coon out of them woods. I know it was a coon. I just know it." The men then loudly drove off. HP waited a full five minutes before he moved.

Once he felt safe, HP stood up, looked around, walked out of the woods, and continued on his journey home. He began walking down the middle of the road. That way, he could see the snakes, possum, or skunk that walked in his path.

HP was engulfed with relief and a burst of energy. He had been tired after another long day of walking, school work, more walking, and then the real threat of death. Now that the danger was gone, all of his senses of excitement were renewed. "I didn't die!" he thought, smiling broadly. He picked up a couple of rocks on the road and threw them into the woods, like any happy kid, from any generation or era playing by himself. He was nearing Petticoat Junction, which meant he was about thirty to forty-five minutes away from the farm. Suddenly, HP realized that he was starving.

He could taste Aunt Rose's greens and mashed potatoes. He loved mashed potatoes and she had promised to cook them for dinner. The way he figured, she would yell for just a few minutes before allowing him to eat. It did not matter. HP was happy to be almost home.

HP's mind was racing as he ambled down the middle of Green Pond road. It was pitch black all around him, but HP could see twenty feet in front of his feet on the red clay dirt road because of the light shining from the night's half moon. As he walked within eyesight of the candlelit main house on the family farm, HP promised himself that he would leave school earlier tomorrow. But if he did not, he thought, still smiling to himself, hopefully it was because the book was just too good.

Just six years later, at the age of fifteen, HP would be the first in his family to go to college. He graduated from South Carolina State University with a degree in chemistry. HP would then join the army and as a Second Lieutenant during the Korean War, would be one of the first African American officers to command white troops following President Truman's order which desegregated the military.

After the war, HP married, settled in Indianapolis, Indiana, briefly attended medical school, and graduated from pharmacy school.

One of the first African American licensed pharmacists in the state, HP owned his own corner drugstore which catered to underserved Indianapolis residents for several years.

In his later life, HP became an ordained minister with a notable expertise in scripture teachings.

Before he died in 2005, HP would occasionally reflect back on those lonely three-hour walks to and from that one-room schoolhouse outside of Aiken, South Carolina. "It was so unlikely that I would go to college and have any professional success, considering where I came from," he would say. "It just goes to show that in life, with an education, anything is possible."

Harold P. Chavous was my father.

Chardi

Chardi grabbed the door handle hard. She grabbed it hard and tight. The car in which she was riding was traveling on a high suspension bridge when the bridge started to open. It was opening from the middle, rising to the sky as bridges do when they allow large boats to pass through.

Chardi was terrified. The bridge kept rising and rising. Chardi was in the right rear passenger seat, sitting directly in back of her mother, Diane. Chardi's best friend, Susan, was sitting next to Chardi in the backseat. Her math teacher, Scott Knowling, was driving the car.

Chardi could not see her mother's face, but could see her right hand grab the door handle, just as Chardi did. Susan was screaming. Mr. Knowling had a look of horror on his face. He gripped the steering wheel with both hands and leaned back in his seat. He was trying to find some leverage that just was not there.

It was all happening so fast, yet it seemed to be in slow motion. As the bridge kept rising, the car was tilting back. Chardi expected the car would slide backwards until it fell back to the bridge's base. Her fear was that it would flip over and they all would be crushed.

Then something even worse happened. They were in the right lane, closest to the side of the bridge. Suddenly, the bridge jerked violently causing the car to flip to the right, smack into the bridge's guard rail. Chardi saw that the car was being hurled toward the guard rail and wanted to cry out, but, for some reason, could not do so. By now, everyone else in the car was yelling or screaming. Chardi felt like she was more of a witness than a participant. She saw the deep, intense fear in Mr. Knowling and Susan's faces. Through it all, she never saw her mother's face.

Surprisingly, the car only lightly touched the guard rail, then careened over it, off the bridge, into the water some sixty feet below. Chardi felt like Dorothy in the Wizard of Oz when her house was flying in the sky.

The car landed in the water with a huge splash and sank rapidly. As the car was filling with water, Chardi tried again to call out, but could not make a sound. In fact, she could not see anyone or hear anything. It felt cold and, in no time, she was surrounded by darkness. The water was everywhere. She wished she could swim, but knew she had to get out of the car first. It was too late. Much too late.

She swallowed water and then it became too much. I am going to die, she thought. Whereupon, Chardi drowned.

Then, Chardi woke up.

The dream was always the same, with usually the same result. Although she stopped dying in the dream a couple of years ago, she still always falls off the bridge and into the water.

Chardi, now sixteen years old, has had the same dream for almost six years.

For the first couple of years, Chardi would have her dream about three to four nights a week. As she got older, the dream happened two to three nights per week. In those six years, however, there has not been a week in which she did not have the dream.

When she woke up, as was her custom, Chardi looked at the digital clock sitting next to her bed. 5:07 a.m., the clock said. "Great," Chardi, thought. At least, I was able to get some sleep. Chardi was never able to go back to sleep after being awakened by "the dream." She hated the nights when the clock told her it was two or three o'clock in the morning.

Chardi then looked over at her roommate, Ashley, who was snoring with her mouth wide open. Ashley was white, blond, and privileged. But she sure looked pitiful and unattractive when she slept. On those nights when Chardi would be awakened by the dream and thus, be sitting at her desk in her room for several hours, she marveled at how consistently ugly Ashley was when she slept. Snoring incessantly, with her hair askance, Ashley also wrinkled her face into a weird expression when she reached that deep sleep level. Chardi had spent hours studying Ashley in sleep mode and came to the conclusion that life would be better if Chardi could sleep like her roommate.

She could definitely use the sleep. Chardi was a junior at the prestigious St. Mary's Academy boarding school for girls. Without question, it is one of the most well known and highly regarded high schools in the nation. Located outside of Philadelphia, St. Mary's caters to girls who come from families of means. Folks who are rich. But the school also has a heart. St. Mary's goes out of its way to recruit girls who come from challenged backgrounds. They believe in diversity and offer scholarships each year to several students who otherwise could not afford to pay the tuition. Chardi is a scholarship student at St. Mary's. No girl in the school comes from a more challenged background than does Chardi.

Chardi knew why she died in the dream tonight. She also knew why this was the fourth time this week that she had been awakened by the dream. It was all because she had visited her mother this past weekend and was worried about her younger sister, Carla. Chardi was afraid that Carla would slip into the life that engulfed her entire family. A life consisting of crime, drugs, and violence. She knew the signs and suspected that Carla was headed in that direction. Part of Chardi's stress was guilt. She made a promise to her father that she would look after her younger sisters. Now, she was in the suburbs at a fancy school, while her sisters were left to fend for themselves. Chardi knows she cannot help her four older siblings. Each are caught up in the life. Her focus is on her three younger sisters. She was determined to keep her promise to her father.

Chardi's mother, Diane, was a drug addict. So was her late father, Emmanuel. Diane has since beat her cocaine and heroine addictions, but still drinks too much. She has also remarried. Her new husband, Vincent McKoy, does not do drugs, has a good job, and goes to church. It bothers Chardi when she sees her mother these days. Diane acts as if her "old life" never existed. But it did exist. Chardi remembers every bit of it. It makes her angry that her mother ignores her past. Very angry.

Chardi said as much to her mother the previous weekend during her visit at her mother's home. Officially, Chardi does not live with her mother anymore. She lives with her best friend Susan's family when she is not at the boarding school. Chardi met Susan Peters at the Philadelphia Math & Science Public Charter Middle School. The school includes students in grades five through eight and has a strong focus on math and science. When Chardi was accepted into St. Mary's, she agreed to the Peters family suggestion that she make their home her permanent residence. Everyone close to Chardi was concerned that the pressure of living with her mother would hurt her as she matriculated through St. Mary's. Looking back on it all, Chardi admits that they were right. She even had to smile as she thought to herself, in the midst of Ashley's snores, "Heck, one weekend with my mom and I am back up to four nights of the dreaded dream!"

Now that she was older, Chardi understands that her parents' marriage never had a chance. From birth to death, the likelihood of either of Chardi's parents leading a productive life was virtually non-existent. They were pretty much doomed from the start. Saddled with family histories of poverty, alcoholism, drug abuse, incest, criminal behavior, and mental illness, both Emmanuel and Diane met and fell in love under a common "hood" cloud: your vices become my vices. As a result, Diane, who came from a family of alcoholics, but shied away from drugs, allowed Emmanuel to introduce her to cocaine and heroine, thereby instantly expanding her addictions. Not to be outdone, Emmanuel, who sold and did drugs, but was not involved in other criminal activity, picked up superior burglary and robbery techniques from Diane and her brothers, all master thieves.

Emmanuel also had a strong family history of mental illness. Two brothers had been institutionalized by the time he and Diane married. In the years that followed, as he increased his drug use, Emmanuel's mental state became more and more bizarre. He also became increasingly violent. His violent outbursts spilled heavily into his drug-dealing world and at home.

At the time they married, Emmanuel had three children by a previous marriage: Carolyn, Junior, and Roy. Together, he and Diane had four children: Andre, Chardi, Carla, and Katie. Following Emmanuel's death and after her marriage to Vincent McKoy, Diane had another girl, Keisha.

Nicely ensconced in an elite boarding school where she has been exposed to normal family settings, Chardi has come to realize that the characterization of her family as chaotic and dysfunctional would be an understatement. By the time that Chardi was born, Emmanuel was immersed in the Philadelphia drug trade. By then, he was also a master thief. The problem was that there was no consistency attached to either of those vices. He sold drugs and stole when he needed money. Most of the time, he was doing drugs with Diane while his children were fending for themselves. With little or no nurturing or oversight, all of Chardi's older siblings were soon lost to the street. Andre, just two years older than Chardi, did show some potential. Andre was very bright and liked school. In fact, his interest in school was a positive influence to Chardi at a young age. Andre was the only one who ever talked to her about school.

Chardi, however, was something special. From the very beginning, it was clear that she was extremely bright. She was reading by the first grade, though no one knows quite how that happened. She went to a preschool and sat on the laps of the day care providers, who read to the toddlers daily. Chardi would dutifully follow the words and somehow just started reading.

When she reached the first grade, Chardi's first-grade teacher, Anna Givens, saw instantly that her new student was wholly unique. Ms. Givens was astonished by Chardi's capacity for learning. The teacher was particularly dumbfounded when she learned of Chardi's background. "How could such a young child know so much without any support at home?" she often wondered.

As a means of finding out just how far along Chardi actually was, Ms. Givens arranged for her student to take a national test. The results floored everyone in the entire school district. Chardi had the fifth best score among first graders taking the exam around the country. Not fifth percentile. Number five. Tens of thousands of first graders took the test and Chardi Crawford had the fifth best score.

Soon, the principal, school district's superintendent, and Mayor all were singing the praises of this smart, poor girl who had bested nearly every other peer in the country. Ms. Givens was now determined to make sure that her prize pupil was positioned as best as possible to succeed. She knew she had to meet and engage Chardi's parents. They never came to the school and were no shows at the school program honoring the six-year-old wonder. First, Ms. Givens started sending notes home to Chardi's parents. No response. Next, she began calling the home phone. Disconnected.

Finally, she decided to do a home visit. Checking the address in the school's office, Ms. Givens trekked to the Crawford apartment one Saturday morning. She was not prepared for what she saw.

For most of her young childhood, Chardi, her brothers, sisters, and parents, all lived in a one-bedroom apartment located in one of Philadelphia's tough west side neighborhoods. Chardi's parents slept in the bedroom. Chardi and the rest of the Crawford brood slept on the floor or crowded on the one bed located in the middle of the living room. By the time Chardi was six, all of Emmanuel and Diane's children had been born, except for Katie. So, in effect, at any given time, six children were left to fight over that one bed. As she got older, Chardi recalled rushing to get home after school to "reserve her spot" on the bed. She knew that the boys would generally get in late—by now, the street life was reeling them each in like fish on hooks—so the girls almost always were able to sleep on the mattress.

That day, Ms. Givens knocked on the door and waited for what seemed like an eternity for someone to answer. When Diane did open the door, the chaos behind her was there for any and all to see. The worn mattress was right in the middle of the floor. Surrounding it were clothes laying everywhere. Empty cereal boxes, dirty dishes, shoes, boxes, and other debris could be seen throughout the room. Along the walls, Ms. Givens saw a few mousetraps. Chardi and a couple of her siblings were sitting on the bed eating bowls of cereal, watching cartoons on an old television.

"May I help you," Diane said.

"Yes, I am Anna Givens. Chardi is my student. She is my best student. In fact, she is the best student I have ever seen. I--I--I hate to bother you, Mrs. Crawford, but, I wanted to meet you and let you know how proud we are of Chardi."

Diane grunted and said, "Well, thank you. None of my teachers ever came to my house growing up, so she must have done something right. Me and my husband believe in education. By the way, can I offer you a drink? I was about to fix one myself."

Diane then turned, leaving the door partially open. Ms. Givens saw her grab a bottle of bourbon off of a table near the kitchen, along with two glasses. It was ten in the morning.

"No, thank you. Mrs. Crawford. I am not staying. I just wanted you to know how proud we are of Chardi."

In recognizing her teacher, Chardi got real quiet. In truth, she was embarrassed. Though only six, she knew that her household was not "right." She wanted to hide.

Diane's response to Ms. Givens was to the point. "Suit yourself." She then took a big swallow.

Ms. Givens begged her goodbyes and left. She had not set foot inside the apartment.

At school, Ms. Givens never talked about the visit with Chardi. She did, however, continue to work with the child. She also tried to engage Diane. Before long, Diane would allow Chardi to visit Ms. Givens at her home. Chardi loved those visits. Her rapport with her teacher helped her in many ways beyond school. Seeing Ms. Givens house, Chardi witnessed how "normal" people live. She was surprised to learn that most people have their own bed in their own room. She asked Ms. Givens a lot of questions and the teacher always answered honestly though sometimes delicately, being ever mindful of Chardi's circumstances. Chardi would talk freely with Ms. Givens and wished that she lived with her. In time, the closeness of their relationship would help destroy it. Neither Diane nor Emmanuel liked the idea of another adult getting close to one of their children.

Chardi was not only smart. She also had a photographic memory and incredible intuition. Her earliest memory was sitting in a car seat in her parents' living room. Chardi recalls looking at a mirror hanging on the wall near where she was sitting. She could not walk or talk and was not yet two years old. With vivid detail, Chardi can recount watching her parents smoking marijuana after drinking for a long period of time. While they were smoking their drugs, baby Chardi remembers seeing the mirror slowly move. Apparently, the nails holding the mirror were weak and the mirror was in the process of falling from the wall. From where she was sitting, Chardi could tell that the mirror was going to fall on her. She recalls feeling helpless. She also was mad at her parents for not paying attention to her. The mirror eventually did fall on her, cutting her young forehead.

Back at Chardi's boarding school, Ashely was beginning to stir. Chardi was already dressed and ready to go to the school library. Ashley blinked her eyes, looked at the clock, which read 6:45 and then back at Chardi. "What time this morning?" she asked.

"5:07," Chardi said.

"That's not too bad. You will be alright today. Have a good one." With that, Ashley rolled over. She was going to catch a few extra minutes of sleep.

Chardi smiled and walked out the door. She really liked her school, her new life. She was excelling in every way. She has been on the honor roll since she began at St. Mary's. She will always be smart. She is captain of the basketball and softball teams and a star on the soccer team. But her true gift is in math. Chardi is one of the more gifted math students in the state of Pennsylvania. She absolutely loves math. Loves it. As she has worked through her family problems over the years, math has helped to save her. At one point, in addition to dealing with the dream, Chardi had a terrible time falling asleep. She felt caught in between. She could not go to sleep and when she did, the dream would wake her up.

One night, while tossing and turning, Chardi pulled out her math book and started to work on some math problems. In doing so, a nice, comfortable calm engulfed her. She soon got sleepy and slept like a baby, without the dream. Now, whenever she has a hard time sleeping, she reaches for her math book. Works like a charm.

She even gets along with her roommate, Ashley. It was rough at first. Both girls come from totally different worlds. Ashley was spoiled beyond belief and Chardi practically raised herself. But the girls have learned from each other and have grown in the process. Though Chardi does not tell anyone the whole story about her background, she has shared certain tidbits with Ashley. It only made sense, Chardi figured, since the dream would affect Ashley too.

Walking to the library, Chardi was reflecting on her conversation with Carla that took place while she was visiting her mother. As smart as she was, Chardi was saddened by the fact that she may not be able to save her sister. But she still is determined to try.

As soon as she walked into her mother's house, she went to Carla's room, grabbed her by the arm and told her she wanted them to take a walk. Chardi was two years older than Carla and had been as much a mother as a sister to her. Carla sneered a little, but followed Chardi out the door.

"What's your problem, Chardi? Why you sweatin' me?"

"You know why, Carla. Don't play me! I hear about who you are hanging out with. If you keep it up, they may kick you out of school. I am not going to let that happen."

Carla was attending a well-regarded charter school not far from where Diane lived. Many of Chardi's classmates from her old charter school are now upperclassmen at Carla's school. Chardi made it clear to her former classmates that they had to look after her baby sister. She gets regular reports and recently those reports were not good. Chardi was told that Carla was beginning to miss homework assignments as well as skip class. She also was beginning to hang out with some of the block boys near the school, guys involved with drugs. Chardi was furious and wanted to get her sister straight.

"Well, it's my life, big sis. I can do what I want." When she finished, Carla put her right hand on her hip and curled up her lip.

Chardi proceeded to remind Carla in graphic detail about all that they had been through. She talked about their drug addled parents, particularly Emmanuel's drug and criminal behavior. Chardi then talked at length about the subject no one wants to talk about, the day their father almost killed them all. She was imploring her sister, pleading with her.

> Carla, you can't go down the road our parent's traveled. You just can't!

Dang, Chardi. You always want to go back to that. I ain't got nuthin to do with that. I was too young. That ain't got nuttin to do with me.

"How could she say that?" Chardi thought.

"It has everything to do with you, Carla." Chardi replied. "It is a part of us, who we are. Mom, Dad, the drugs, the no good relatives. It is us. But you, me, Katie and Keisha can be different. Remember, we promised each other. We would be different."

Carla remembered. But she also did not want the burden of keeping a promise that did not relate to her life. She liked hanging out. She liked having fun and she was liking school less. Chardi would just have to accept that. She rolled her eyes and walked back toward the house.

When she got back to the house, Chardi began to engage her mother. Diane hated when Chardi had that assertive look in her eye. It always put her on the defensive. Sure, she had made mistakes, but sometimes her daughter was too smart for her own good. Chardi was already boring in.

"Mom, you need to talk with Carla. She is missing school and starting to hang with the wrong folks around her school."

"What do you want me to say?" Diane answered. She actually had a twinkle in her eye. Chardi had never asked her to counsel one of her children, so Diane knew this must be serious. At least it was serious to Chardi. But that was the problem, according to Diane's thinking. Chardi thinks she is better than everyone else. Carla is getting old enough to make her own decisions. Diane had no inclination to press Carla about her activities.

Instead of answering Diane's question, Chardi went straight for the jugular. "Mom, do you ever feel bad about all the things you and dad did to us? Do you ever think about it?"

Diane recoiled, then said, "Your father was a sick man. I'm sorry bout the way he died, but we are all doing better now that he is gone."

Chardi just walked away.

In the library just before class, Chardi thought about what her mother said to her the previous weekend. "Better off? Now that's a matter of opinion," she thought. Yes, she is in a great school and has a bright future. But as crazy as her father was, he was her protector. More than anyone, she sometimes misses him and feels ashamed to admit it.

Make no mistake about it, Emmanuel Crawford was an out and out scoundrel. A crazy one at that. One of the reasons why Chardi's relationship ended with Ms. Givens was because Chardi would tell her teacher stories about her father's exploits. True stories.

Emmanuel Crawford came from a family of drug dealers. Unlike the smart ones, he often used his own merchandise. As a result, he was always coming up short with his suppliers and forced to supplement his shortfalls through thievery. Plus, he had six kids to feed, along with a junkie wife to supply.

When things got real tight, he would give his street runners a hard time. He would accuse them of stealing from him and plotting against him. Of course, much of that deception is part of the business. On those occasions when Emmanuel had proof that one of his lieutenants was stealing from him, his reaction was lethal. Literally.

Of all the people in his household, Emmanuel loved Chardi the best. He never said he loved her, it was just apparent. Chardi was the only child he never beat. He also took her with him regularly on his drug and thievery runs. By the time she was five years old, Chardi was used to seeing her father pistol whip drug runners, curse out suppliers and steal from business establishments. Once, Chardi waited in the car while Emmanuel broke into a convenience store safe. They drove off with the alarm blaring in the background.

Having heard Chardi talk of these activities, Ms. Givens was generally not surprised by what she was told by the young phenom. Except when Chardi casually told her teacher that she saw her father shoot a man in the head and kill him "many times." Ms. Givens did not know quite how to respond. Emmanuel did not give her much time to figure it out. When Chardi told her daddy what she had shared with her teacher, Emmanuel paid Ms. Givens a visit. Ms. Givens remained encouraging to Chardi, but no longer engaged her in talk about after-school activities. Soon thereafter, Emmanuel moved his family from their apartment and put all of the kids into new schools. Chardi never saw Ms. Givens again.

Chardi was almost seven when Emmanuel moved his family from that one-bedroom apartment. For the next two years, he continued to move them from one place to the next, trying to stay one step ahead of the law and other enemies. The kids grew accustomed to police raids, threatening phone calls, and even gunfire in front of their residence, wherever it happened to be. Though he never sought medical attention or treatment, Emmanuel was slowly descending into madness. And he seemed bent on taking his family with him.

It all came to a head just before Chardi's ninth birthday. Two weeks earlier, Diane had just given birth to Katie, her parents' youngest. The pregnancy was especially difficult and Katie was delivered by cesarean section. Emmanuel and Diane were arguing and fighting regularly those days. It did not matter that Diane was pregnant.

On this day, Chardi saw her father begin to beat her mother. He beat her about the face, arms, and stomach. Diane winced every time Emmanuel punched her on her stomach, which was full of surgeon's staples from her cesarean section. Suddenly, Emmanuel demanded that the whole family get into his old Lincoln town car. He said he wanted them to all go see his sister, who lived just a few miles away in Camden, NJ. Emmanuel's sister also was a heavy drug user.

As soon as Chardi squeezed into the car with her parents and her siblings, she knew something was wrong. Her father was acting more and more bizarre. He was weaving back and forth down the street, even bumping into a few parked cars. The kids started to scream and cry, all but Chardi. By now, Emmanuel was back to punching Diane. Diane was sitting in the front passenger seat, with two-week-old Katie in her lap. Emmanuel was driving with his left hand and swinging wildly at Diane with his right, sometimes striking the newborn with flush punches. In order to protect her baby, Diane placed Katie on the floor. While her siblings were crying and pleading with their father to stop, Chardi, who was sitting in back of her mother in the back seat, closest to the door, began to think that they all were going to die.

Emmanuel was out of control. A dysfunctional life of mental illness and drug abuse had sent him over the edge. He drove onto the Walt Whitman bridge, which crosses the Delaware River from Philadelphia to Camden, NJ. The Walt Whitman bridge is a high suspension bridge.

Emmanuel began to recite over and over the same expression: "Before me there was none and after me there shall be none." He said it over and over. Chardi will remember that expression and the way her father was wildly reciting it for the rest of her life.

As they were nearing the top of the bridge, Emmanuel increased the car's speed and made a hard right turn, heading straight for the guard rail on the side of the bridge. Chardi then knew why she thought she was going to die when they all got into the car. Her father was about to kill them all by driving off of the bridge!

As Emmanuel pointed the car toward the rail, the crying inside the vehicle rose to a fever pitch. "Daddy, please don't kill us!" "Daddy, don't drive off of the bridge."

In the midst of it all, Chardi did not say a word. She kept looking at the guard rail and was preparing for the worse. She knew that even if she survived the fall into the water, she could not swim. She was going to die.

The Walt Whitman bridge is one of the most fortified bridges on the east coast. The side guard rails can withstand enormous amounts of force and pressure. The bridge designers would have been proud that day. Emmanuel rammed into the side of the bridge full force. The rail did not budge!

The crying stopped for an instant. Taken aback, but determined nonetheless, Emmanuel put the car in reverse, backed up a few yards and accelerated as fast as he could toward the same spot.

Other bridge patrons were honking their horns, some even stopped their cars, trying to divert the attention of the madman attempting to drive off of the Walt Whitman bridge with a carload full of screaming kids.

The car hit the rail again. "Bam!" The rails still held.

Emmanuel tried a couple more times before he gave up. He finally sped off the bridge and continued to his sister's house, which was located less than a mile away.

Chardi could not believe it. She was going to live.

When they arrived at Emmanuel's sister, everyone jumped out of the car, quickly. Diane told Chardi to take her siblings upstairs to her aunt's bedroom and to lock the door. Chardi dutifully complied, but after locking the door, she went back downstairs and out on the front lawn where Emmanuel was arguing with Diane. Emmanuel's sister, Janice, was trying to calm her brother down, but he was not having any of it. Emmanuel pushed Janice aside and began hitting Diane again. Chardi stood on the front porch, watching the whole scene.

With all that had happened, several people had called the police, including Janice, who did not take kindly to her brother coming to her house, pushing her around, and acting like a fool. The police arrived in force, ready to take on Emmanuel.

Emmanuel was well known within police circles. He was viewed as a borderline psychopathic drug peddler. They knew of his violent tendencies and many on the force did not like him at all. The first two officers who arrived at the scene were familiar to Chardi. They had been to her house to roust her father in the past. It took them no time to subdue Emmanuel and place him in the back of the squad car.

As Emmanuel was being placed in the car, Chardi recalls being overcome by a weird sensation. She was looking directly at her father, who was trying to kick open the rear police door. Unable to do so, Emmanuel started to rhythmically rock back and forth in the back seat. Seeing her father do that reminded Chardi of the story her father had mentioned to her several times about her grandmother, Emmanuel's mother. Emmanuel told his daughter that the last time he saw his mother, she was sitting down, staring straight ahead rocking back and forth.

Chardi intuitively knew that this would be the last time that she would see her father. In a panic, she ran down from the front porch and begged the policemen to let her hug her father one last time. Diane quizzically looked at Chardi, while the police were trying to convince the eight-year-old that she had no need to worry, her father would be alright. Chardi, however, was insistent. She knew that she would never see her father again. She wanted to hug him.

The police finally relented and let Chardi hug her father. Emmanuel, still in handcuffs, let his favorite hug him and kissed her cheek. He then simply said to her, "Be strong, don't cry and take care of your brothers and sisters. I am counting on you for that."

Two days later, Emmanuel Crawford was found dead in his jail cell.

No one knows for sure how Emmanuel died. The autopsy said blunt trauma, but no one was charged with any crime associated with his death. A couple of officers were suspended for neglecting their duties, but the death remains somewhat of a mystery. Chardi has no doubt that the police killed her father. One of Emmanuel's cousins was in the cell next to Emmanuel. The police, however, had no idea that the two men were related. The cousin told Diane that the night before Emmanuel died, several police grabbed him from his cell in the middle of the night and took him somewhere. When they returned in the morning, Emmanuel was beaten badly and semiconscious, according to the cousin. Hours passed before anyone checked on him. He died that night.

Oddly, things did get worse for Chardi following her father's death. From the time she was five, she was used to taking care of Carla. Now, with her mother always high, grieving over Emmanuel, Chardi, the responsible one, had to fashion meals and take care of Katie. She did diapers, fed Carla and Andre raw hotdogs, and ate a lot of cereal. Even to this day, Chardi took to heart her father's request that she look after her brothers and sisters. In her mind, she has rationalized that she cannot do anything about the older siblings, but she must save those younger than her.

At first, she had hopes that Andre would stay on track. He was two years older than Chardi and almost as smart. Before Emmanuel died, Andre began to hang with guys on the street. Close when they were younger, Chardi began to try to distance herself from her brother. Soon after her tenth birthday, Andre raped Chardi. He continued to do so for the next year. Each time, Chardi kept a blank expression and tried to shield Carla from Andre. Her candid view was better me than Carla. I can handle it.

Through it all, she continued to do well in school, her only place of refuge. She was picking up honors left and right. Ironically, she learned about the Philadelphia Math & Science Charter School when the principal came by the house to recruit Andre. Eavesdropping on their conversation, Chardi then popped into the living room declaring, "I think you need me at your school." Later that week, the principal and his best math teacher gave Chardi a bunch of math to solve. She did them in no time. The math teacher, Scott Knowling told the principal that Chardi was like Matt Damon's character in Good Will Hunting. "This kid may discover the formula for travel to Saturn one day," Mr. Knowling said, tongue in cheek. Mr. Knowling became Chardi's math mentor and friend. He helped her get into St. Mary's, found a psychiatrist to assist Chardi with the emotional trauma she has experienced, and guided her through the transition from living with her mother to being with the Peters family. Mr. Knowling feels honored that he has made his way into the dream as the driver of the car.

As they say, life happens. Chardi lives it every day. She tries not to look back. She constantly talks with her younger sisters; she is comfortable at St. Mary's and she knows that she will go to college and beyond. She feels better about her life and knows or hopes that the dream will go away in a matter of time. But she still feels the need to honor her promise to her father.

Four months after the weekend visit to her mother's house, Chardi decided to take matters into her own hands. She took three bus transfers and went to Carla's school. By now, Chardi's sources made it clear to her that Carla was now fully entrenched with the kids going nowhere. She was using drugs and had stopped going to class. When

Chardi asked Carla about her activities during their telephone calls, Carla would say that Chardi's nosey friends were making things up. Chardi needed to see for herself.

When Chardi arrived at Carla's school, one of Chardi's former charter school classmates met her and pointed her in the direction of Carla's hangout spot, a corner about a block away from the school. Chardi walked down the street and, in no time, saw her sister standing on the corner with some friends.

"Carla! Come here." she yelled.

Carla looked down the street, saw her sister and was visibly nervous. She whispered to her two friends and walked to where Chardi was standing, both hands on hips, waiting for her baby sister.

As Carla got close to her, Chardi first saw the redness in her eyes. Then she smelled the smell. She remembered that smell when that mirror fell on her head when she was a toddler. Carla had been smoking marijuana.

Carla, understanding that her sister could tell what she and been doing, just froze and said nothing. After all of these years, Chardi thought, I just cannot keep that promise. I have lost my sister. She then sat on the sidewalk, put her head in her hands and cried. Carla merely watched her.

After a few minutes, Chardi picked herself up, walked to her sister, hugged her, turned around and walked to the nearby bus stop. For some strange reason, she felt free. She would never look back, and never worry about unkept promises or bad families. She would forever focus on the future, her future. The burden had been lifted.

Chardi continued to excel at St. Mary's, where she graduated and is now going to college. She maintains contact with her mother and her younger sisters, including Carla.

Andre is in jail for an attempted murder charge. Chardi harbors no bitterness for all that she has endured in her young life. She remains positive about her future. Chardi also insists that she will always love her father and forgives him for his actions.

Ronnie

The applause was thunderous. The ovation was deafening. The crowd was going wild. At least, that is how it felt to eleven-year-old Ronnie Stevenson when he heard his name called. Ronnie had just been announced as the sixth-grade poetry winner in the annual Baltimore Elementary School poetry contest. He was ecstatic.

In truth, as Ronnie walked onto the stage to receive his award, the applause was generous, but polite. The crowd consisted of about one hundred people, mainly participants, from every elementary school in the city. Since Baltimore had junior high schools from the seventh to the ninth grades, all of the elementary schools stopped at the sixth grade. As a result, the most coveted award went to the sixth-grade champion.

And that was now Ronnie.

When Ronnie's name was called, there were no shrieks or screams as was the case when the fifth-grade winner was announced. That girl happened to attend a better school. A school with a student in the final group for every grade competition. That school, Theodore Roosevelt Elementary, had college students as coaches, who help the kids with their poetry writing. They were the New York Yankees of Baltimore schools poetry-writing competitions. They always had winners in the citywide contest.

In contrast, Ronnie came from Harriett Tubman Elementary, located in the middle of two housing projects on Baltimore's west side.

Ronnie was attending the finals as his school's only representative. He was accompanied by his teacher, Mrs. Joan Tillman, the person who introduced Ronnie to poetry writing. Mrs. Tillman was a tiny, petite woman, who had been teaching at Tubman for ten years. She had a graduate degree in English. Ms. Tillman loved the English language and everything about writing. She met Ronnie in her fifth-grade class and knew right away that he had a natural proclivity for putting words together. Sitting in the audience that day, she was proud beyond words.

More than that, she felt vindicated. As far as she was concerned, Ronnie had the contest won as soon as he entered it. She intuitively knew that no other student in the city would be able to write poetry to match Ronnie's work. His writings were one of a kind.

When Ronnie grabbed his award, he turned to the audience and threw both his arms in the air as high as he could, just like Magic Johnson, his favorite basketball player. He also had a smile on his face that could rival Magic's.

This was the first time in Ronnie's life that he had won anything. And to win a school-related contest? He felt strangely validated. He knew his grandfather would be proud. His mother? Well, that's another story. To Ronnie, though, this was huge. At that moment, he believed he knew exactly how Magic felt when he won the NBA championship the previous year. Man, it felt good.

At about the same time that Ronnie was equating himself with Magic Johnson, his public housing project friend, thirteen-year-old Moon Miller, was smoking a joint in an alley three blocks away from Charles Drew Junior High School, where he was an eighth grader. Like Ronnie, Moon was smart and engaging. He was a natural leader who, also like Ronnie, received very little support at home. Unlike Ronnie, however, Moon was more drawn to the streets. The pull was magnetic and intoxicating, even when it was obvious that the attraction could have dire consequences. Like a moth to a flame, Moon was headed toward a certain inevitability he just could not stop.

That day, Moon had cut class. No matter. The school year was almost over. Next week would mark the beginning of summer. Moon was more focused on organizing the John Holmes housing project junior football team. John Holmes would be entering a team in the Jackson-Stewart Football league. Jackson-Stewart was a city-wide football league designed for kids between the ages of ten and thirteen. Any neighborhood recreation center, school or public housing project could enter a team. An adult affiliated with the applicant had to sign and submit the application. Usually, there we are about fifteen to twenty teams in the league each summer.

Jackson-Stewart was a big deal for kids all over Baltimore. Not surprisingly, high school and even a few college coaches would watch some of the games. It was never too early to fawn over real talent.

Moon was the leader of the kids under the age of fourteen in the John Holmes projects. He had this way about him that suggested that he was in charge. You felt it when he walked into a room. Adults even deferred to Moon. Occasionally the John Holmes security guards, also known by the residents as the fake cops, would hassle the kids if they were making too much noise playing in the street or hanging around the building entrances. If the fake cops saw Moon in the group, they would instinctively back away.

Moon was smoking his joint with No Neck and Sugar Spoon. To understand these assorted names, one has to appreciate hood life. It is rare that a boy is called by his given name his entire life. At some point in time, a nickname will be born. Often, the nickname comes from the way you look or something you have done. There is no guarantee that a nickname will stick, but when it does, it's yours for life.

Moon got his name when he was born. He had a perfectly round head, like Charlie Brown. So his cousin called him Moon. Very few people know that his name is Steven. As Moon got older, the big, round head was more noticeable. Unlike other big round-headed boys, Moon was tall and rail thin. His head really did not look like it fit his body. At all. Anytime he met someone new and gave them his name, the other person would always smile. The name fit him to a tee.

No Neck, well, is obvious. Overweight, dark skinned, and greasy looking, Demetrious Jones would never be called by the name he was given at birth.

Fred Sears had the funniest story of all associated with his naming. He was the best skateboarder in the projects, both John Holmes and Murray Dwellings, which was located on the other side of Harriet Tubman Elementary. Every day, Fred could be seen skating through the two projects at breakneck speeds.

As would be expected, huge territorial rivalries existed between John Holmes and Murray Dwellings. Not just kid rivalries. This was the early 1980s in west Baltimore. The drug epidemic was in full bloom. Marijuana, heroin, powder cocaine, and other chemicals were sold every hour of every day. Drug dealers marked their territories like dogs mark their spot. The New York Jamaican dealers controlled the drug sales in John Holmes. The local Baltimore west side crew owned Murray Dwellings. Drug boys on either side would beat boys up visiting from the other side just for "GP" or general principle. Each wanted to send the message: stay on your turf, this one is ours. Kids from both projects knew they had better think twice before leaving their public housing community to venture over to the next one. Not Fred Sears.

Fred was legendary for making skateboard dashes from John Holmes, through Harriet Tubman, into Murray Dwellings and back.

He would often make his runs on a dare. He was so fast and so agile on his skateboard, that the Murray Dwellings boys could never catch him. He had even been shot at a couple of times, but always made it back.

At any rate, Fred had gotten so good on the skateboard, that he could eat a sandwich or manage a bunch of schoolbooks while riding at fast speeds. Fred also loved eating raw sugar from his mother's sugar canister. When he got good enough on his skateboard, he would come out of his house with the canister in one hand and a spoon in another. It was one unique sight watching a twelve-year-old skateboarder continuously pouring sugar with his left hand onto a spoon in his right hand, while riding a fast moving skateboard, all without spilling a drop. Fred Sears eternally became Sugar Spoon.

No Neck and Sugar Spoon were Moon's lieutenants. They would also play on the John Holmes football team. Moon pulled them out of class to smoke a joint and talk about "who our twenty two players should be on the team." Moon would be the quarterback while Sugar Spoon would be a running back. No Neck would play on the line as center. While passing the joint, they would name names and positions and match them accordingly. Ronnie, though two years younger, would play tight end. Ronnie was a medium size thick kid, with huge hands and feet. Only in the sixth grade, Ronnie already wore a size nine shoe. He had a perfect football body.

When Ronnie's name came up, Sugar Spoon said, "Yo, Moon, you know that Ronnie is up for that poetry award today. Whaddya think of dat?"

Moon took a long drag on his joint and said, "Ronnie's a good kid, real smart. I'm happy for him. He needs to understand though that school ain't gonna get him nowhere. He's from John Holmes, period! Ain't nobody gonna respect nobody from John Holmes or Harriet Tubman. That's why we got to get ours now. I got me some plans and there ain't no need to waste time in school."

"True dat," Sugar Spoon said. "He'll be a good tight end on our team. He can catch good."

Ronnie, by now, was heading back to Harriet Tubman with Ms. Tillman. She was just as excited as he was. "Now, I am certain that you can get into that literary media arts program at the Eastside Academy for the Arts," she said. "Harriet Tubman has never had a student go to Eastside, Ronnie. You will be our first. I am so proud of you."

Ronnie was proud, too. He wanted to go to Eastside. He wanted to write more poetry. He wanted to be better. More than anything, Ronnie wanted to make something of his life. He did not want to be in John Holmes forever. He wanted more out of life. Much more.

He could not wait to tell his grandfather. Next to Ms. Tillman, his grandfather was his biggest support base. Grandpa, or as he was called, Big Rod, would have been at the poetry finals if he was not sick. Cancer was eating his body away, but Grandpa remained upbeat. He was no doubt a man's man.

Ronnie lived with his grandfather and had since he was eight years old. Ronnie's mother, Katy, did not want Ronnie. Ronnie did not know his father. Katy had two children; Rose and two years later, Ronnie. Katy was not a good mother to either child, but had major issues with Ronnie. From Katy's perspective, he was too needy. Early on, he would ask her to help him with homework, participate in school activities, and inquire as to whether he would ever see Baltimore's downtown. Too much! Rose never asked for much. She just did her thing and left Katy alone.

Katy felt that she was too young to be bogged down with kids. She was short and attractive with a body guys in the hood craved. "Phat" is what she was called. Katy wanted the good things in life, at least from the perspective of a woman who grew up in the hood around poverty, pimps, prostitutes, and drug dealers. She wanted to be taken out to nice places, driven in a fine car, and hang out with a man who has a wad of cash in his pocket.

Katy had a fondness for drug dealers. She hung with those who were at the top of their game. Her world revolved around pleasing them and being at their ready. She had no time for her kids.

When Rose and Ronnie would come home from school, Rose would cook dinner. The two children would then do their homework. Katy might be home or may be somewhere else. She would leave the house almost every night and often would not be back home by the time the kids got up to get ready for school.

When she was at home, she generally had a couple of girlfriends at the house who shared Katy's view of the world. They would smoke marijuana, do each other's nails, and cackle among themselves.

By the time Ronnie was eight, Katy was tired of him trying to get her to act like a mother. Ronnie would always ask his mother where she was going and when was she coming home. He also, though just a small boy, would challenge the numerous men she would bring into the home. Katy hated Ronnie's inquisitions and his over protectiveness.

Finally, Katy said to eight-year-old Ronnie, "You know, I never wanted you. You wouldn't be here if your father wasn't so cheap. I needed money for an abortion, but your cheap bastard of a father never gave me the money. Now, you all in my bizness. You need to leave here, if you gonna be askin me all them questions. You need to live with your grandfather."

Katy then called her father, Big Rod, who lived in the same complex, a few buildings over. Big Rod was six feet, four inches tall and muscular, even for seventy years old. He was the top maintenance man for John Holmes and had been so for over twenty years. Prostate cancer was knocking him down a bit, but he still was Big Rod. He also hated the fact that Katy, his only child, was just no good.

Big Rod loved his grandkids, but took a basic hands-off approach to their rearing. He believed that they were Katy's responsibility and that he could not allow himself to be sucked into the day-to-day upkeep of Rose and Ronnie.

Big Rod knew his daughter all too well. If she had her druthers, both kids would be living with Big Rod. He resisted all efforts to push them on him.

But Big Rod had a soft spot and sensed that Ronnie was different. Though at first he figured that Ronnie would eventually be lured into the street life that gets all the other boys in this area, he had been rethinking his original fatalistic view of his grandson.

Big Rod had noticed Ronnie a lot playing with the other boys. Ronnie was indeed different. Yes, he was part of the in crowd at John Holmes and, like Moon Miller, he was a natural leader. But he was different. He might make something of himself.

So when Katy called her father to ask him to take in her bothersome son, Big Rod relented and said yes.

Even Katy was surprised. "Somebody does want you," she said to Ronnie. "You are going to live with your grandfather."

The first thing Big Rod said to his eight-year-old grandson when he moved in with him was, "Boy, I ain't got a lot of money, so you gonna have to find a way to get your own money, but I do have time and I will give you plenty of that."

And he did. For the next five years, Big Rod showed Ronnie how to be a man. He encouraged Ronnie when he did his homework, attended school events, and generally reassured Ronnie wherever he could.

Big Rod's encouragement really made a difference when Ronnie was introduced to poetry writing by Ms. Tillman in the fifth grade.

Ronnie will never forget the day Ms. Tillman told him to see her at the end of the school day. Ronnie assumed that she wanted to go over an English homework assignment. Instead, she told him that she wanted him to read something. She then handed Ronnie a small pamphlet entitled, "The Poems of Langston Hughes." Ms. Tillman had book marked a page that had the Langston Hughes poem "I, too, Sing America."

That poem changed Ronnie's life forever. He had to read more. Ronnie took the pamphlet home and read every poem. While reading the words, he viscerally understood the messages that Hughes was trying to convey. He was blown away. Nothing had ever affected him like that. When he mentioned the poems to Big Rod, his grandfather offered the timely support that he needed. "I don't know much about poems, boy," he said. "But, I do know that a lot of smart people write poems. There can't be nothing wrong with you learning more about 'em.'"

Big Rod's biggest lesson to Ronnie was on self-sufficiency. True to his word, he did not give Ronnie much money, but pushed him to get work on his own. He constantly drummed into Ronnie that a man had to find a way to make an honest living. Without directly bashing the drug dealer's life, Big Rod used examples of money-making alternatives. He talked about entrepreneurs like Henry Ford and Lee Iaccoca. (Big Rod liked Fords.) "You gotta think like a businessman, boy," he would say.

Fact was, all around Ronnie, his slightly older peers were acting just like businessmen. The cross-fertilization between drug trafficking and urban education is stark and real. The fast life has always presented an attractive alternative to the studious book life, but in the eighties, the vast majority of our urban males saw street life as their only option.

This happened for three primary reasons. First, public education in our urban areas became a disaster. Although there were exceptions, by and large poor resources, lackluster teachers, inadequate facilities, and a commitment to a one size fits all approach left most urban schools with a product not designed to address urban kids' needs.

Second, selling drugs became a realistic way of supporting your family and achieving material success never dreamed of. Most urban male teenagers come from single mother-headed households. Over time, many of these boys saw the dollars associated with drug trafficking as a way to "help mama."

Finally, Congress passed the mandatory minimums criminal legislation. Promoted by the Reagan administration in the early eighties, this federal legislation significantly increased the penalties for certain criminal offenses and took away judges discretion in the imposition of those penalties. An unintended consequence of mandatory minimums is that sophisticated drug dealers started to recruit juveniles to serve on the front lines of the street dealing business. At the time, if someone under eighteen years of age was arrested for a felony, they often would be treated with kids gloves, released to a guardian, and face a far more lenient juvenile system. Drug trafficking leaders had no problems using juveniles as street mules selling drugs while they were virtually insulated from the effects of the mandatory minimums bill.

The business behind the urban drug trade was as finely tuned as any major successful corporation. The essence of the street drug trade revolves around the basic business principles of buying for less, selling for more, keeping overhead low, understanding profit and losses, and always monitoring the bottom line. The business model resembles a pyramid. The runners sell the drugs on the street. Each runner is responsible for a block or corner. Runners report to area captains, each of whom may have five to ten runners working under them. The area captain then reports to the neighborhood leader, who is, in effect, the king of that community. The chain of command moving upward gets more and more narrow, such that it is easy for one or two people to control the drug trade in an entire city. Similar to the approach used by the mafia, buying and selling, corporate executive recruitment, and takeovers often involved brazen violence.

While Ronnie was writing poetry, his friend Moon was plotting more than who would play what positions on the neighborhood football team. Moon wanted to be the undisputed drug kingpin of John Holmes.

Similar to Ronnie, Moon did not have support from his parents. In fact, both of Moon's parents were heroin addicts. Moon had been fending for himself for as long as he remembered. Though Moon was smart and had the potential to be good in school, he unlike Ronnie, he did not have one teacher or mentor who took to him or went out of their way to nurture his natural academic abilities. Part of the challenge he faced was that he, like Ronnie, was a project kid. From kindergarten on, some kids who come from public housing are unfairly typecast and systematically assumed to be academically deficient. Of course, not all teachers do this, but far too many do. More than

Ronnie, however, Moon had that edge about him. He was a tough kid and it showed. He was easily intimidating, even to adults. Folks did not warm to Moon Miller.

As far as Moon was concerned, school did not offer him any future. Instead, he saw the man who sold both his parents' drugs dressing nice and driving nice cars. Moon saw that image as a role model to which he could aspire.

Though Moon was two years older, he and Ronnie bonded when both were very young. When Ronnie was in first grade, he realized that Moon was the best reader among any of the kids in their age group. That led to Ronnie going to Moon for clandestine tutoring sessions that lasted for several years. Moon made sure that no one knew about these sessions and would often meet Ronnie late at night at Ronnie's grandfather when no one was around. Moon even heard Ronnie recite his poems and offered his thoughts about them. As Ronnie got closer to the citywide poetry competition, he secretly longed for Ronnie to win, but also insisted that Ronnie not tell anyone about their private sessions. It was almost as if Moon could envision Ronnie succeeding in school and in school-related activities, but was resigned to the fact that he could not.

As much as Moon liked Ronnie, and one of the reasons why he has been quietly tutoring him over the years, is that Moon viewed Ronnie as a threat. He intuitively knew that Ronnie was the only kid who, if he put his mind to it, could compete with Moon for control of John Holmes. Moon would much rather see Ronnie in college than fighting in the inevitable future neighborhood turf wars.

Over the previous few months, Moon was observing and learning the drug game from a business point of view. He knew that Jamaican Winston Franklin was the king of John Holmes. Franklin began by selling heroin and helped to get Moon's parents hooked. Moon did not like Franklin at all.

Franklin had five captains under him who supervised about twenty to twenty-five runners. All the runners were between thirteen and nineteen. Having known Franklin since he was very young, Moon saw how he rose to the top. He also knew where he was weak. Though just thirteen, Moon planned on befriending Franklin's younger runners and developing the right relationship with them. Everyone knew that Franklin treated his people like dirt, so Moon was confident that he could gain the youngest crew members' trust. A key step in that strategy was the football team he was organizing.

Next, he would engage a couple of Franklin's captains. Fortunately, the two responsible for his immediate area were also shaky with their boss. By getting the runners on board, Moon would go to the captains from a position of strength. He would then offer them more money.

Moon's secret weapon was his unknown relationship with the local boys who ruled Murray Dwellings. They hated Winston as well. Moon had been talking with them about his plans and they would provide him a steady supply of drugs, as well as weapons. Their view was if this cocky kid could pull it off, the better for them.

Moon understood buying, selling, mergers, acquisitions, corporate raiding, hostile takeovers, employee benefits, and a better work environment. It sounded like wall street. If his accident of birth had been different, Moon Miller would have been a CEO of a Fortune 500 company.

Moon had no need to worry about Ronnie. Big Rod, Ms. Tillman, and Langston Hughes sealed that deal. Ronnie would never sell drugs. But he still had to grapple with his environment. Big Rod was very sick with cancer and Katy had made it clear that Ronnie could not move back in with her. Ronnie was too young to get his own place, plus he needed money to live on. So far, his natural industry and entrepreneurial talents had served him well. Ronnie made more money than any kid ever could in the projects, without selling drugs. First, he delivered newspapers on his paper route. When he moved in with Big Rod several years ago, Ronnie realized that he had to buy his own clothes. Being only eight at the time, his money-making options were limited. Then, one day, he noticed twelve-year-old Mookey Mims struggling with the stack of papers he was trying to deliver while riding his bike. Ronnie offered to help. Mookey let the kid deliver papers on a couple of blocks and gave him a dollar. A couple of days later, Ronnie, who was waiting for Mookey, stopped him and told him that he could handle the four blocks around his area everyday for half of what Mookey was being paid. Mookey never really like delivering papers anyway, he was only doing it to help his mother pay the rent. Mookey's mom unusually kept tight reins on him which prevented him from selling drugs. Now that Mookey was getting older, he was beginning to navigate around his nosey mother. He jumped at the chance of getting Ronnie to help him with the papers so he could ease into the hustler's life. Within a year, Ronnie had control of all of Mookey's route.

Soon, Ronnie began to expand his operation. By the time he had picked up his poetry award, Ronnie controlled the paper routes for all of John Holmes and Murray Dwellings. Ronnie had ten boys working for him between the ages of eight and thirteen. He was making a lot of money and he was building an army of workers. That growing army of workers was the thing that concerned Moon the most.

But Ronnie did more than manage his budding paper franchise. Ronnie found unique ways to take advantage of the ghetto environment and make money, all without selling drugs. He always had a scheme. The older guys joked that young Ronnie would always find a way to make a dollar out of fifty cents. In one scheme, Ronnie bought five bootleg porno movies and strategically charged admission to selected young boys for exclusive viewings. By purposely limiting the number of viewers, the market demand and cost went up. Ronnie also doled out the movie showings sparingly. He made a lot of money on that one. By the time a couple of other boys tried to copy his idea, Ronnie was also serving pizza and coca cola at his showings. He remained ahead of the competition.

As Big Rod became more ill, Ronnie started to help him more with his building maintenance responsibilities. In doing so, Ronnie noticed several older women struggling while carting their trash to the dumpsters. Unfortunately, in the hood, chivalry is sometimes dead. Ronnie, with all the charm that he could muster, began to offer to dump these ladies' trash for them. At first, he did it for free. Then, one by one, they began to give him money for his trash runs. Ronnie found ways to engage people and make money.

Recognizing all of this made it only natural for Moon to expect that Ronnie may, one day, decide to transfer his entrepreneurial spirit to the drug game. As much as he liked Ronnie, he continued to see him as a future rival.

These various dynamics were taking place as the school year was ending and Ronnie picked up his treasured award. After getting back to Harriet Tubman, Ronnie gave Ms. Tillman a hug and walked home to his grandfather's. When he arrived, Big Rod was in the bed, obviously having a rough day. Big Rod's face lit up like a Christmas tree when he saw the plaque that Ronnie was carrying. "Boy," he said, "You are on your way!" The two hugged and smiled at each other.

Later, Ronnie walked to the John Holmes basketball courts. Like all public housing projects, the John Holmes basketball was the ultimate gathering spot, a community staple. John Holmes had two full courts.

One was for the younger kids, one for the older kids and young men. Every kid growing up in that development felt it was a rite of passage to go to the court for the older, more skilled players. Ronnie, Moon, and their respective peers were still on the young kids' court, but they would soon make the transition to the main court.

Moon, No Neck, Sugar Spoon, and others were playing a game when Ronnie walked up. "Hey man," Sugar Spoon said. "How'd you do?"

"I won!" Ronnie yelled.

"You go, boy," Moon said. High fives were being given out all around. One kid was not celebrating. In fact, while Moon and the others were patting Ronnie on the back, he was glaring at Ronnie with a curled lip the whole time.

"Yo Ronnie, don't girls write poetry?" said Wayne Robinson. Every smart kid from the hood has a neighborhood nemesis. That someone who may be jealous of their success in school or who just may not like them. Wayne Robinson was Ronnie's nemesis. He was a year older and always messed with Ronnie. They have fought only one time and Ronnie beat him up pretty bad. So, Wayne generally resorted to sarcasm and cutting remarks when he went after Ronnie.

"Some do, Wayne," Ronnie said. "Like your mother. She was there cheering for me today!"

Everyone started to laugh and join in with the oohhs and awwws. Wayne continued to curl up his lip. He grabbed the basketball and started to shoot at the basket.

Later, Moon and Ronnie walked back toward Ronnie's grandfather's apartment alone.

"Thanks man, for all of your help," Ronnie said. "I couldn't have done any of this without you."

"Look dog, you my main man. Just keep doing what you are doing. You going places." The two shook hands and Ronnie watched Moon walk down the path toward his apartment.

Moon had actually put together a pretty good football team for the Jackson-Stewart boys football league. He had a decent arm, but more than anything, had a knack for directing the team. Sugar Spoon was as fast on his feet as he was on his skateboard. He was one of the best running backs for his age in the city. High school prep school scouts came to the game to watch him play.

Moon served essentially as player-coach. John Holmes recreation center director Joshua Young signed the entry forms, but everyone knew that this was Moon's team. Mr. Young deferred to Moon on who was in the game and what plays were called.

The team did well. They won all but one game, and more importantly, crushed project rival Murray Dwellings. They lost in the semifinals during the citywide playoffs in early August.

Moon adroitly had five drug dealers, all from Franklin's crew, on the team. Three of them were older than the no older than age thirteen league limit. Everyone knew it, even with their fake birth certificates. Coincidently, four boys who worked on Ronnie's paper delivery team also played.

Moon had accomplished what he wanted, except one thing; he needed to have a heart to heart with his top dog, Ronnie.

Moon came to Ronnie's grandfather's late one Sunday evening. When Ronnie answered the door, Moon asked Ronnie to come outside. The two friends then sat on the small porch by the front door of the four-unit building.

"Ronnie," Moon began, "you had a great season, Dog."

"Thanks, Moon. You were our leader."

"Well, in a way, Dog, that's what I want to talk with you about. You see, you and me represent the future up in here and I need to know that we on the same page. I got plans, Dog, big plans. And I need to ask you if you gonna get in my way."

Moon was sitting on the top porch step, while Ronnie was leaning against one of the porch's support pillars. Ronnie was about five feet from Moon and both were looking toward the street while they were talking.

Until then.

When Moon finished his question, Ronnie turned his head around hard to the right and looked dead in Moon's face. Upon seeing this, Moon, who was sitting down, quickly stood up and looked back at Ronnie.

"What you mean, Moon? What are you talking about?"

"Look, Ronnie, I see how you making a name for your self, round here and at school. You got folks working for you! Well, I plan on being the king around here and I need to know if you are going to get in my way."

Ronnie then understood. Although both boys were incredibly young, growing up in the streets made them more savvy than some men twice their ages.

"Moon, you know where my head is. I am getting out of the projects. I am going to make something of myself. You know how much I like school. Man, I'm going to college one day. Nothing is going to stop me from that!"

Moon said nothing for at least thirty seconds. Finally, he said, "My fault, Dog. I just got to know where everyone is. One day I'm movin in on Franklin. I got to be sure that my boys are with me."

"Moon, I know what you're doing. But I think that you should focus on school. Man, you smarter than me."

"School ain't for me, Dog. Plus, you go ahead and be something in your world. I'm going to stay right here and be something in mine."

With that, they shook hands and Moon left.

Ronnie knew Moon better than anyone. He knew what Moon was going through. Because he was smart, Moon needed something more. Since he felt he could not get it in school, he was going to get it in John Holmes. If he was going to be a project dweller, then he would be the baddest one around.

Ronnie also knew that the issue of Moon's parents played a big part in Moon's life. Moon was embarrassed and angry about both parents' addiction to heroin. Though he covered it well, Moon could get very emotional. Later, when he became a big drug dealer, the word was that when Moon got drunk, he started crying. When he got mad, he started shooting.

That night made everything clearer for Ronnie. He was already on track to go to a good high school and on to college. But he vowed that night to never fall prey to a life of crime. As time passed, he had to do everything he could to keep that vow, but his determination was solidified that night.

Nearly three years later, Ronnie's grandfather died. He hung on much longer than was expected, but the disease had left him a shriveled shell of himself.

Ronnie was fourteen years old and had been preparing for that day. By then, he had received his scholarship to Eastside Academy and was starting in their literary media program that fall. Knowing that he could not live with his mother, Ronnie had it set up to live with his sister Rose's boyfriend, Duane and his family. It would be awkward, but he needed to be somewhere, at least temporarily, until he found a permanent spot.

Those plans unraveled at Big Rod's funereal. Rose came to him at the repast and said that Duane's mother had changed her mind. Apparently, she had heard that Ronnie was up late at night studying a lot and she did not want him using up her electricity like that.

Ronnie was floored and did not know what to do. When Rose asked him that very question, he just shrugged his shoulders and walked away. He thought about going over to Duane's house and chat with the mother, but then thought the better of it. "No need for me to go live where I am not wanted," he reflected to himself.

Ronnie went through his options. He had cousins throughout John Holmes and Murray Dwellings. But he had tried hard not to lean on his family. Most were caught up deep in the street life and he did not want to get sucked into one of their battles.

He considered speaking to a couple of his teachers, but just did not know how to broach the subject. Plus, he was still very much a minor. If he went to the wrong adult, he could end up in the foster care system.

He could pay rent somewhere, because all of his business hustles were doing well. He still had the paper route, in which he then controlled the paper delivery for four different public housing communities. He had thirty-seven boys working for him. Only a few of them knew that Ronnie ran the business. Each thought he was the delivery boy who dropped off their papers to them and brought them their money. Some of the workers were as old as seventeen. They would be shocked to know that Ronnie was running the whole thing.

Ronnie also had enhanced his trash take out service. In John Holmes and Murray Dwellings, he worked out a deal with the company responsible for trash clean up and disposal whereby Ronnie and his crew would sweep and clean the areas the contractors did not like to touch. Places like around the dumpsters, cubby holes where the rats hung out, and so on.

Ronnie had money.

At fourteen, however, he could not sign a lease for his own place. He had only one person he could ask for help. He went to see Moon.

By then, Moon was well along the way with his plan to run the John Holmes drug trade. At sixteen, Moon was number two behind Franklin. Moon had dropped out of school the previous year. Having seen how Moon nurtured relations with several of his best runners, Franklin decided to approach the ambitious young man and offer him a deal. Franklin would train Moon to be his number two and give him nearly full reign on the street activity if Moon joined him. Moon agreed, knowing that this would be a short-time arrangement. He still was intent on being number one. Franklin's troops were mostly all loyal to Moon. It was just a matter of time.

As Moon and Ronnie began to get older, their peers began to get killed in the neighborhood drug wars. Five of the twenty-two players on the Jackson football team Moon had organized were now dead. No Neck was the most recent.

When Ronnie saw Moon, he began the conversation by offering condolences for No Neck.

"Sorry about No Neck, Moon."

"Yeah, he was a good man. He always had my back." Indeed, No Neck served as Moon's pseudo bodyguard. Interestingly, Ronnie's nemesis Wayne Robinson was now assuming that role.

Moon continued. "You ready for that fancy arts school, man?"

"Yep," replied Ronnie. "I am real excited about it."

"Well, I give you this, Dog. You stuck to your word. You still ain't gotten in the life."

"And I won't my brotha. I just want to go to college."

"I hear you. Sorry about you grandfather. Big Rod was a good man. Wish I had someone like that around me." Moon was getting that far away look in his eyes. Ronnie needed to bring him back.

"That's partly why I'm here, Moon. Rose's boyfriend has reneged on me. You know I can't go back with my mother, but I need a place to stay. Can you help me?"

"You wanna stay here in the Holmes?" Good question, Ronnie thought. Rose's boyfriend lived in the John Holmes projects, but his family was not involved in the street life. Ronnie knew that it would be hard to find many other families like that.

"Honestly, I would prefer living somewhere else. Close to Eastside. Right now I gotta go clear across town and take two bus transfers. Do you know anyone closer to Eastside I could go see?"

Moon put his right hand to his chin and his left hand on Ronnie's shoulder. "Tell you what, Dog, I'm going to give you an address and a Jewish guy's name. You tell him that I sent you. He will give you a place to stay."

He then smiled at Ronnie. "Plus, I need you otta here anyway. You still might try to steal my business." Then, for the first time in their lives, the two boys embraced. They hugged like old friends.

Ronnie smiled back. "I told you, man. I'm going to college. You're going to need some friends downtown one day."

Moon let out a strong laugh. "I will always need friends, but I already got friends downtown. I just gave you the address to one of 'em.'"

They said their goodbyes and parted ways.

For many, it is inconceivable that a fourteen-year-old and a sixteen-year-old would have the wherewithal and life experiences necessary to speak with each other like Moon and Ronnie did that night. But it happens every day among similarly situated boys in assorted cities across the United States. Many feel that the crisis among boys of color has reached epidemic proportions. Too many are dropping out of school. Too many are filling our prisons. Too many are being killed. By the time that Ronnie was twenty-five years old, only four of the twenty-two boys who played on the Jackson-Stewart football team were alive. Eighteen had been killed. Of the four who were living at that time, two were in prison. One was strung out on drugs. Ronnie was the only one who ever set foot on a college campus. The only one who "made it."

The day after talking with Moon, Ronnie took a bus to downtown Baltimore to the address Moon had given him. The location was in a seedy section of the downtown area, full of prostitutes, homeless folks, and junkies.

Ronnie knocked on the door, which was quickly answered by a short, balding Jewish gentleman with horn-rimmed glasses. He looked at Ronnie with a blank expression.

"Yes," he said.

"Afternoon, sir," Ronnie said. "I would like to rent a place from you. Moon gave me your address."

The man looked Ronnie up and down, rolled his eyes and said, "Ok. I know you are eighteen, right? One hundred dollars per week. No drugs. You got the money on you?"

Ronnie said, "Yes. Ok." and "Yes, I do," in response. He then pulled out a hundred dollar bill and gave it to the man.

The man snatched the bill and led Ronnie down a hall and up some stairs. This was a rooming house reconstructed from three separate Baltimore row houses. These properties were reconfigured into sixteen separate one-room apartments, complete with a roll away bed, cooking plate, sink with running water, and small refrigerator. Some of the rooms also had a toilet and tiny shower. Luckily, Ronnie got one of those.

Ronnie then caught the bus back to John Holmes, grabbed some essentials and slept in his new home that very night. It was not until two in the morning, after being awakened by people walking up and down the hall, that he realized that most of the inhabitants of the rooming house were prostitutes.

For the next two years, Ronnie lived in that makeshift, prostitute-laden rooming house.

In spite of it all, the honors and accolades kept coming in for Ronnie. He graduated from high school in the top ten academically of his class, was Class Vice President, and won a scholarship to Howard University in Washington, DC. He continued to write poetry and was awarded a supplementary college scholarship by a prominent writers' guild.

Eventually, Ronnie moved out of the rooming house and stayed with a middle-class schoolmate during his junior and senior years. While living in the rooming house, however, he developed a close, almost motherly relationship with Renee, a thirty something prostitute who lived on his floor down the hall. He found that he could talk freely with Renee, and she with him. Ronnie had never had a meaningful relationship with a woman prior to meeting Renee. She helped him understand the emotional and practical aspects of a woman's mind. Try as she might, she could never offer Ronnie a good reason why his mother treated him the way she did.

Ronnie also did very well in college. Frankly, he viewed college as easy. He had already grown up a long time ago. Showing up in class and writing essays was a breeze. Ronnie readily admits though that he was not ready for the world, even with his worldly life experiences. He possessed many insecurities, even after he graduated from college. In spite of his intellect and his accomplishments, he often felt totally inferior to his peer work colleagues. Similar to some experiences he had in college, Ronnie would quickly change the subject when friends started to talk about their childhood or families. After undergoing some counseling, Ronnie realized that even with his insecurities, he was not alone. He came to realize that everyone has insecurities, not just the kid from the projects. Today, when he walks into a room for a business meeting, he knows that he is not the only one in the room with hang ups. "Everybody has issues of some kind," he is fond of saying.

While at Eastside and at Howard, Ronnie would occasionally visit the old neighborhood. He would generally visit his mother and his sister for a brief period of time and then go to the John Holmes basketball court, the one for the big boys. He would play a few games, talk trash with the fellas, and head on back across town. He still had respect among his own peers. In fact, he was proud when the recreation center director, Joshua Young asked him to speak to some of the twelve- and thirteen-year-olds who Mr. Young thought had the potential to go to college. Ronnie now had a reputation as the kid who made it from the neighborhood.

Moon made it to number one. He ruled John Holmes and then later Murray Dwellings. While Ronnie was finishing up at Howard, Moon was being labeled as one of the two or three most notorious drug dealers in Baltimore. Some nights, Ronnie would finish his homework, turn on the TV and hear reports about the new crack epidemic in the city and the underground operation of drug kingpin Moon Miller. The stations would then show the same file footage of Moon adorned in gold chains with silk suits at a local hip hop concert or a Vegas fight. Moon had only been arrested for a couple of misdemeanors, but it was universally known that he had a happy trigger finger.

Not surprisingly, Moon took over Franklin's John Holmes operation when Franklin was found in a trash bag near a John Holmes trash dumpster with three bullet holes in the back of his head. To this day the crime remains unsolved.

As Ronnie watched these periodic news clips, he often wondered why Moon could not have made it in school like him, especially since Moon was smarter than Ronnie. Ronnie came to the conclusion that no one celebrated Moon's smarts or his potential. Not his teachers, family, or friends. Ronnie also strongly believes that some people cannot overcome who their parents are. In contrast, Ronnie learned not to associate with his own family, especially his mother.

Not long after Ronnie graduated from college, Moon was finally caught. Typical story. Someone snitched. Then the prosecutors pieced together enough charges that added up to a lot of time. Moon did not get a murder beef, but he was convicted of selling crack and possessing a lot of weapons. After they did the math, he got forty-four years to life.

Before he was busted, Moon stepped up for his top Dog one more time. Just prior to his college graduation, Ronnie went back to the hood to visit his mother and play ball on the neighborhood court. As usual the games were intense, with a lot of trash talking. Some of the old crew was playing along with Ronnie. Fate being what it was, Ronnie was on a team opposite his old adversary, Wayne Robinson. When the game started, Wayne immediately declared that he was going to guard Ronnie. Despite the pushing, shoving, and obvious fouling, Ronnie was "lighting Wayne up." Ronnie was a much better basketball player and he kept hitting shot after shot over Wayne.

By now, Wayne had a reputation as a big enforcer type. He was Moon's muscle. He did not take kindly to the college kid he hated embarrassing him in front of the fellas. To his credit, Ronnie did not talk trash. The boys on the sidelines, however, were riding Wayne hard. After Ronnie called a foul on Wayne for blatantly striking his arm while he was shooting, Wayne yelled, "That wasn't a foul. You ain't getting the ball, college boy."

"C'mon, man," Ronnie said. "It was obviously a foul. I got ball."

That was the response Wayne was waiting for. "Take it then, punk!"

The whole court got quiet. Even the little kids playing on the other court stopped playing. All eyes were fixated on Ronnie and Wayne.

Ronnie said, "Look, Wayne. It's not worth all of that. Give me the ball or we should just stop playing. Now, give me the ball!"

Hearing Ronnie raise his voice, Wayne walked to the sideline, reached into his duffel bag and pulled out a glock. He then cocked the gun and marched straight to Ronnie.

"I said take it, punk!"

Ronnie had lived long enough in the hood to know that no matter what happens, you have to go out like a man. He could not show fear. Upon seeing the gun, his first thought was, "Damn, I'm not going to graduate from college."

As Wayne approached him, with gun cocked, Ronnie softly said, "No matter what you do, Wayne, it was a foul. Everybody knows it. You want to take it to that level, go ahead. I'm not going to run."

Just then, a car horn sounded from across the street. It kept blowing and blowing. Looking in the direction of the horn, everyone saw Moon getting out of his gold Mercedes and walk toward the court. He had on brown tailored slacks, with a cream collared shirt. The shirt had several top buttons unbuttoned so as to showcase his three thick gold chains.

Moon was walking slowly and deliberately toward the court. Everyone had seen that look before. Moon meant business.

Wayne saw the look too. He nervously blinked his eyes and the hand carrying the gun began to shake a little. Seeing that, Ronnie was fearful that the gun would go off on a fluke, killing him anyway.

A path cleared for Moon as he entered the playing area. No one said a word.

Moon kept his eyes directly on Wayne. He had not looked anywhere else since leaving his car.

When Moon got within four feet of Wayne, Wayne lowered the gun and acted like he wanted to say something. Moon, continuing to walk toward Wayne at the same pace, finally stopped right in front of him, raised his right hand and slapped him hard against the left side of his face. Real hard. The sound of the slap was so loud that everyone audibly gasped.

The gun fell to the ground, but fortunately did not discharge. "Take your butt home," Moon said to Wayne.

Wayne strolled quickly to his car, looking like a kid whose mama caught him doing something wrong and then embarrassed him in front of his friends.

The crowd was still silent.

Moon then turned around, looked at Ronnie, and then, as if nothing else had happened said, "There's my top Dog! What's up, college graduate?"

Everyone breathed a sigh of relief.

Ronnie hugged Moon for the second and probably last time in his life, saying, "Hey, Moon. It's good to see you, man. Really good."

Everyone was smiling and then, oddly, some started clapping. Ronnie and Moon walked arm in arm back toward Moon's gold Benz.

Standing by the car, Moon was brief. "Let's not talk about Wayne. I am just glad to see you. I am really proud of you, Ronnie. You have made us all proud."

"Moon, I couldn't have done it without you, man. You have always been there for me."

"And always will, my brotha. Look, the heat is on me strong. I am glad that I got to see you graduate. You keep making us proud."

"Thanks, Moon. Hey, man, do you need anything?"

Moon smiled and said, "Just don't forget me, alright?" With that, Moon jumped in his gold Mercedes and drove off.

After graduating from college, Ronnie worked for the city of Baltimore, did part time work at a local recreation center, then later for a real estate development firm. He still visits his mother periodically and remains healthy and happy.

Ms. Joan Tillman retired from Harriett Tubman after teaching English for twenty-five years to fifth and sixth graders.

Wayne was shot and killed about a year after the basketball court incident. Sugar Spoon never played football in high school or college. He dropped out of school when he turned sixteen, continuing to be one of Moon's key lieutenants. He was shot and killed a year before Ronnie graduated from college.

Moon is still in jail, incarcerated for life.

Zina

Zina was crying. And she could not stop. She kept crying and crying.

While crying, she was sitting on the edge of her new bed with her head in her hands. At one point, she laid down, but that small act reminded her that this was not her bed and she wished she was back home. So Zina cried harder.

Funny thing is that Zina is not a sad person by nature. Quite the contrary, she was always upbeat and kept a smile on her face. Those that knew Zina marveled at her consistent positive, cheery attitude, particularly because of some of the challenges she had experienced during her childhood.

But now, Zina was not cheery. She was not upbeat. She was scared. She was lonely and she was sad.

Zina's favorite teacher, Joy Albertson, had just dropped Zina off at Villanova University outside of Philadelphia, Pennsylvania. College was a dream come true for Zina. In many ways, it was an impossible dream. But here she was. As proud as she was to be in college, she just did not feel right. She missed her mother and also missed her brother and two sisters. They had all been through so much. Many families could not have survived the way they did. They stuck together, supported each other and she was in college. Alone.

"So this is how it feels?" Zina thought.

She stood up from the bed and walked to the window in her dorm room. This is a pretty campus, she thought. It has a lot of trees.

She watched students meander along the walking path in front of her dorm. A group of frat guys (obviously a jock frat!) were talking loudly and pushing each other back and forth as a basketball moved among them. Each of the five boys had on shirts with greek letters on them. Zina knew some greek, but did not understand the fraternity concept. "It must be an important club," Zina mused.

She then saw a couple of smart-looking kids with glasses on and books in their hands. They looked like they were arguing, or at least debating about something important.

Behind the smart kids was a couple of young lovers. They were holding hands and would stop to kiss every few steps. "Ugh!" Zina said out loud. "Americans are so 'public.' We would never do that in my country."

The thought of her country led Zina to burst out crying again. She looked at the door and hoped that her two new roommates would stay away for just a little while longer. They seemed nice enough. Debbie, an African American girl, was from Brooklyn, New York, while Sheema was of East Indian descent, but grew up in Connecticut.

Since Zina was an Afghani of Pashtun and Persian descent, she wondered if they put all the minorities in the same dorm room. She had been in the United States long enough to be conditioned to ask those kind of questions.

As soon as she met her new roommates, she began to cry. Joy Albertson had helped Zina bring her bags up from the car and was eager to get back on the road. Los Angeles, where Zina lived, was a long way from Philadelphia.

Debbie and Sheema introduced themselves to Zina and Joy, smiling the whole time. Joy said she had to get on the road and Zina started to cry.

While Joy and Zina were hugging their goodbyes, Debbie and Sheema said they were going to the student center and would catch up with Zina later.

After they left the room, Joy placed both of her hands on Zina's shoulders, looked her squarely in her eyes and standing four inches from her face said, "Zina, this is your time! You have been through too much and have too much to do to be weak. Your family, your friends and your school are proud of you. We all love you. I love you." At that point, Joy started to cry as well.

"Just be yourself, Zina. Just be Zina."

With that, Joy Albertson, Zina's favorite teacher, walked out of the door and left Zina alone in that room to cry all by herself.

Watching those other students almost brought Zina back from her sadness. But thinking about her country led her to think about her father, and, naturally her journey. From Afghanistan to Philadelphia. Thinking about her journey usually did not make her sad. It was what it was.

But, Zina, now nineteen, was becoming more acutely aware of the impact of not having a father around. She did not quite miss "him." She was only seven years old the last time she saw him. But she missed what he represented, what he meant to her mother. She missed the sense of security and support that fathers bring to a household. She missed the idea of not having a father to go to with problems. That, Zina thought, was not quite fair. Zina then found herself getting that guilty feeling she sometimes gets when she thinks of her father. "Stop!" she thought. "It's not your fault."

Plus, Joy was right. This was Zina's time. Zina believed in her destiny and believed in her purpose. She also believed in the value of an education, even when it made no sense for her to hold on to that belief. Indeed, as Zina pulled herself together in that Villanova dorm room, she began to think about her journey in more reflective terms. She felt her sadness being lifted from her. Zina started to think back to that time not so long ago, when she was not even allowed to attend school. After the Taliban took over, no girls were allowed to attend school. But that did not stop Zina. She always knew she would get her education; she always knew.

Many people can point to one moment in time when their life changed forever. Most remember the intimate details of the incident or chain of events that ultimately became fixed in their mind as uniquely noteworthy. Very few, however, can point to an event as dramatically life changing as what Zina experienced when the Taliban took control of Afghanistan in 1993. For Zina, the difference between "before the Taliban" (BT) and "after the Taliban" (AT) was as stark to her as before Christ's birth (BC) and after Christ's death (AD) was to the Christian world.

Afghanistan in the early nineties was a far different place than it is in 2011. Prior to 1993, Afghanistan was emerging as a fairly progressive Muslim nation. While maintaining its traditions, the country was also open to growing the roles of women in their culture. As a result, Afghanistan had more educated women than nearly every other nation with a large Muslim influence.

The Bashir family, of which Zina was the third oldest out of four children, reflected the best of the progressive pre-Taliban-controlled Afghanistan. Before the Taliban, Zina's mother, Karina, was a respected and well-educated professor of Persian Literature at a local university. Her father, Rahim, was an influential government worker, as was her grandfather.

The Bashir family had a nice life for many years. Rahim and Karina strongly believed in education and expected that each of their four children would be college educated. Those hopes and dreams were shattered when the Taliban overthrew the government in 1993, beginning a reign of terror that continues, in many ways, today.

When the Taliban took control of the country, everyday Afghani life was turned topsy turvy. The Taliban strongly believed that Muslims should live the way Muslims lived 1,400 years ago. This core belief led to the issuance of rules by the new government, which were designed to end the influences of the modern world in Afghanistan. There were a wide variety of banned activities included movies, television, movies music, dancing, kite flying, and possession of depictions of living things, whether drawings, paintings, or photographs, stuffed animals or dolls.

Zina felt the difference instantly. Her parents were forced to gather up all of her toys, including dolls and burn them. Zina vividly remembers seeing her favorite doll go up in flames.

It was, however, the Taliban's restrictions regarding women which were the most odious. Women could not work or go to school, nor could they wear clothing considered stimulating or attractive. All women had to wear burkas, a traditional dress covering the entire body except for a small screen to see out of. What's more, Taliban patrols roaming the streets would randomly beat women found to be violative of these and other restrictions on women. Countless women would be beaten or stoned for infractions as seemingly insignificant as having a hole in their burka which allowed the possibility of someone being able to see part of the woman's leg.

Shortly after seizing power, the Taliban issued an edict stating that women were not allowed to work or receive an education. Zina's mother Karina, lost her job at the university while Zina and her sisters had to drop out of school.

At the time the edict was issued, Zina was in the third grade and loved school. She did not understand why she had to stop going to school, but things got worse soon thereafter.

The Taliban organized roving militia patrols who periodically raided neighborhoods and homes to stamp out subversives or those who questioned their rule. During one of these random raids, the patrol threatened to kill the entire Bashir family when Zina, in her childhood innocence, mistakenly suggested to the raiders that there was a gun in the Bashir home. This was an emotionally jarring event for Zina, particularly when, a few weeks later, her father disappeared. Soon thereafter, so did her grandfather.

Though details are sketchy in her mind since she was only seven years old, Zina remembers her father always being present and then one day he was gone. Just like that.

In fact, many Afghani men who were in the government and who worked for the previous administration disappeared when the Taliban took control of the country. And these men were not sent to prison. Most were brutally killed.

In addition to her father and grandfather, the Taliban systematically killed every male member of Zina's extended family, except for her younger brother, Fareed.

To this day, Zina does not know what happened to her father. Nor does she know what happened to her grandfather, or other male family members. The lack of closure has been devastating to the family. More than anyone, however, Zina still harbors guilt over the gun statement during the Taliban raid of their family home. It is something she cannot seem to reconcile.

For years, while the family struggled to make ends meet, they each speculated privately as to the fate of the male leaders of their family. The speculation intensified as they heard the stories coming from fellow refugees about the Taliban death squads and the horrific methods they used on their victims.

This loss was further exacerbated by the reality of not having the primary male family members around. Afghanistan is one of the most male-dominated societies in the world. Even prior to the Taliban taking over, men were the clear and absolute leaders of their families according to Afghani culture and tradition. Men made the important family decisions and even professional women, as few as there were in the country, were conditioned to fall in line behind the family male leader.

When Zina's father and grandfather disappeared, her mother was initially somewhat ill- equipped to deal with the sudden change of reality for her family. She also missed her husband. Zina's parents really loved each other. They apparently had a solid marriage, by any standard and Rahim was secure enough with himself to support his wife's professional career in a country where such careers were rare.

For Karina, losing her husband in the way that she did, so suddenly and swiftly, without any forewarning or preparation, was just too much. She continued to tell her children that their father was probably being held in a camp somewhere and that he would be home one day. Years later, even while Zina was in high school in Los Angeles, the telephone would ring at her house and Karina would look at it wistfully. Zina and her sisters would knowingly look at each other, but would not say a word. They knew that their mother was hoping that this was finally the call that she had been waiting for informing her that her husband had escaped the Taliban and was on his way to the United States to be with his family.

But, in spite of it all, Karina was a remarkably resilient woman. Through intelligence and guile, she found ways to navigate around the new government in ways that would benefit her family. Though she was stripped of her job as a professor and was left to compete with other similarly situated women for menial jobs, she remained upbeat and positive. She began to sew and make hats, which Zina and Fareed would sell on the street so that the family would get some income. As the situation in the country went from bad to worse, however, Karina knew she could not stay in Afghanistan. The Taliban was out of control, she could not make a living and her children were always hungry. Walking the streets in her once stable neighborhood, Karina saw people she knew starving right before her eyes.

Karina decided to do what many others had done. She had to make sure that her family made it's way across the border to Pakistan. Pakistan had several refugee camps set up for Afghani citizens leaving their country to flee the Taliban rule. There, the family settled into a refugee camp where they would stay for two years. Karina would then move her family to the city of Quetta where they would live with relatives.

For Zina, the impact of all of these changes and family challenges did not hit her at the time as hard as it did her mother and older sister. She was too young. The biggest impact was her not being allowed to go to school. The Taliban banned girls from attending school, so the only family member going to school was her brother, Fareed. Zina and her two sisters had to stay home. Though she was young, it bothered Zina immensely that she could not go to school with her brother.

She was a bright, cheery, and precocious child, with an amazingly inquisitive mind. She had a craving for learning.

When her father was around, Zina recalls asking him questions about any and everything. The kind of "why is there air?" questions that bright four- and five-year-olds ask that lead to other questions, which lead to more questions. Her father would patiently answer all of Zina's questions, which, in turn, would encourage her curiosity.

The family upheaval took place just as Zina was really enjoying school. She looked forward to going to school everyday and longed to be able to read books like her parents.

While in the refugee camp, in the morning Zina used to watch her brother get out of the cot he slept on, get dressed, grab his school books, and go to school. As much as she loved Fareed—even today he is her best friend—she envied his being able to go to school.

It just did not make sense to her. And, it was not fair. During those years, Zina would pester her mother repeatedly about school. In the camp, while the men worked and the boys went to school, the women and girls did domestic cleaning, cooking, sewing, and so on.

Zina asked her mother every morning about school. Since her older sisters had been to school for a brief period before the Taliban takeover, they had some reading skills. Over time, Karina and her older daughters would sneak in opportunities to teach Zina how to read. However, this was a dangerous undertaking. If Karina was caught teaching Zina how to read, both could be killed.

Over time, Zina appreciated and understood the risks associated with her mother's private tutoring of her. But her desire to learn was insatiable. Once, when she and her mother were almost caught with an open book by one of the camp guards, Karina sat Zina down on her cot and told her she could not teach her anymore. The risks were too great, Karina told her young daughter. Zina just could not accept this reality. "I want to learn, too!" Zina insisted. It was at that moment that Karina realized that her spunky child was going to find a way to learn with or without Karina's help. She might as well be the one to teach her, Karina thought.

During those two years in a Pakistani refugee camp, Zina continued to fret over not being able to go to school. Though the family was living in Pakistan, the extremist influences of the Taliban were still evident, particularly as it related to views on the role of women. Near the camp, there was a school for girls, but it was located in a very unsafe area. Many girls were beaten or raped while going to and from school. Karina continued to quietly and discreetly teach Zina within the confines of the camp, where girls were not allowed to go to school. Because of her mother's consistent commitment to teach her, Zina learned how to read, write, and count.

Zina would read anything she got her hands on. She read her brother's books, her mother's books, old magazines that she found in the trash, anything. While her mother tried her best, the instruction that Zina received was spotty and unstructured. These sessions often occurred when everyone in the camp was sleep. Karina had to put the lamp on the floor to hide their activity.

As a result, Zina learned far more than any other girl of her age in the camp, but still was far behind boys of her age who benefited from daily structured schooling. Zina was just glad that she was getting some exposure to teaching and learning. Like most precocious children, the more she got, the more she wanted. Karina's best efforts could not satisfy the thirst for knowledge that existed in her daughter.

While Zina was getting used to her life in the camp, Karina was focused on one thing: getting her family to the United States. But first, Karina had to get her family out of the refugee camp. The camp was increasingly unsafe and Karina could not afford to get by on the sales from the items she sewed and had her children sell on the street.

Finding a way to get to the United States was going to take time, but she had to get her children out of that environment. Karina decided to reach out to relatives in Quetta, the capitol city in the Balochistan Province of Pakistan. Quetta was a far more progressive city than other cities in Pakistan. It had several well-known schools for girls and many institutions of higher learning. Plus, Karina liked Omar, her cousin Samira's husband. He was a good man and he reminded Karina of Rahim. Omar had a high position in the government and worked very hard for his family. Through intermediaries, Omar made it clear to Karina that she was welcome to bring her family to live with them in Quetta. Nearly two and a half years following the disappearance of her husband, Karina smiled to herself for the first time. She knew that she and her children would be living in a safe, clean environment; that her girls may have a chance to go to school; and that she could sleep for once with both eyes closed. She began to sob because for the first time in over two years, she was actually happy.

The basic unit of Islamic society is the family and Islamic law defines the obligations and legal rights of family members. The father is seen as financially responsible for his family and is obliged to cater to their well-being. Modern Muslim men, like Rahim eschewed the extremist teachings of the Taliban and had more of a partnership relationship with their wives. While still the unquestionable leader of their households, these men treated their women with the utmost respect and encouraged their daughters and other female family members to obtain as much education as possible. Omar was the epitome of the modern Muslim man.

Married to Karina's first cousin, Samira, Omar had strong views about the empowerment of women in the Muslim world. He and Samira had two children, a boy and a girl. Omar made certain that his daughter received the same educational opportunities as his son. He also spent time encouraging his daughter and talking with her about college and a professional career which was not the usual custom among Pakistani fathers.

After all that Karina and her children had been through, Omar was the perfect patriarch for the Bashir family. He welcomed the family with open arms. Although his household had more than doubled, he went out of his way to make each new house guest feel a part of the home. He was especially taken with Zina. Omar had never met a more inquisitive child in his life. She asked questions about everything and her thirst for knowledge was unmatched. After spending some time with Zina, Omar immediately thought that she needed to go to college. In spite of all that she has been through, he believed that Zina could have a very bright future. But first, she would have to get into school.

As progressive as Quetta is, it is still located in Pakistan. Over the past twenty years, Pakistan has not been able to make up its mind about what it wants to be. In some years, Pakistan acts like a progressive Muslim country trying to build an alliance with the west. In other years, the country seems sympathetic to extremist groups like the Taliban and Al Qaeda, often harboring terrorists wanted by the rest of the world.

The country is equally schizophrenic about its treatment of women. Legally women can attend school. But practically, it is harder to get girls in school than it should be.

It did not take Karina long to face these conflicting realities. Getting her girls enrolled in school became a virtually impossible task. To begin with, fathers had to endorse their daughters' education plans. The government did not accept the excuse that Zina's father had been killed or captured by the Taliban. Then, Karina learned that each of these schools for girls had enrollment caps and waiting lists. This was exacerbated by the influx of Afghani families into the city. The Pakistani government decided that it would respect the new Taliban regime and not allow Afghani girls to go to Pakistani public schools. Now, even Omar's status could not help. Weeks turned to months and soon, Karina was back to teaching Zina on her own. Omar would also help. But Karina's brief stay in Quetta underscored for her that this region of the world would never work for her and her daughters. It also made Karina more determined to move her family to the United States.

Because she was educated and intelligent, Karina became aware of all of the programs available for families like hers, those acutely impacted by the Taliban's atrocities. She began to research them all, trying to find the right one for which she could qualify.

In early 2000, Karina learned of a United Nations-sponsored program for displaced Afghani citizens through Global Missionaries. The program allowed widows and their remaining family members to apply for immigration to the United States. The program was highly competitive. It was understood and accepted that only the "right" families should have access to the opportunities found by living in America. Omar, Karina, and Samira spent hours learning about the program and preparing the family for the evaluation process.

After months and months of filling out forms, having family interviews and finding supportive allies, Karina and her children were finally accepted into the program. To Karina, this was the chance she needed to give her children the future they deserved and to break free from the horrors that plagued her homeland. As she prepared her family for the move, Karina continued to think about her husband and all that she had been through. This was a dream come true. The family was going to America. Zina was happy as well. Now thirteen years old, she was going to be able to go back to school. No longer would she have to sneak to read. She could sit in a classroom with other students, even girl students! She was so excited that she could hardly contain herself. Karina, Zina, the entire family circled the date on the calendar when they were scheduled to take their first plane ride and go to the United States. Omar, who had given so much support to the Bashir family, even prepared a little surprise party for the family the day before they were supposed to leave. He gave each family member a personal gift that would help them in America. He gave Zina a little pocket dictionary, written in English which remains one of her most treasured possessions.

After the party, they all watched Omar cross off the last date on the calendar. Everyone went to bed excited and happy. Little did they know that the date they had circled would become as important to Americans as it was to them, for vastly different reasons. The departure date for the Bashir family's trip to America was September 11, 2001.

Needless to say, Karina and her family were vastly unprepared for what awaited them at the airport. No one in the family had ever been on a plane. Or even seen a plane. Each person shared an equal amount of fear and excitement about their journey. Zina, by now fourteen years old and having been out of a classroom for six years, was totally focused on one thing. She could not wait to be in school. It would be a mammoth understatement to say that Zina was obsessed with learning. Her inquisitive nature, which was instantly recognized by anyone who met her, was only fueled by the unfortunate circumstances presented to her at such a young age. In recent months, both Omar and Karina had to fashion responses to Zina's growing curiosity about the politics and religious zealotry which led to her father's disappearance and the uprooting of the family. It made no sense that girls could not go to school or that women could only hold menial jobs. As Zina said to Omar one day, "My mother was a professor in a college. Doesn't it help a country to have educated people help others be educated?" Karina and Omar had to coordinate their responses to Zina, which led to several late-night discussions among them, often with Samira. The adults were very concerned about Zina asking the wrong person the wrong question, thereby inciting the ire of the government. As refreshingly naïve as Zina was, she was also razor sharp and direct.

Holding her dictionary at the airport, Zina was sitting at the gate marveling at the size of the plane she would be boarding. Her brother Fareed, now fifteen, was trying to look brave, but Zina knew that he was more scared than she was. Fareed kept asking about the mechanics and operation of the plane. He could not grasp how something so big and heavy would be able to get off the ground. Remember, he had been going to school pretty consistently for the last several years. But he was stuck on the notion of gravity. Zina thought it was funny. "I bet if I had been going to school the last six years," she surmised, "I would understand planes better than Fareed."

The family had been at the airport for a couple of hours when a lot of frenetic activity began to take place. Airport personnel were running all over the place. Some people who had boarded planes scheduled to take off were now coming off of their respective planes. Planes on the runway waiting to take off were coming back to their gates. Zina noticed that Karina was looking worried and scared. Karina stood in line to speak to the airport officials, but they would not give her any information.

Finally, Karina decided to call Omar on one of the few pay phones near the gate. Twenty people were in line to use the phone. By the time Karina was able to make her call, she had already gotten word that there had been a bombing in New York and Washington, DC. Although the details were sketchy, she had been told by others that Arab extremists were bombing America and that all flights would be canceled. Omar told Karina to stay calm and to remain at the airport until things could be sorted out.

Taking Omar's advice, Karina and her four children sat at the airport and waited. For over twenty hours. Eventually, a representative from Global Missionaries came to them to tell them that the program was temporarily suspended and that they should go back to their home. With hopes, dreams, and aspirations dashed, Karina assembled her family and their luggage and went back to her cousin's house.

Over the next several days, Omar was able to provide better clarity about the September 11 attacks on America. Like most Muslims, Omar detested Al Qaeda and saw all of this as a huge setback for Muslim–Christian relations. More personally, he wondered if Karina and her children would ever make it to America. The Global Missionaries program was in jeopardy and he knew of no other way to help Karina get to the United States. Within a couple of months, however, the Global Missionaries contact told Karina and Omar that the program would continue and that those families that were given approval before 9/11 would be allowed to enter the United States in January and February of 2002. The Bashir family was given a January 22nd date and the family endured an agonizing two months as they waited for that day to arrive. This time, there was no marking of the calendar, no parties, no gifts. Just the nervous energy that engulfed everyone. In fact, what was most noticeable was that no one even talked about the trip. It was clear that no one wanted to get their hopes up again only to see them destroyed. Silent, lonely expectation was the approach leading up to that January date.

On January 21, Karina gathered her family together for a prayer. Shy by nature, she rarely held family meetings or spoke at all in a direct way about their challenges over the years. But on that day, she wanted to assure her children that their future was in God's hands and this was all His will. Her words were noteworthy for their clarity and brevity. Zina went to sleep knowing that everything would be alright.

The trip went according to plan. The family boarded the plane on time and took in all aspects of the plush seats, loudspeaker system which allowed the pilot and flight attendants to talk to the passengers, and the food which was organized on plastic serving trays. It was pretty impressive.

After landing in JFK airport in New York, they all walked off the plane feeling like they were on another planet. The Bashir women were all wearing the traditional burkas that Afghani women wear. Fareed was also dressed in Arab attire. Everyone in the airport gawked at them, some even pointing. Karina could not believe what the women were wearing. American dresses showed women's legs and some women actually showed parts of their breasts! Allah be praised. Every American woman would be stoned to death by the Taliban patrols if they saw this.

A representative from Global Missionaries met the family and took them to a hotel where they gave each of them a set of American clothes and then, the next day, had them sit through a three-to-four-hour orientation session with other families new to America. Zina loved the clothes. She had never seen jeans or the type of sweater they gave her. But they were great. They were practical too, since it was January in New York and bitterly cold. They all would need to get used to the weather.

At orientation, however, they were told that they would be getting on another plane in the morning and that they would be living in Los Angeles, California. They were also told that Los Angeles had a very warm climate, unlike New York. Zina took this and the other information that was given as evenhandedly as possible. Her focus was on getting to her new home and going to school. She was told that she would be starting school in a couple of days. She just could not believe it. This was truly a dream come true.

When Zina and her brother walked into the Los Angeles middle school that first day, all of her heightened expectations were quickly mitigated. Her school was a challenged public school in an equally challenged neighborhood. Many poor Latino and African American students attended the school. Though Zina and her brother did not speak English, they knew that something was wrong with the school from their very first day. The atmosphere was unruly and undisciplined. Everyone was loud, both teachers and students. Zina wondered how any learning took place in this environment. Keep in mind that for Zina and her family, the United States has been a mythic place in their psyches. The United States was the land of opportunity and the home of the free. Zina would not have been surprised if the streets were paved in gold. As it related to education, it was assumed that every American schoolchild, including the girls, received a good education and that the teachers were the best in the world. Imagine the shock experienced by Zina and her siblings when they realized just how bad some American schools really are. Zina's older sisters went to a public high school and they came home that first day trying to understand the role of metal detectors and weapons in schools.

Though Zina had not been to school since the third grade and she did not speak a word of English, it was decided by the Los Angeles school officials that she should be in the ninth grade since she was fourteen years old. They placed her in class and told her to try to follow the best she could. There were no interpreters, no extra support. Nothing. To say that she was lost would be to put it mildly. For weeks, she sat in her various classes and tried to pick up bits and pieces of English. It was clear that her teachers did not care; they saw her as nothing more than an annoyance. None went out of their way to help her. In one class the students were told to write a journal. During one of the few times that she was engaged by a teacher, she was told to write her journal in her own language and try to find someone to translate for her. That was it. The only real help that she received was from a classmate, Hana, who was from Afghanistan and got to the states several months earlier because her family was also part of the Global Missionaries program. Zina's new friend would try to help Zina translate some of her lesson assignments from English to Farsi, their native language. The language barrier was only part of the problem. Since Zina had been out of school for six years, she was virtually lost in all substantive academic areas. Still, Zina could not believe the inattention paid to her and her classmates by most of her teachers. Hana told her that she actually overheard one teacher talking to another about not expecting much from "these kids." The teacher said, "We don't need to teach them higher vocabulary since they aren't going to learn it anyway."

After a month of U.S. schooling, Zina was frustrated beyond belief. She could not make friends, because she was different, an oddity who spoke a crazy language and, according to the thinking of some classmates, probably had relatives who participated in the 9/11 attacks. She also was not learning a thing. Zina had mythologized so much about American schools that she unrealistically had expected to be speaking the language and learning something new in class on a daily basis.

Zina's siblings were having similar experiences, but it did not affect them as deeply. Zina knew she was always different in that way. She hungered for an education. Longed for it. Obsessed over it. While her siblings were also frustrated, they were, in many ways, just happy to be in a new country away from the instability of the middle east. Zina was past all of that. Why be in the United States if she could not learn?

The family's transition was also being impacted by Karina's difficult adjustment. Even though she had fought, schemed, and maneuvered to get her family to America, she still was an Afghani woman through and through. She knew that this environment was best for her children, but she missed her country, her husband, and her friends. Karina was incredibly homesick. The issue with her husband's disappearance continued to bother her and always will. There was never any closure. She loved him so much and missed him each and every day. Coming to America brought those emotions to the forefront for Karina. Yes, she was in America, but she would never be American. She did not want to learn English. She did not want to assimilate. She was doing what was best for her children, but she was proud of her Afghani heritage. Plus, in her heart, until she hears otherwise, Karina believed that there was still a chance that the Taliban would be run out of the country; that her husband would call her and that her life would return to normal. She would forever wait for that day.

All of this left Zina to fend for herself. But how? The Global Missionaries contacts would periodically check in, but their main thrust was to get the families to the states and make sure that they were oriented and, in the case of the adults, employed. With respect to the Bashir family, Karina was placed in a very good job—she was working as a supervisor in a clothing manufacturing company in which nearly fifteen Afghani immigrants worked under her—and each of the children were in school. The Global Missionaries was not concerned about education quality issues.

But Zina was restless and she was determined. She was going to get her education one way or another. In early spring, Zina saw an advertisement on the back of a city bus about the Community College Prep Academy Charter School. In the ad, the children were all dressed in the same uniforms and they were smiling. Really smiling. At her school, none of the people smiled. Not students. Not teachers. Not staff. Zina kept seeing this ad and wanted to learn more about this school and how she could get into it. She talked to Hana about the charter school, first trying to understand what a charter school was and then how one gets to attend it. Zina discovered that these schools were also public schools with an open enrollment policy. Exhibiting her mother's stick-to-it-ness, Zina finagled her way to Community College Prep with Karina, Fareed, and a representative from the Global

Missionaries in tow. Soon, it was agreed that Zina and Fareed would enter Community in the summer, so long as each would commit to working above and beyond what was expected in order to catch up. It was also conveyed to them that both students would have to be tested to assess where they are academically, though it was clear before any testing that Zina would have to repeat the ninth grade and may need to placed back to the eighth grade.

As happy as Zina was with the outcome of her efforts to get to a new school, she was also stunned by the reality of her academic situation. She was so far behind. "Would she be playing catch up her whole life?" she thought.

That summer marked a new beginning for Zina. For the first time in her life, she was doing what she always wanted to do. She was a real student, in real classrooms with real teachers, who were helping her learn. But it was not easy. It was amazingly hard work. She had so much to learn, so much catching up to do. At least the approach at Community was nurturing and encouraging. Her test results showed she was far behind, but her mother's consistent tutoring had helped. School officials believed that she could make up what she had lost by not attending school if she followed an aggressive plan which included summer school from 9:00 until 1:00 p.m., with follow-up tutoring sessions from 2:00 until 5:00 p.m. During the school year, she would follow the same schedule as the other Community students: 7:30 a.m. until 5:00 p.m., with a study hall three times per week from 5:30 until 7:00 p.m. She would also have Saturday school during the school year from 9:00 until 1:00 p.m. She would repeat the ninth grade when classes started in the fall.

Importantly, Zina was fitting in well socially. Though reserved by nature, she began to feel comfortable around her fellow students. She developed a few friendships and was not treated like an outcast. Zina started to dress like American high-school girls with jeans and colorful blouses. She was fascinated by American television and the movies. And she had never seen anything like MTV. Soon, hip hop and pop music began to grow on her.

Zina also noticed the stark differences between her first American school and her new charter school. The biggest obvious difference was with the teachers. Many of Community's energetic teachers worked around the clock to make sure that their students learn. These teachers viewed the teaching profession as a calling, not a job. That approach was critical for students like Zina, who needed more time on task because they were so far behind.

When Zina started summer school, her teachers immediately supported her and pushed her to maximize on her potential. They employed creative ways to work around the language gap. Drawings and pictures were used to help accelerate instruction when the language barrier was in the way. Several of her teachers spent time with her after class and during the evening study hall to make sure she understood the day's lesson plan. The charter school teachers were young, energetic, and demanding.

The more Zina learned, the more she wanted to learn. Unfortunately, the more she learned, the more she also realized how much she had missed by not going to school. It was very frustrating for her. In time, she would pick up on the basics of math, English, and sentence structure. The pictures and drawings had helped immensely. Zina also learned how to study, how to read a passage and glean the important points from it. But the gaps remained. She was told by her teachers that her analytical skills were excellent, they just had not been used. So Zina continued to work harder and harder.

Socially, Zina was being accepted by her classmates and other students at Community. She developed a reputation as a hard worker, somewhat of a nerd. It was impressive to her classmates how quickly she was picking up the English language, which allowed her to participate more in class. Although Community was not really a school with a lot of cliques, Zina always felt as though she did not quite fit in. Her experience was so different from everyone else's, a reality she faced every day. There were so many instances where Zina had no frame of reference in passing conversation or in class. She did not "get" George Washington, Abraham Lincoln, the civil rights movement, baseball, Justin Timberlake, Tom Cruise, television programs, nothing in American folklore. American History and Government classes were completely new for her. She did appreciate how her teachers took the time to give her the appropriate context with each lesson plan, context that was obvious to everyone else.

Slowly, yet ever so surely, a fledgling, young, thinking adult was being hatched in the Community classrooms. Zina was developing her own opinions, with the benefit of life experiences and a growing knowledge of history to fortify her emerging beliefs. Her instinctive strong views about the treatment of women were growing stronger.

She was fascinated by the women's liberation and the civil rights movements in America. Though just fifteen, Zina was beginning to think of the world view about women's rights issues. More and more, she felt as though she had something to prove. Increasingly, she saw herself as an example of a girl from Afghanistan who can overcome the odds and get an education. Some nights, after studying late, Zina would stay awake and think about all of the girls in her country who were needlessly consigned to a life of ignorance and poverty. This is when she began to have her crying bouts. Sometimes when the pressure was intense, she needed to be alone so she could cry. Most of the time, these bouts lasted around ten minutes, but she found them to be releasing. She could always feel them coming on. The stress from her work habits would build and she would begin to feel out of sorts. Then she would think about all that she and her family had been through, the perennial sadness in her mother and the loss of her father. She would then find a quiet place where she could cry alone. Fiercely prideful and unwilling to burden anyone with her sadness, Zina, to this day, keeps these moments to herself.

Zina did exceedingly well during her ninth grade at Community. She had a 2.6 grade point average, with only one D, which was in math. She had worked hard and gained a lot of confidence. Zina had similar success during her tenth grade year, though the deficits still plagued her. Hard work remained the centerpiece of her personality and reputation.

As she was coming into her own, Zina began to believe that she was being prepared for a purpose bigger than herself. It was during this time that she met Joy Albertson, who would become her favorite teacher and most trusted friend. Joy was an Arizona native who had graduated from Arizona State University before getting a graduate degree at Harvard. She had a missionary spirit. After spending a year teaching in Kenya, on the continent of Africa, Joy joined Teach for America and eventually joined the Community staff.

Zina met Joy while taking the Psychology class that Joy taught to Community juniors. Prior to taking psychology, Zina had never really thought about the brain or how it worked. After a couple of weeks in Joy's class, she liked what she was hearing from her new teacher, but did not quite understand it. True to the form that she had from the time she was young, Zina went to Joy after class one day and asked a lot of questions. After much back and forth, Joy resorted to the technique that had worked well for Zina in other classes. She drew pictures. In a methodical, descriptive manner, Joy drew the outline of the brain, using different colors for the various brain parts. She then explained the functions for each part and related how human behavior emanates therefrom. Zina was fascinated by all of this. She and Joy took to each other quickly. Joy became Zina's mentor and counselor.

Zina did well in Joy's class and did much better overall in her other classes. As she was about to enter her senior year, Zina was more focused than ever on her ultimate goal of going to college. Her grades were getting good enough for college, but Zina and her teachers knew that her challenge was her performance on standardized tests. It was on these tests where the gap in her learning experience was most evident. Zina's SAT scores were nowhere near where they needed to be for her to go to a good college. It worried her that she might not be able to make up for these deficits through hard work alone.

Zina and Joy talked about college every week. Joy knew Zina was smart enough, but also knew that colleges were placing more and more emphasis on test scores. Joy began to look at colleges that had special programs designed for young people who have overcome difficult odds and are ready for college, but whose test scores may not be as strong as what the college requires. Villanova University had such a program, which was tailored for minorities. Those accepted into the program would have to enter into an intensive remedial summer program at the school and then pass the final exams for each course at summer's end. The students would then start their freshmen year, but would be required to participate in ongoing tutoring classes throughout their freshman year. The students would have to maintain a 2.0 average. Following their freshman year, the program participants would have to attend summer school again and pass the finals at the end of the summer. By then, the start of their sophomore year, the tutoring sessions will continue, but they are more sporadically scheduled. Once the student successfully completes their sophomore year, the remediation period ends.

As Joy spelled out the program requirements to her, Zina could not help but think that she was destined to be a "remediation girl" or "special case" for her entire education life. Of course, she did not mind the work, but she was concerned about going to college with the NEEDS HELP sign plastered on her back. But Zina also knew that this may be her one chance to get into a good University and succeed. Zina applied for the program and was accepted.

On the day that Zina was accepted into college, she went home and gave her mother a tremendous hug. She was so happy that she could not contain herself. As pleasant as she was as a person, Zina was also very restrained. She just did not show her emotions. On this day, all emotional restraints were released. For the first time in her life, she cried in her mother's arms. Karina cried too. And they continued to hug a long time.

Finally, Karina cupped Zina's cheeks with her hands, looked in her eyes and said, "Your father would be so proud of you! He knew you were smart and destined to do great things. Now you go to that American college and do what you are here on this earth to do."

Zina looked at her mother and let the tears flow, totally unashamed.

Zina adjusted well to the summer college program and her room-mates, who have become her surrogate sisters. She graduated from college with a double major in Sociology and Women's Studies. She picked Sociology because she remains fascinated with how society works, how various societies interact, and why people do the things that they do. She admits that she is constantly trying to understand why things are the way they are. Zina is revered as a poster child for the Global Missionaries program. Zina plans on working on women's rights issues. She is committed to getting involved in women's issues in Afghanistan. Though she is always positive and upbeat, Zina still finds the need to be alone so she can cry.

Zina's brother, Fareed, is a student at a midwest college and an active member of a college fraternity. Her two sisters have attended college and have also adjusted well to life in the United States. Zina remains in contact with both Joy Albertson and Omar, who are equally proud of what she has accomplished. Karina still works everyday, but has not learned how to speak English. She still looks at the telephone wistfully every time it rings.

Daniel

For twenty-nine-year-old Daniel Big Eagle, this was the moment of truth. As he sat in the Black Cadillac Escalade that he stole several days ago, Daniel watched the lone county sheriff get out of his cruiser and walk toward Daniel's vehicle. Being on desolate Interstate 29 around midnight, sixty miles south of Sioux Falls, South Dakota, several random thoughts came to Daniel, even though he was high out of his mind. He could press on the accelerator and speed away, which would result in the high-speed chase for which he had been preparing; he could ram the police cruiser; or he could relent, allow the deputy sheriff to arrest him and get ready for his life in prison. While none of those options seemed particularly appealing, Daniel seriously contemplated all three as the officer got within ten feet of the Escalade.

Daniel's thoughts were interrupted by the panicked whining of Sarah Three Feathers, who was sitting in the passenger seat of the Escalade. Sarah was not really a friend of Daniel's, more of a get high buddy. Over the previous six days, Daniel had been moving from one druggie friend's place to another, literally on the lam from the police. On day two of his fugitive status, he was with a cousin in a small town off of Interstate 90, when he saw his picture on TV, along with a photo of the Escalade. He was a wanted man. Though high as usual, Daniel knew he was facing a showdown with the police one way or another. He decided that he would continue to move around from place to place and let things play out as long as he could. He also kept the gas tank full. Daniel fully expected that he may have to run from the police.

On the night he was pulled over by the deputy sheriff, Daniel had been getting high with Sarah and a few other friends in Vermillion, South Dakota. They were all hanging out at George Fast Horse's place. George was notorious for having great marijuana and even better marijuana parties. For some reason though, on that night, George was running out of drugs. Daniel decided to drive to Sioux Falls to get more drugs. Sarah said she would ride with him. The two were not necessarily close, but Sarah thought Daniel was cool. Plus she knew that he really liked to get high and so did she. She figured once they got the drugs, they also would get first dibs. Now, having seen the officer force them off the road, Sarah started to whine and cry incessantly. She kept telling Daniel that they could not afford to get arrested with the amount of the marijuana and meth amphetamines they had in the car. "If he arrests us, Daniel, we will get a minimum of ten years," she said over and over. In actuality, Sarah was right. South Dakota has one of the toughest drug possession laws in the country. If the two of them were arrested, they would not see the light of day for a long time.

Daniel made a snap decision. As the officer got close to the Escalade's driver's side window, Daniel looked over at the crying Sarah, shifted the car in reverse and floored the accelerator, burning rubber the whole time. He then sped around the momentarily stunned officer and headed up the highway toward Sioux Falls. Through his rear view mirror, he could see the officer unholster his revolver as he half stumbled, half ran back to his cruiser. "Yeah," Daniel thought, "They may kill me tonight. But, I am going to make them work for it." With that in mind, Daniel pushed the truck to a speed of over 120 miles per hour and soon could not see the cruiser in his mirror. Daniel knew, however, that it would not take long for the officer to get backup support. Vermillion was only a few miles to the south. Reinforcements, namely other white police officers, would be champing at the bit to capture the crazy Indian in the stolen Cadillac. Sarah, though still crying, started to throw drugs out of the car window. Upon seeing that, Daniel angrily grabbed what was left of the twenty cocaine-laced prerolled marijuana blunts on the Cadillac's console and placed them in the side compartment located on the driver's door. He then grabbed the fifth of gin from the backseat and took a swig. In the process, he had unwittingly slowed down the speed of the Escalade. Both he and Sarah were alerted to that fact when they heard police sirens coming up behind them. Now navigating one of the few curvy stretches of the South Dakota highway, Daniel counted four police cruisers heading his way about a mile behind him and gaining fast. Daniel took another swig, winked at Sarah and made a hard right hand turn into a cornfield. As Sarah screamed, Daniel laughed. "Come and get me, you bastards," he yelled. The chase was on.

It was not supposed to end this way for Daniel. It was never part of his destiny to be a statistic. Daniel had strong Lakota Sioux roots from both his mother and his father. His mother's great-great-grandfather was a tribal chief. Daniel's great-great-grandfather on his father's side was at Wounded Knee with Sitting Bull. Early in his young life, Daniel embraced the value of acquiring an education. Much of this was drilled into him by his mother, Mary. Mary, by all accounts, is a remarkable woman. A member of the Rosebud Sioux tribe and the Bad Wound family, Mary learned the value of an education from her grandfather, who insisted that his heirs be schooled in the western ways. Such views were a departure from many traditional Native American cultural purists who strongly believe that Indians should shun western civilization and teachings and instead, focus on preserving the tribal customs and mores nearly destroyed by oppressive whites. These purists gained significant support for their perspective when the U.S. government placed many Sioux in boarding schools as a means of "purging" them of their traditional cultural values and imbedding a more "civilized," western lifestyle on them. The boarding schools became notorious for their aggressive and insulting tactic of indoctrination, which included, among other things, the cutting of Indian hair, viewed as a sacrilege in traditional tribal circles.

Mary's grandfather, and some like him, adopted a more practical view of Indian tribal life in the United States. "Preserve your culture and customs," he would preach to his heirs. "But learn the western ways, as well. Our people would be wise to become educated in western schools and know all that the white man knows. That way, we can always win the battle of the mind."

True to her grandfather's teachings, Mary excelled in both tribal customs and American schools. Mary was attending the University of South Dakota in 1973 during Wounded Knee II, in which members of the American Indian Movement (AIM), long frustrated by years of racism inflicted on Lakota Indians, seized and occupied the town of Wounded Knee. The AIM controlled the town for seventy-one days while the U.S. Marshall Service and other law enforcement agencies cordoned off the town. Eventually, the AIM and the U.S. government negotiated an agreement which ended the occupation and later led to laws protecting the rights of Native Americans. An immediate result of the occupation, however, was the antiwestern education sentiment which gained momentum among assorted Indian tribes. Catching this fever, many of Mary's University of South Dakota Indian schoolmates dropped out of the university. Mary stayed. She stuck to her guns, followed her grandfather's teachings and graduated with a degree in biology. Later she obtained two master's degrees, in guidance counseling and social work.

While in college, Mary met and married Daniel's father, Sam Means. Sam also was part of the Rosebud Sioux tribe and came from a family with strong beliefs in traditional Indian culture. Unlike his wife, Sam did not have a rabid commitment to getting an education. But he was not hostile to it, either, as were other Native American tradition purists.

Quite simply, Sam met Mary, fell in love and was content to accept all of her, including her progressive views on schooling. Sam and Mary's first of four children, Daniel, was born in 1974, one year after Wounded Knee II. At his birth, Mary proudly proclaimed that baby Daniel would be a future tribal chief and that he would use his knowledge of his people's customs and his superior education to honor the legacy of forward-thinking Lakota ancestors like her grandfather. Daniel was expected to do great things from the moment he was born.

As Daniel meandered through that southern South Dakota corn-field, however, wildly zigzagging and trying to elude the police, he presented as the exact opposite of a tribal chief or a leader of his people. He looked awful. Unshaven and unkempt with baggy eyes, Daniel looked like the druggie he had become. He had been using regularly for nearly nine years, ever since he had dropped out of the University of South Dakota. All of the hope and promise placed in him was a distant memory. Daniel Big Eagle had hit rock bottom.

As is often the case, the unraveling of one's life is not the result of one incident. It usually comes from the accumulation of bad acts, bad decisions, and bad luck. While a young teen, however, Daniel was well on his way to becoming the man his parents wanted him to be. Daniel was always a good student, but Mary wanted him to be the best. When he was thirteen, she enrolled him in a highly competitive math and science camp at the University of North Dakota. The camp essentially served as a college preparatory summer camp for Native American students with potential. It was a great experience for Daniel, who met and established friendships with bright Indian students from North Dakota, Minnesota, Wyoming, South Dakota, Nebraska, and Montana.

Daniel also was deeply immersed in learning and understanding Lakota history and tradition. He benefited greatly from having both great-grandfathers in his life until high school. Both lived well into their nineties and Daniel would spend hours sitting with them and soaking in all of the knowledge they could impart. From them, as well as from his mother, Daniel came to understand and appreciate his

Native American and Lakota spirituality. Native American spirituality differs greatly from traditional western religion. Whereas western religion tends to be monotheistic, with ceremony serving as the servant of a particular theology or belief, for Native Americans, their whole culture and social structure is infused with a spirituality that cannot be separated from the rest of the community. To that end, ceremony plays a vital and central role in the spirituality of Native Americans. As theology scholars recognize, unlike the Euro Americans, Indian people do not choose which tribal religious traditions they will practice. Rather, each of them is born into a community and its particular ceremonial life. For the Lakota people, as Daniel learned from his great-grandfathers, ceremonies like the sun dance and the sweat lodge represent a renewal, both of the tribe and the people and also, of the earth. The Lakota believe strongly in destiny and in the oral tradition of passing history from the elders to their youth. Daniel was constantly reminded of his destiny as a future leader of his people by his mother and his great-grandfathers.

Daniel's great-grandfathers were particularly proud that Daniel eschewed the chemical vices and negative mindset that plagued Native American men for decades. It is common knowledge that alcohol and drug abuse among Indians far exceeds such usage in other communities. In elementary school, Daniel noticed that some of his friends were beginning to drink before and after class. By the time he entered high school, the drinking was supplemented by cocaine, heroin and, more universally meth amphetamines, commonly known as meth. In the Rosebud and other tribal Lakota communities, meth usage was becoming an epidemic. Similarly, suicide among Native American men also took place with increasing frequency. As Daniel grew older, he saw how badly Indian women were treated by many of the men. Even middle-school peers began beat on and rape some of the girls. All of these self-destructive tendencies reflected the inherent hopelessness and despair found on many Indian reservations.

In high school, Daniel would speak out against these tendencies. He would counsel his peers against alcohol and drug use and he would try to get them to better understand the laws of nature, destiny, and tradition as ordained by God. Soon, Daniel was forced to follow his own advice as his parents' marriage crumbled around him.

Daniel's father Sam was a laborer by profession. Like most Lakota people, Sam was nomadic by nature. It was hard for him to stay in one place. During his young life, Daniel and his brothers and sisters had lived on reservations in South Dakota, Minnesota, Wisconsin, Iowa, Nebraska and Colorado. Not surprisingly, Sam began to develop a drinking problem. A bad drinking problem. What's worse was that Sam, usually even tempered by nature, was a violent drunk. Most days, he would come home from work, get drunk and pass out. But on a few occasions, he would get drunk and start slapping Mary. Then he started hitting her with his fists. Each altercation seemed to get worse.

Since the abuse took place late at night, Daniel's younger brothers and sisters were sleep. But not Daniel. He was always wide awake, covering his head with a pillow, agonizing over why his father would beat his mother. It became too much to bear.

Soon after Daniel's great-grandfather on his mother's side died at age ninety-three, Mary and Sam separated. Daniel was fourteen. He immediately had to take on the role of father to his younger siblings. And though he took to it well, his parents' separation and eventual divorce affected him deeply. Daniel was especially affected by the way he saw his father treat his mother. That treatment mirrored what he saw in other Indian men. Having had the benefit of his great-grandfather's spiritual teachings, Daniel felt mortified by the self-destructive behavior of his people. More sensitive and spiritual than most, it was all hard for Daniel to reconcile, especially coming from his own father.

Daniel persevered, successfully completed high school, and enrolled in the University of South Dakota where he planned to study in the field of medical technology. It was in college that Daniel was introduced to meth and alcohol. It began innocently enough. Daniel first started to drink as a way of engaging his friends socially. Then came the marijuana. Next the meth. Then Daniel came to the realization that while high, he did not feel pain or have any problems. When he was high, he did not stress about his mother or his siblings. Nor did he obsess over why his father treated his mother the way he did. Drugs were the perfect escape.

Before long, Daniel was totally caught up in the drug world cesspool. He attended class his freshman and sophomore years and got by just because he was naturally bright. By the time he started his junior year, however, Daniel was a total druggie. He dropped out of school and, true to his tribe's nomadic roots, drifted from reservation to reservation in various states with no goal or life plan. He never had a job, except for selling drugs from time to time. He just existed to get high. Daniel lived this way for nine years.

During his travels, Daniel would periodically go home and visit his mother and siblings at Rosebud. Each visit broke his mother's heart. She would cry on sight and immediately pray her prayer of redemption. Mary's faith was deep. She had seen a lot and made tremendous strides in her life. Growing up, she had no running water, no electricity, no extravagances whatsoever. She did have the desire and focus to get her education and did just that, being the first in her family to go to college. From the time of his birth, she had high hopes for her eldest son. Though he had lost his way, she was convinced that he would turn his life around. So during these visits, Mary would remind Daniel how smart he was, how much of a natural leader he was, and how it was his destiny to do good work for the Lakota people. Daniel was stoned during most of her tirades, so he took them in stride, patiently waiting for her to finish so he could eat and then be on his way.

Intuitively, Daniel knew that his lifestyle was not right. He would dream about his great-grandfathers and their teachings. He would get emotional at the thought of his numerous friends who were lost to drugs, alcohol, suicide, or prison. Like most addicts, Daniel did not see himself as having a problem. He was just in a slump. He could stop whenever he wanted. At least that is what he told himself.

In life, years can pass quickly, while some moments seem to move in slow motion. For the six months prior to the chase, Daniel's life moved in slow motion. In spite of the drugs and the reckless behavior, something was gnawing at Daniel. That something was telling him to stop. Maybe it was his mother's constant pep talks. Maybe it was the memory of his great-grandfathers. Or maybe it was Daniel's inner spiritual voice of reason. Whatever it was, Daniel was feeling more and more restless about his life, more wracked by guilt about his actions. He knew he could be better. He knew he was better.

Still, Daniel was an addict. As he grappled with these inner feelings and began to envision turning his life around, he was generally in the midst of popping a pill, smoking a joint, or taking a drink. As a result, thoughts of reconciliation were fleeting. By then, Daniel was spending more and more time with lifelong friend, Joe Running Bear. Though Daniel had always been popular, he was, by nature, a loner. He had many acquaintances, but few really close friends. During his drug years, Joe became his closest friend.

Joe was also a Lakota, who grew up on the Pine Ridge Reservation. Joe had personality plus. Where Daniel could be reserved and somewhat analytical, Joe was in your face. He was the quintessential life of the party. The two bonded while they were in high school, playing many sports and chasing girls together. Joe was always wilder than Daniel, but he also went to great lengths to encourage Daniel about school and his future. In many ways, Joe would sound like Mary in the way he spoke to Daniel. "Man," he once said, "you don't realize how talented you are. All of us look to you for our future."

When Daniel went to college, Joe supported his friend by helping him move onto the University of South Dakota campus in Vermillion. By then, Joe was heavy into using drugs and even deeper into selling them. Joe tried to shield Daniel from that life somewhat, though they would occasionally smoke a joint together after Daniel settled in on campus.

Ironically, it was Daniel's college friends with whom he began his heavy drug usage, particularly his use of meth. When Daniel decided to drop out of school his junior year, Joe, like many other family members and friends, was disappointed. The two friends began to hang out more and more, but Joe continued to suggest to Daniel, even while they both were high, that he was destined for a different life.

For that reason, Joe always kept Daniel away from his increasingly gang-styled drug dealing. During Daniel's nine-year binge, as he wandered from reservation to reservation, Joe settled in the Minneapolis area, where he became a drug lord of sorts with one of the city's drug-selling gangs. Daniel knew about Joe's activities, but never participated in that aspect of drug life. Daniel might sell marijuana to a few friends, but he was never into the hardcore violent drug gang life.

Since Joe was in Minneapolis, Daniel made Minneapolis part of his traveling rotation. He liked spending time in the city and through Joe met Kimi Littlejohn. Kimi was a pretty, smart Lakota Sioux, who grew up in a privileged family in Minneapolis. Kimi's father had blended well in Minneapolis business circles, so the family was much better off than many.

Joe, who had been dating one of Kimi's friends, introduced Kimi to Daniel and the two began to hang out. Like Daniel, Kimi liked to get high. Before long, Daniel would indulge in drug binges with Kimi in the house her father bought for her. Sometimes those binges would last for days, sometimes weeks.

Several weeks before the police chase, Joe was gunned down in a bloody drug-related shoot-out in Minneapolis. Daniel was devastated. So was Kimi. The two of them became drug-induced zombies, alternatively crying over the loss of a friend and finding solace in each other's arms. Kimi owned a Black Cadillac Escalade. She had given Daniel a set of keys to the car. By then, Joe's death, coupled with all of the subconscious voices telling him to get off of his self-destructive merry go round, led Daniel to get more and more restless. One night, Kimi invited several friends over to her house to get high. Everyone passed out in and around the pit couch located in her basement. Daniel dreamed about his great-grandfathers that night. He cannot remember the specifics of the dream, but he woke up in a sweat during the middle of the night. Something was telling him to get out of that house. He took a shower, grabbed the keys to the Escalade and left. Kimi was passed out on the floor. Daniel's fugitive status began that night.

Presently, however, Daniel had to deal with the police and his get high buddy, Sarah, at the same time. Once he made the hard right turn into the cornfield, Daniel lit another marijuana blunt. Sarah was intent on throwing all of the drugs out of the car, while Daniel was determined to smoke them all before being caught or killed. Daniel whipped the car in a semicircle, eventually bringing it back on I-29, this time heading south toward Vermillion. The cloud of dust coming from the cornfields as a result of five speeding cars looked like a mini nuclear explosion mushroom. The dust provided Daniel with just the cover he needed to momentarily keep the officers disoriented.

Daniel headed south on I-29 for just a couple of miles before making another right onto a small country road. Sarah was now apoplectic. "I can't take this, Daniel," she shrieked. "I want out. I can't go to jail."

"Fine," Daniel replied calmly. "Get out."

With that, Daniel jammed on the brakes, reached over her to open the passenger door and gave her a shove on her left shoulder. "Leave," he said.

Sarah, with tears in her eyes, glared at Daniel and got out of the car. Daniel floored the gas pedal and saw one of the cruisers pull over where Sarah was standing. Sarah, a stout young woman with long, coal black hair, had her hands high in the air. Looking at the scene in his rear view mirror, he felt shame for bringing her into his drama. That feeling passed quickly. "At least," he thought, "she won't die tonight." Daniel sped on.

Usually, police car chases of fleeing suspects lasts for a few minutes, if not seconds. Rarely do such chases last more than fifteen minutes. That night, Daniel eluded the police, much of the time while in their sight, for nearly forty-five minutes. After Sarah got out of the car, the number of police chasing Daniel grew from four to eight to twelve to finally, fifteen squad cars. Since he was in a far superior vehicle and knew the terrain like the back of his hand, Daniel was able to easily avoid capture. He did jumps, went down back roads, traveled over farmers fields, and even skirted around a couple of police blockades. In fact, he could have kept the chase going longer, but reality began to set in; his subconscious was bringing him back to center.

As Daniel bypassed one of the blockades, he noticed that one of the police cars tried to ram the Escalade. He also saw several officers with their weapons drawn. "Was he really ready to die like this," he thought. Even in his drug-riddled state, logic and common sense started to impact Daniel. His death wish subsided. He thought about his mother. He thought about his siblings. He thought about his ancestors. He thought about his people. He thought about the education he could have had, but walked away from. Then, he thought about how he could get out of that situation alive.

Daniel was well aware of the tension existing between Indian youths and white policemen. Even if he was not killed, he was likely to be beaten, especially after embarrassing them with the night's playful chase. It occurred to Daniel that he needed to be caught in an area where other citizens were present. Multiple witnesses were always a deterrent to aberrant police behavior. He decided to head to the small town of Canton, South Dakota, off of state road 44, approximately twenty miles from Sioux Falls.

Daniel was unaware of the fact that the police were working hard to anticipate his every move. Because he had operated so erratically, it was hard for them to predict where he would go next or what he would do. They knew he would run out of gas sooner or later and they expected that he would begin to steer away from the main interstate highway and start to use smaller highways which led to small towns and villages. Using this logic, the state police set up barriers in several small towns within a thirty-mile radius of Sioux Falls, including Canton. Having been outfoxed by Daniel at other roadblocks, the state police decided to lay a set of spikes across the main roads leading into these small towns. Similar to the spikes used by rental car agencies at their car return entrances, all of the Escalade's tires would be immediately punctured and go flat as soon as the spikes were crossed. The police were tired of dealing with this crazy young Indian.

As he got within a couple of miles from Canton, Daniel realized how tired and worn out he was. He was still high, though all the cigarette blunts and alcohol were long gone. Being an experienced drunk, he could tell that he was about to pass out, but strangely, he suddenly became concerned about wrecking Kimi's car. Looking down the road, he saw police cars located on both sides of the street near the town's only traffic light. He also saw the spikes laid out across the street. Daniel kept looking around and felt relief when he saw a bunch of bystanders gathered in back of the police cars. Obviously, Canton was not used to police barricades in their town at 1:00 a.m.

Daniel slowed down his speed to twenty mph, then ten mph. He deliberately and dramatically wanted to show the police that it was his decision to end the chase. The machismo in him wanted something to hang onto.

Daniel then methodically drove over the spikes, allowing all four tires to be punctured. He then got out of the Escalade, raised his hands high in the air and assumed the position by sprawling his body on the hood of the car. In no time, the law enforcement officials had him in handcuffs and whisked him away to jail.

As the night's events unfolded, few involved expected Daniel to live. Not Sarah. Not the police. Not even Daniel. At some point in time during those forty-five minutes, however, something happened. The seed planted by his mother, his grandfathers, and Joe's death began to bear fruit during that midnight police chase. Not only did Daniel want to live. He wanted to do what he was called to do. The nine years of drifting were over. He was, indeed, a different man. To this day, he points to that night as the night he was changed forever.

But change is easier said than done. He was facing a variety of felony theft, drug, and eluding charges. And, he had a drug and alcohol habit he needed to kick. Once the prosecutor sorted everything out, Daniel was facing over twenty years in prison for his reckless behavior. Here, however, is where the hands of his ancestors intervened. Through inexplicably good fortune, luck or destiny fulfillment, an assortment of factors combined to keep Daniel from receiving a long-term prison sentence. Even today, it is hard to believe that all of those factors held together in the way that they did to Daniel's benefit.

The first critically important development involved Kimi and the Escalade. Although her father pushed her hard to press charges, Kimi decided not to do so. Since Kimi was the only listed owner on the car, she had the final say. She would not press charges. That development meant that the prosecutor had to drop all of the theft charges. A guilty finding on those charges would have led to longer jail time.

Another critical factor was that no drugs or alcohol were found in the car. Both Sarah and Daniel were clearly high and Daniel did receive a DUI charge. But Daniel's decision to run from the first officer and Sarah's insistence on throwing the drugs out of the window served them both well when charges were being considered. By the time Daniel surrendered, he had smoked the remaining marijuana blunts and thrown the empty alcohol bottles out of the window. The police could find no evidence of any drugs.

For her part, Sarah gathered her wits and stayed strong after being picked up by the police when Daniel told her to get out of the Escalade. While being transported to the police station, she confirmed Daniel's identity, but was pretty much closemouthed thereafter. She did not face any major charges or fines.

Finally, it was fortunate that Daniel decided against ramming any of the officer's vehicles. The prosecutor went to great lengths during his various interviews to find evidence of a possible assault by Daniel on the police. It just was not there. Consequently, Daniel avoided another string of possible charges that could have led to more jail time.

While all of this was going on, Daniel was being held without bail in the Minnehaha County jail in Sioux Falls. His case was transferred to that county and within forty-eight hours he was feeling the effects of drug and alcohol withdrawal. His mother, Mary came to the jail as soon as she saw the reports of his arrest on television. As usual, Mary was a rock. She stayed in a hotel near the jail and saw Daniel whenever it was allowed. As he was visibly going through his withdrawals, she would rub his forehead, beaming from ear to ear, thanking God for bringing her son back to her. She repeatedly told Daniel that he could now live up to his destiny by finishing college and helping his people. Mary was glad to see Daniel being forcibly weaned off of drugs.

As happy as Mary was about that process, Daniel was suffering. He realized that he had not spent two days in which he was not high in nine years. As the forty-eight hours turned to one week, two weeks, and more, Daniel experienced constant mood swings. He would curse the guards and fellow inmates, who just ignored his ranting. It finally occurred to Daniel that those in the system were used to the new folks coming in going through their period of adjustment. One guard said to him: "You will settle down soon enough Sonny boy. After a few years, you will be quiet as a mouse."

It was also during those first few weeks that Daniel admitted to himself that he was an addict. When the most intense withdrawal period subsided, Daniel immersed himself in books his mother brought him on addictions and addictive behavior. He also read incessantly about his Lakota ancestors and sacred tribal teachings. Slowly, he felt his spiritual strength return. It was just a start, but it was an important first step.

Within sixty days of his arrest, Daniel's lawyer had worked out a plea bargain which would allow Daniel to plead guilty to felony eluding and a DUI. He would serve ninety days and then be released on three years probation. He would also have to participate in a rigorous drug and alcohol treatment program. The plea would be taken by the judge on the eighty-seventh day following his arrest. Mary was ecstatic. Daniel was numbed by it all. He could not believe that he was getting out of jail as soon as he was.

On the day when the judge was to issue Daniel's sentence, Mary beseeched Daniel's lawyer to request that Daniel be released the next morning, which was Saturday, two days earlier than his scheduled Monday release. Ironically, that Saturday represented a holy day for Lakota Indians. Many were taking a pilgrimage to Bear Butte mountain in the Black Hills, located about thirty miles outside of Rapid City, South Dakota. The pilgrimage represented a reaffirmation of each Lakota's spirituality and connection with the earth and each other. Mary was insistent that Daniel go on the pilgrimage. The trip would "set him on the right path," she maintained.

Daniel's lawyer was hesitant to make the request of the judge. From the lawyer's point of view, Daniel was getting an unbelievable break with the sentence he was receiving. The lawyer was fearful of over-reaching in a way that may lead to rethinking by the judge.

Mary, however, would not let it go. Waiting outside of the court-room just before the court clerk called the case, she prevailed upon the lawyer to let her speak to the judge and make the request herself. "Young man," she said, "let me speak to this judge. I will make him understand how important it is for my son to enter his new life the right way." Mary had her arms crossed and her eyes made it clear that she was not going to take no for an answer. The lawyer relented. "As long as you know that by making this request, you are risking everything, go ahead," he said. "If it backfires, it is not my fault."

Judge Lawrence Hendrickson had served on the bench for nearly fifteen years. The judge was a tall, beefy, red-faced man of

Scandinavian descent. Universally known as tough but fair, Judge Hendrickson dispensed justice the same to everyone, irrespective of race, creed, or color. There was one thing that the judge insisted on, that he looked for. Honesty and contrition. If he gave a defendant a break during sentencing, sometimes he would press the defendant about his or her sincerity. He would regularly ask, "Can I trust you to live up to this deal?"

On some occasions, he would actually make the defendant walk to the bench, whereupon the judge would extend his hand and ask the defendant if he was prepared to shake on the deal, man to man. That handshake turned out to be a double-edged sword. For those who shook hands with Judge Hendrickson only to violate their probation or parole later, a maximum sentence was waiting for them. No exceptions. In Judge Hendrickson's world, he was providing criminals with their last chance to be honest law-abiding citizens. If they broke a deal with him, they deserved to be locked up forever.

Of course, Mary knew nothing about the judge or his proclivities when she asked Daniel's lawyer to let her speak in court. She was merely following her own path.

Soon after Daniel's lawyer acceded to Mary's wishes, the judge took the bench and Daniel's case was called. Daniel walked into the courtroom and smiled at the sight of his mother as he was led to stand next to his lawyer. As the prosecutor began to lay out the terms of the agreement, Judge Hendrickson began to shift in his seat. Once the prosecutor finished and before Daniel's lawyer could speak, the judge blurted out, "This is one heck of a deal, counselor. Does your client know how lucky he is after all of the havoc he has brought to our community?"

Daniel's lawyer began to nod his head and stammer at the same time. "Uhh, why, yes...of course, your honor. Mr. Big Eagle is well aware of that fact and sees this as a chance to get his life back on track."

The judge was not impressed. Still, it was clear that the deal made some sense, especially since Kimi would not press charges. All Judge Hendrickson said in response was, "I sure hope so!"

Though he thought better of it in the wake of the judge's question, Daniel's lawyer mustered up the courage to ask the following. "Your honor, if it pleases the court, would you allow the Defendant's mother the opportunity to speak with the Court concerning a special request?"

The judge looked shocked. "This is quite unusual, counselor. Can't you make the request?"

"I believe that it is important that you receive it from the mother, your honor."

"All right. If you insist, counselor. Ma'am, please step forward."

Daniel did not have any idea what was going on. He looked confused. Both the prosecutor and Daniel's lawyer sat down.

Mary walked to the center of the courtroom, nodded at the lawyers, and began to speak.

> Mr. Judge, my son is a good boy, who lost his way. Based on all that has happened, he could be getting more time in jail, but he has a path that he must follow. I recognized that he had a special path when he was born. The bad is now behind him. He is ready to move forward. Even though he is scheduled to be released on Monday, I am asking that you release him to me tomorrow morning. We Lakota have a pilgrimage to the Black Hills tomorrow. My son must go and walk with me and my other children to Bear Butte. He needs to be there so his reaffirmation and renewal is complete. Please let him go with us tomorrow.

Judge Hendrickson placed a forefinger to his cheek and was obviously weighing all that he had just heard. Mary did not break eye contact with him. It was as if they were the only two people in the courtroom.

After several seconds of silence, the judge waved his right hand as if he had made a decision. "Ok, ma'am. I am going to release your son to your custody tomorrow morning at eight am. You are instructed to bring him back to the jail by six pm on Sunday. At that time he will undergo a drug and alcohol test. If he is drug and alcohol free, he will be released for good and his probation will begin forthwith. But, ma'am, you need to know this. If he fails the drug test Sunday night, I will treat it like a probation violation. That frees me to give him more time in jail. Do you understand?"

"Yes, your honor, I understand. I will bring my son back to the jail by Sunday at six pm. He will be drug and alcohol free. I thank you, sir."

Judge Hendrickson then stood up and said, "Ma'am, would you please step forward so we can shake on our agreement?"

"I would be honored to shake hands with you, your honor."

Mary then seemingly waltzed to the front of the judge's bench, reached up, and grabbed his extended hand. The handshake lasted longer than most and both participants smiled warmly at each other during the ritual. Mary then turned around and walked out of the courtroom. During the whole time, she never once looked at Daniel. Daniel, the two attorneys, the court reporter, the courtroom clerk, and those sitting in the courtroom all looked like they had just witnessed a historic meeting between two world leaders.

At 8:00 a.m. the next morning, Mary pulled her van in front of the Minnehaha County Jail. She had three of her children in the van and was ecstatic about being able to pick up her oldest child. Daniel walked out of the jail beaming like a little boy about to go to an amusement park. Mary and Daniel's siblings all gathered around him for a long family hug.

In truth, Daniel was happy to be out of jail, but was nervous about the pilgrimage. Yes, his spirituality was strong, as was his belief system. But Daniel was still shaky. He was not sure about his sobriety and he felt a tremendous amount of guilt for all that he had done and for his lifestyle over the past nine years. Seeing his younger brother and sisters added to the guilt. During the end of his parents' troubled marriage, Daniel was, in effect, raising his younger siblings. Then, when he left for college and got caught up in the chemical addiction world, he literally dropped off of the planet as far as they were concerned. For that, Daniel felt an immense amount of shame.

As they neared Rapid City, Mary pulled over to get some gas. Daniel dutifully started to pump the gas, while Mary and Daniel's siblings went into the convenience store. As soon as they all walked away, a car pulled up adjacent to Mary's van and Daniel saw a familiar face behind the wheel. George Fast Horse! George had hosted the drug party Daniel attended the night of the police chase.

"Hey, dude," George yelled. "I didn't think I would see you for years. You must have beat the rap, huh? Good stuff, man."

"Hi, George. Actually, I am on probation, starting Monday, but the judge is letting my mom take me to Bear Butte."

"That's cool. Say, man, I've got some good stuff with me." George then reached into a backpack on the passenger seat of his car and pulled out a bag of marijuana. He had a huge smile on his face. "Man, with all that you have been through, have a freebie on me!"

Daniel could not believe it. Of all the gas stations to pull into, he had to be in one with a former drug-using friend. He felt himself begin to sweat. He knew his mother was risking a lot by asking the judge for the early release. Now he was really being tested. Looking at that marijuana in George's hand made Daniel fidget.

George picked up on Daniel's hesitancy. "Hey, man. I know you been cooped up for a while. Maybe you need to ease back into it. Tell you what. Forget the bag. Take a couple of rolled blunts for use later." George extended his hand, in which were three perfectly rolled marijuana cigarettes.

Daniel looked in the direction of the convenience store. His mom and siblings were still inside. He looked down the street and around the gas station parking lot. "It would be easy," he thought.

Now dripping wet with sweat, Daniel started to shake his head violently from side to side. "George, I am on a different path now. I just can't do it anymore."

George began to frown. "You stuck up now, man? You know how much this stuff is worth. I am giving it to you becuz you my boy!"

Though weak in the knees and on the verge of hyperventilating, Daniel remained strong. "My brother, I am on a different path. My old life is no longer part of my new life. I hope you find your path, too."

The two old druggie friends stared at each for a few seconds. George then saw what he had never seen in Daniel before. A different Daniel. Without saying a word, George shrugged his shoulders and drove off.

Daniel replaced the gas cap and leaned on the back of the van trying to pull himself together. Mary and the kids were walking toward the car. After ushering her younger children into the van, Mary gently, yet knowingly grabbed Daniel by his collar, kissed him on both cheeks and, with a twinkle in her eye, said, "My son, I think that you are ready for your pilgrimage." No longer sweating, Daniel smiled back at his mother.

Within a year of his pilgrimage to Bear Butte, Daniel had re-en-rolled into the University of South Dakota. Through much effort and determination, he was selected as a prestigious Udall scholar. For several semesters, Daniel made the Dean's list and graduated with a double major degree in American Indian Studies and Alcohol and Drug Studies. He is now enrolled in a graduate program and plans on pursuing his PhD. Ever committed to his spirituality and native customs, Daniel has been honored to train as a Sun Dancer during the spiritual Lakota Sun Dance, a time of renewal of the tribe, the people, and the earth. When his education is completed, Daniel plans to return to his Rosebud home where he will dedicate his life to counseling others in his community and leading by example.

Mary continues to support and praise her son for his fortitude and determination. She is proud that he is following his path.

Daniel has not spoken with Kimi since the night he stole her Escalade. He acknowledges that he owes her an apology and a thank you.

Daniel has not taken a drink of alcohol or any nonprescription drugs since the night of the police chase. He has been sober and drug-free for over six years.

Jamie

Twelve-year-old Jamie was at wit's end and did not know what to do. She had just finished her chores on the family farm and was gazing into the sky. "What a night!" Jamie thought. The sky was clear and the air was fresh. "The stars will definitely be out tonight," Jamie predicted, enjoying the diversion from the issue that had consumed her for weeks. Just then, Jamie's mother, Laura, opened the door to the farmhouse and yelled out to Jamie, who had been standing by the gate to the entrance of the pen where the pigs were located. A larger fenced in area amounting to approximately an acre contained the cows, goats, sheep, and donkey. Another smaller fenced in area contained the goats, sheep, and cows used for 4H show events. Rabbits were also grown and nurtured on the Turner family livestock farm located near Zeaning, Iowa, near the middle of the state. Jamie helped her father maintain the farm and keep all of these animals properly fed, groomed, and cared for.

"You done, honey," Laura yelled.

"Just about mom. I might run to the Peacocks for a bit," Jamie replied, as she began to run down the hill away from her house.

Artie and Joan Peacock are the Turner's closest neighbors. Their property adjoins the Turner's nearly ten-acre land. Artie and Joan's three children are all grown and living with their own families. Sometimes, when Jamie needed her own quiet time, she would run to the Peacocks, roust them out of the house, and sit on their front porch just to talk. Jamie was the oldest of the Jake and Laura Turner's four children. Jamie's siblings were Marie, nine; Susie, five; and Lincoln, one. Jamie was the quintessential "oldest," helping to cook, clean, and parent along with doing her regular homework and farm chores. Both Laura and Jake understood Jamie's need to get away. It helped that the Turner house was situated high on a hill at the peak of their land. They could easily see the Peacocks' house from theirs.

"Ok, Jamie. Don't stay long. You gotta get up early for school to-morrow."

Jamie did not respond, but angrily thought to herself, "Duh, mom. I know I have to go to THAT school tomorrow. That's the problem! Why do I have to keep going to a school that I hate? One that's doing nothing for me."

To Jamie, the problem had reached the point of no return. In truth, she was not going to the Peacocks that night. While grooming some of the farm's goats, she had resolved to do something that night to make her mother understand that Crooked Creek High School was a terrible school. Talking did not help and Jamie's mind was a jumble of thoughts about what to do. Since she knew she could not think inside the house, she was going to run in the field on the farm, find a good spot, lay on the ground with her head facing the sky, and come up with a plan. Tonight. She just could not take it anymore.

The best way to describe Jamie Turner is to think "Scout" in the classic Gregory Peck movie "To Kill a Mockingbird," with long red-dish blond hair and glasses. Same determination. Same spunk. More smarts. Everyone who knows Jamie knows that she is a hard-working, independent free spirit. Wise beyond her years, she does not shy away from responsibility or challenges. And she is fair to a fault. In fact, her innate sense of fairness is part of the reason why she was so disap-pointed in her school. In her view, the school was not being fair to her or any of the other kids. Since Crooked Creek was the only school in a nearly twelve-mile radius, Jamie, like the other students, was trapped. They had no where else to go. "That's why they can treat us badly and not teach us," Jamie thought. "We are all trapped."

Crooked Creek Elementary and Crooked Creek High School services approximately 700 children in and around the Zeaning, Iowa area. Half of the kids are in the elementary school, which includes kindergarten through grade six. The high school, housed in a separate building, starts grade seven through twelve. The two school buildings are located next to each other right across the river from the Turner farm. It only takes Jamie ten minutes to get to school.

Jamie had been attending Crooked Creek Elementary since kinder-garten. At the time that she was contemplating what to do about her school, she was in the seventh grade, near the end of the school year. During her sixth grade year, Jamie began to think that her school was not that good and that not all of the teachers cared. For the most part, she kept those feelings to herself, but vowed to speak up if she began to feel the same way as she entered seventh grade at the Crooked Creek High School. It did not take long for things to indeed get worse once her seventh grade year started. Basically, the administrators and teachers at Crooked Creek let the older students do what they wanted. There was little, if any, discipline in the school and teachers walked around the building with bewildered looks and hopeless shrugs as students disrupted classes and acted like the hallways were playgrounds. Though not a prude, Jamie tired of hearing bad language, witnessing aggressive behavior, including a few fights and weathering occasional teasing by schoolmates. She also heard students boast, within earshot of some teachers, about the drug and alcohol parties they attended on the weekends. More disturbing was the virtual lack of response to these problems by the adults in the school. From Jamie's vantage point, the kids ran the school and as a result, no one was learning.

As a student, Jamie was considered bright. Her report card reflected as much because she regularly received nearly all A's. To Jamie, how-ever, that was a problem. She was getting grades that she knew she did not deserve. And it bothered her.

Jamie knew that she was receiving good grades because she was quiet, cooperative, on time, and participated cogently when called upon in class. Not because she knew the material.

Early in the school year, Jamie sat down with her mother and shared her concerns. Laura also suspected that something was wrong at Crooked Creek, but, frankly, she did not have the time or energy to devote to fixing the problem. Laura and Jake have a great marriage, run a stable livestock farm, go to church regularly, and are raising four young kids. Jake believes he is paying taxes for his kids to be educated and Laura has her hands full with Jamie's siblings. Before Lincoln was born, Laura would go to Crooked Creek from time to time to complain about one matter or another. But as Jamie entered the sixth and seventh grades, Laura was just too busy to follow behind Jamie's teachers. Plus, Jamie was always getting A's and a few B's. Everything seemed alright.

When Jamie sat her mother down that day, she did not bite her tongue.

"Mom, you can't trust those folks! No one is learning at my school. I am not learning. You have to do something. I am afraid that I will fall too far behind to catch up when I am in high school. I will never be able to get into veterinarian school with a bad foundation."

Suffice it to say that Jamie's experience around and love for animals made her desire to become a veterinarian a natural. She was determined to go to veterinarian school. Jamie knew the anatomy of the animals on the family farm better than any of the other Turners, including her father. The family regularly slaughtered some of the cows and pigs for their own food and Jamie often took charge of that chore. She also would skin eight to ten rabbits every Friday and sell them to neighbors for extra money. Jamie was smart enough to realize, however, that such knowledge alone would not get her into vet school. She had to have book knowledge.

"I don't disagree with you, Jamie," Laura said. "I will go talk with your principal and your teachers. But, what other options do we have? Crooked Creek is the only school around here for miles. We really don't have any other choices."

"There has got to be something you can do, mom," Jamie insisted. "How can you let your child go to a school that is not teaching her?"

That one stung. Laura merely nodded and promised she would go talk to the folks at Crooked Creek.

For the next several months, Laura, being true to her word, regularly visited with and spoke with Jamie's teachers and monitored the activities taking place at the school. At first, Laura was somewhat mollified by the assurances relayed to her by the principal. Over time, however, as she paid closer attention, it was clear that something was not quite right with the academic instruction that Jamie was receiving. For instance, even though Jamie always received A's in English, her written sentences were poor. She also had a habit of adding an "e" at the end of certain words. Increasingly, it became apparent that Jamie was having a harder time grasping what she would read. Laura tested this by having them both read something and then discuss it. Clearly, Jamie could read the words, but could not explain what was going on in the passage. Additionally, Laura noticed that Jamie had a difficult time sounding out many vowels, particularly "u." Try as she might, Jamie could not seem to read words with a strong "u" sound in them.

When Laura raised these concerns to Jamie's teachers, they said she was overreacting. "Jamie's grades say it all, Mrs. Turner," one teacher said. "There really isn't any need for you to worry about Jamie."

As it related to the discipline problems, Crooked Creek's principal said that school officials had limited power to discipline the students. He indicated that if they were too hard on the students, the parents would complain. In short, he rationalized, their hands were tied.

Neither Laura nor Jamie could accept that explanation. Jamie was particularly incensed when a couple of her classmates began to engage in long French kisses in the hallway in between classes. In front of the teachers. Other than gentle urgings to hurry on to class, the teachers did not try to stop the students from what they were doing. Again, when Laura mentioned this incident to the principal, he made light of it, emphasizing the fact that no one was getting hurt by such activity.

Soon, Jamie began to feel like a pariah. Her classmates knew that she was pushing her mother to be more involved in the school and some of the main troublemakers in her class started to give her a hard time. Whenever Jamie would speak in class or respond to a teacher's question, some would snicker, taunt, and sneer at her. Even some of Jamie's closest friends tried to get her to "just accept things the way they are." Though she stayed close to her friends, Jamie came to accept the fact that many of them just did not care about their education the way that she does. Jamie honestly began to question whether she fit in with her school peers. Never a social butterfly, Jamie began to feel increasingly removed from the other students at Crooked Creek.

In truth, Jamie had always been a bit of a loner. More introspective than most kids of her age, she always felt the need to have chunks of time to herself. Living a rural life contributed some to Jamie's solitary leanings. Once the dominant lifestyle of our nation, rural living has been firmly supplanted by the urbanization of America. Jamie knew that living on a farm was different than most American kids existence. Though the United States began largely as a rural country, with most people living on farms or in small towns or villages, today most people live in or near urban areas. It is extremely rare to see single-family farms similar to the Turner family farm. Indeed, how many twelve-year-olds does one know in today's urbanized America who regularly slaughters pigs and skins rabbits. Jamie remembered when American Idol's Carrie Underwood was viewed as a unique commodity for singing to pigs on her family farm in Oklahoma. Slowly, she has come to understand that her loner tendencies and independent spirit represent a core centerpiece of the American culture. Interestingly, while Jamie is fine with who she is and where she lives, she grew increasingly frustrated with the go along to get along attitude of many of her schoolmates. She felt that many of them had huge identity problems.

Another more personal event impacted on Jamie's psyche as a young child and, as a consequence, exacerbated her loner tendencies. The death of her older brother, Chad. Although only three at the time of Chad's death, Jamie misses his presence even today. Chad was born with a rare heart ailment, which required numerous doctors' visits and various treatments. None of that deterred Chad from being an active, fun-loving child. He and Jamie had a special relationship. He was the consummate big brother, constantly looking after Jamie, who was two years younger. Chad would bring Jamie food, toys, whatever she needed. He doted on her incessantly. One day, while riding his bicycle on the farm, Chad went into cardiac arrest and died. Young Jamie was devastated. When Laura told Jamie that Chad "rode his bicycle to heaven," Jamie started to beg her mother to get in the car and go find him. That began periodic country road sojourns in which Laura and her three-year-old would gaze throughout the neighboring countryside ostensibly looking for Chad. This went on for several months. Looking back, Laura realizes that she should have established better closure for Jamie on the issue of Chad's death. The end result, however, centers on Jamie's longstanding need to have a big brother, someone to rely on to look after her. As her younger siblings began to come and as Jamie's day-to-day farm responsibilities grew, she would often reflect on how much easier life would be if she had her big brother. That feeling has never left Jamie.

Several weeks passed and things did not change at Jamie's school. Laura had tried, but school officials refused to acknowledge any problem whatsoever. She told Jamie to finish out the year and they would work something out. To Jamie, her mother's suggestion was not good enough. Since she had been repeatedly told that there was no other school around, she knew that once the summer was over, she would be pushed back into Crooked Creek.

While staring at the stars that clear night, Jamie decided to press her mother about homeschooling. Jamie understood that her mother had her hands full with her younger siblings, but Jamie could help by working hard and having the curriculum and lesson plan laid out for her mother so it would be easier for her to administer. Thinking to herself, Jamie decided that she could not just talk with her mother about her idea. She needed to write about it. "That's what I'll do," Jamie thought. "I will write mom a letter. Then, she will know that I am serious." Whereupon, Jamie jumped up, ran to her house, bounded up the stairs to her bedroom, grabbed a pencil and paper and began writing.

Dear Mom,

Well, there is no other way for me to say this then. Will you home school me?!?! That would be sooo much better for me! I strongly dislike the high school. If you home schooled me I would be a lot smarter. I also would not have to hear what every body says or what they do at home (sometimes not so fun to hear about!) I don't like the enviroment I am in eather! It fells like the bus dumps me into a sene of an R rated movie sometimes. Trust me I try to ingore them but that doesn't make them go away! If you home schooled me I would still be around people! I mean I am always with people! I would never have to wast hours wating for the class to be quiet or wating for the bell to ring because that's all the teacher had for us to do. We could move right along with our day. I would also get the 1 on 1 addition that I need/deserve. I want to do good in school, I want to be rally smart, I want people to look up to me, and I want to follow my dreams! To go to collage, get a good education (I spelled that right, Yes!) And get a good job. I know it starts with my education NOW! And we would olny go 1 year at a time. So if it went down hill then we won't do it next year and we could get someone to put me back where I need to be! Yes, I am awar that we will gave stuff we will have to go around by that's ok! I want this sooo bad that I will find a way to get money to buy the equement needed. Please, please help me secude in this. I am willing to make sacrafices (If necesery)

Love,

Jamie xoxo

P.S. Please!

A cursory reading of Jamie's letter reveals obvious academic challenges. Challenges anyone can see. Anyone except, of course, Jamie's teachers and administrators at Crooked Creek High. Just prior to writing the letter to her mother, Jamie had been inducted into the National Honor Society by her school. Jamie had been pleading for help about for months and was tired of getting A's when she knew she did not know the subject matter. To her, the National Honor Society induction was the last straw. By nature, Jamie was full of grit, moxie, and determination. Whatever she got, she wanted to earn. But she could not learn on her own. She had to be taught. She was not being taught at Crooked Creek.

Actually, by speaking out, Jamie was exposing great myth. Jamie and many of her peers had been led to believe that bad schools are primarily an urban problem. Not so. In fact, the reality is that many of our historically good public schools are not quite as good as they once were. Jamie was insulted by the fact that her teachers and some of her school colleagues acted like they were in a good school, when they really were not. From Jamie's point of view, if most schools were like hers, the whole country was in trouble.

Jamie left the letter to her mom on Laura's nightstand before she caught the bus to school. Laura read the letter and cried. Laura then had a long talk with Jake about how they move forward. Jake, who was also a part-time bricklayer, had been supportive throughout Jamie's difficult school year. Working twelve-hour days, however, prevented him from being hands on in finding a solution. He did remind Laura of a church friend, George Peterson, who homeschooled his child. Laura decided to chat with George after next Sunday's church service. She also vowed to take the whole week to learn as much as possible about homeschooling.

Laura had much trepidation about homeschooling Jamie. Laura had graduated from high school and was a decent student, but she knew that Jamie needed more than what she could give. Laura also understood that her daughter would not hesitate to point out Laura's shortfalls, just as she had pointed out the deficiencies with the Crooked Creek teachers. Still, if the only choices were homeschooling and Crooked Creek, Laura would have to homeschool.

The following Sunday, Laura spoke at length with George Peterson about his homeschooling experience with his son. As George recounted the challenges and the effort he expended, Laura began to feel the tears come to her eyes. It was all too much for her. She could never make it work and raise the rest of her kids at the same time.

George, sensing the sadness, said to Laura, "Hey, Laura. You don't HAVE to home school. Have you heard of charter schools? One has opened in our area. My brother sends his child to it and has raved about it from day one!"

Laura had never heard of a charter school, but was intrigued to know that another educational option may be available for her daughter. "Can I talk to your brother?" she asked George.

"Of course. I will set it up."

Eventually, Laura met George's brother, Irvin, who told her about the Iowa Academy Public Charter School. Irvin could not say enough good things about the school. Like Laura, Irvin had grown dissatisfied with Crooked Creek. His daughter was not getting the support she needed and Irvin was afraid that she would drift toward the wrong crowd. Everything changed, Irvin recounted, when his daughter enrolled in the Iowa Academy. "The teachers actually care," Irvin said over and over.

Irvin introduced Laura to Jim White, the founder and principal at Iowa Academy. Tall, tanned with a beard and head of hair reminiscent of the Muppets Jim Henson, Mr. White was focused on one thing: the education of the children who have been entrusted to him. Laura spent the better part of ninety minutes with Mr. White and had never met anyone quite like him. His passion for kids was unmistakable and unshakeable. Mr. White showed Laura around the school, which was located only fifteen minutes from their farm. He then introduced her to several teachers and constantly talked about creating an education plan to meet each child's needs as opposed to forcing each kid to learn in the exact same manner. Laura had never heard talk like this. She was blown away.

Within days, Laura took Jamie to Iowa Academy for a visit. Although, this was the alternative school that she had been clamoring for, Jamie was extremely nervous. Seeing this, Laura smiled. For all of her feisty daughter's bravado, she was still just a little girl.

The folks at the Iowa Academy loved Jamie. They eagerly accepted her into the eighth grade for the upcoming fall semester. By then, it was the end of the school year. Mr. White suggested that Jamie attend summer school at the Iowa Academy. Laura had shown him the letter Jamie had written to her and had shared her observations about Jamie's reading and comprehension problems. Mr. White believed that they would be able to accurately access Jamie during the summer and, thus, have an education plan in place for her by the fall.

While nervous at first, Jamie quickly warmed to her new education environment. The teachers did really care and there were virtually no disciplinary problems. The other children in the school wanted to learn and class was actually fun. Halfway through the summer, Jamie came home from school one day and gave her mother a big hug.

"Thank you, mom! I am so happy at the Iowa Academy."

Laura beamed.

What neither of them knew at the time was that the hard work was just beginning. By summer's end, Mr. White and his team had completed their assessments and sat down with Laura and Jake to explain their findings. Jamie had a Learning Disorder (LD), as do fifteen million other American children, adolescents, and adults. Jamie's specific LD diagnosis was a Non Verbal Learning Disorder (NVLD). Children, like Jamie, with NVLD are typically good students with average to high IQ's that excel in auditory processing and retention skills, which means they learn better through hearing, rather than seeing. As these students progress through school, they develop trouble reading, have difficulty with problem solving, peer interaction, organizing their homework, and writing thoughtful essays. NVLD is totally treatable, but, sadly, is often misdiagnosed or not recognized at all. Proper assessment of NVLD is crucial to the students' success. Without it, they are sure to fail. As she listened to the presentation, Laura felt a sense of relief. Now, she had a explanation for why Jamie had challenges with reading comprehension and nonverbal expressions. More revelatory was the awkward socialization aspect of the diagnosis. Though Jamie clearly had legitimate complaints about the goings on in her school, recognition had to be given to her NVLD social deficits.

The presentation made by Mr. White and his team was thorough and professional in every respect. One of the teachers leading the discussion was Sandi Thompson, who had worked closely with Jamie during the summer. The two had developed a special teacher–student bond and Laura was pleased that Ms. Thompson was leading the discussion about her daughter. At the end of the meeting, Mr. White explained the education plan that they would put in place for Jamie, with Ms. Thompson leading the effort. They also set up a time for both Jake and Laura to be trained on how to effectively help Jamie with her homework. Even though it was a positive meeting in every respect, Jake and Laura felt drained by the experience.

On the way home, Jake said what Laura had been thinking halfway during the meeting.

"Do you realize how bad it would have been if you had started to home school Jamie? You would not have had the right knowledge or tools. It wouldn't have worked and it wouldn't even be your fault."

Laura was shaking her head from side to side.

"We were so lucky, Jake. Just think about all those people out there with smart children, who aren't learning because their schools aren't doing what they should be doing."

They rode in silence for the remainder of the drive back to the farm.

Jamie calls her eighth grade year at the Iowa Academy a perfect year. Working closely with Ms. Thompson, she advanced two grades in one year. Jake and Laura were satisfied beyond belief.

Unfortunately, Jamie's experience at the Iowa Academy would only last for one school year. The charter school ended in the eighth grade. The Iowa Academy had no high school in the area. Therefore, Jamie would have to go back to Crooked Creek for her remaining high-school years. Needless to say, the Turner family feared that all of Jamie's progress would be lost once she reentered Crooked Creek's doors.

Jamie was not going to let that happen. Having gained the confidence based on knowing her LD and still progressing two grades over the past school year, she was not going to be stopped now. Jamie and Ms. Thompson set up a tutoring plan, so that the teacher could supplement what Jamie does not get in school. Also, the fully comprised Team Turner—Jamie, Laura, Jake, Mr. White, and Ms. Thompson—have explored making use of virtual education models to ensure that Jamie receives the foundational courses to prepare her for college and veterinarian school. Jamie Turner will be just fine.

After Jamie had officially left the Iowa Academy, Mr. White asked her to help him. Just before the new school year, Mr. White gathered all of his teachers together for a retreat in Des Moines, Iowa, to reinforce the importance of a kids-centered approach to education. He insisted that his teachers remember why they were in the classroom. Mr. White has these retreats every year and usually invites a reasonably well-known educator or motivational speaker to help inspire and encourage his teachers.

For this particular gathering, Mr. White asked fourteen-year-old Jamie Turner to give the keynote address. Jamie wrote and delivered the following speech.

> Hello, my name is Jamie Turner. I am from Zeaning, Iowa. I want to tell you about my experience at Iowa Academy and how it has changed me. The Iowa Academy has made a huge impact on my life. The last school year was the best school year I have ever had. Iowa Academy has truly done miracles for me! At the beginning of the school year, I took placement tests. I then realized why I needed Iowa Academy. I was a year behind in Math and English! I thought that I would never get caught up. By the end of the school year, I was where I needed to be in both subjects! Because I went to Iowa Academy, my self confidence has gone up. I never thought I was capable of doing anything on my own. I just thought I would graduate like everybody

else. I had no goals for myself whatsoever. I started doing extra things to catch up to my grade level. For example, I did two to three math lessons a day. At the end of the school year, I reached my goal. I was at grade level. Now, I have many long term goals because I know now that anything is possible with hard work and the support of my teachers and family. I became very independent. I was responsible for all of my school work while I was home. Before I came to Iowa Academy, I would never rely on myself. I thought I needed my mom right there all the time to direct me. I discovered self reliance. It has also helped me academically. At my previous school, I was getting good grades, but I believe now I got them because I was quiet and listened during class. The grades I earned at Iowa academy were due to my hard work and perseverance. I believe those grades are a more accurate reflection of my abilities. When I went to Iowa academy, I never complained that I had to go. I was always excited to learn. Last year was the only time I have EVER received perfect attendance. While at Iowa Academy, I met two very good friends who love school as much as I do. Together we came up with a recycling program for the school. I will always keep in touch with them. I also made two other unique friends; my principle: Mr. Jim White and my teacher: Mrs. Sandi Thompson. They both have given me strength and encouragement that I will take with me throughout my life. Because of the fact that I was able to call or email Mrs. Thompson whenever I needed her allowed us to have a relationship that means the world to me, as a result I attained a job; babysitting for her three children. Unfortunately, Iowa Academy is not going to the ninth grade. So I am going back to my previous school. This time I am more prepared and ready. I am self reliant and motivated to learn. Overall, I can't say enough about Iowa Academy, the teachers and staff. It has been a great school for me. It definitely changed me. I loved going to Iowa Academy.

As Jamie finished her speech, the whole room erupted. Jamie felt proud, especially since she had written the speech on her own.

Later, when asked about the problems in our schools, Jamie expressed her sentiments in the manner to which she is accustomed. Practical. Blunt. To the point.

"As a kid, I shouldn't have to fight with my school to get a good education," she said. "All kids deserve that. If the adults don't get it right, many kids won't have a choice but to get into trouble. That's not good for anyone."

Jamie is progressing well at Crooked Creek, though Jamie and Laura feel they must constantly monitor the instruction Jamie receives from her teachers. Always a hard worker, Jamie maintains a 3.75 grade point average, scores well on standardized tests, and has earned a selection to the National Honor Society. Jamie has also begun to integrate better with her classmates and is on her school's tennis team. Team Turner remains in place and is making sure that Jamie gets all of the support that she needs.

Javier

Dr. Roger McDonald is an excellent surgeon. Yale-educated. Board-certified. On every "Top Ten Texas Physicians" list in the state.

As good as Dr. McDonald is, he was no match for Alberto Morales.

Dr. McDonald was on call to support his colleague, Dr. William C. E. Roberts, the treating physician for Alberto's eleven-year-old son, Javier. Javier was very sick. The boy needed multiple organ transplants, but his body was not waiting for donors. In awkward layman's terms, Javier's lungs were cannibalizing themselves and taking the boy's heart along with them.

Once extremely active, Javier was now confined to a wheelchair and could not walk five feet without feeling completely exhausted. Many, like Dr. McDonald believed Javier's days were numbered. But not Alberto Morales.

Alberto and his wife Fatima were in the El Paso General Hospital emergency room in El Paso, Texas, when Dr. McDonald came into the waiting area to talk with them about their son's condition. They had brought Javier back to the hospital two hours earlier following another one of his violent coughing episodes.

In order to stave off, or rather, slow down the multiple organ deterioration in the boy's body, Dr. Roberts and his team of cardiac and pulmonary physicians had prescribed an assortment of comprehensive medications for Javier. These doctors had only one objective in mind. To buy time. They knew that time was not a friend of Javier Morales. In fact, at a meeting of Javier's team of doctors that took place a few days before the emergency room visit, the team agreed that Javier's prospects were slim at best. Without the transplants, he would die. The chances of him getting the transplants were less than 10 percent.

The Javier Morales medical team, led by Dr. Roberts was doing all they could to buy the boy time.

As is often the case, however, multiple medication usage has its side effects. For Javier, popping twenty different highly toxic, somewhat incompatible pills three times a day, proved more than the boy could sometimes take.

Having been on the medication for three months now, there were days when Javier just could not take it. Usually, those were the days when he would have the violent coughing spells.

For some reason, the various medications would prompt a need to cough. Though it did not happen all the time, it occurred with more and more frequency over time. Most of the coughing spells would last for a few minutes, then they would subside. On a few occasions, however, the coughing would become violent and uncontrollable.

Javier could quickly tell when he was on the verge of a bad coughing spell. Within minutes of taking the twenty pills, he would feel a tickle in his throat. At first, he would try to get rid of it by clearing his throat, then make a few short coughs. If that did not work, if the tickle got intense, he would start to cough harder. He would then shake uncontrollably and the violent heaves would begin.

During these spells, it felt to Javier as if membranes were being ripped from his lungs. He could almost feel lung tissue being destroyed.

At these times, Javier's mother, Fatima, would try to make her son comfortable by placing a cold towel on his forehead, and force him to sip the warm water, as was suggested by his doctors. On the day they were briefed by Dr. McDonald, both Fatima and Alberto realized that the coughing episode experienced by their son that day was the worse one they had seen. They rushed to El Paso General as soon as they could.

Both parents were determined that their son was going to make it, especially Alberto. He refused to pay attention to the odds or the circumstances presented by his son's medical problems. Ever since Javier's condition was known, Alberto was the consistent voice of hope. On that, he never wavered. "Dios salvara a mi hijo." (God will save my son.), he would say. "Ya esta escrito." (It is already written.)

Dr. McDonald was now standing before them, however, with a message that suggested that there was no need for hope.

Well over six feet, two inches, with an authoritative booming voice, Dr. McDonald clearly looked like the reputation he had earned. He was one of the best at what he does and knew it. Problem was, he had no bedside manner. As good as he was as a physician, he would never be considered great because he did not know how to talk to his patients. His authoritative, clinical manner left them feeling informed but cold. They also felt intimidated. That image instantly came to mind to anyone watching the tall, distinguished white-haired doctor leaning over to speak with the five-foot, four-inch Alberto and four-foot, eleven-inch Fatima.

Standing in that waiting area listening to Dr. McDonald, both Alberto and Fatima were wishing that they were talking with Dr. Roberts instead. The Morales' really like Dr. Roberts. He was not as seasoned as Dr. McDonald, but just as respected. Born in Ohio, educated at Howard University in Washington, DC, the young African American doctor was considered a top-notch surgeon. He had performed several successful organ transplants. After Javier's condition was diagnosed, his parents were referred to Dr. Roberts, who practiced in Houston. That was three months earlier.

One of Dr. Roberts' strengths was his commitment to the team approach in solving patients' problems. As knowledgeable as he was, he genuinely believed that he could learn more from colleagues looking at an issue from a different perspective.

On Javier's case, Dr. Roberts included Dr. McDonald on his team and valued his opinion. Dr. Roberts regularly consulted with Dr. McDonald about Javier and his condition. Since Dr. McDonald practiced in El Paso near the Morales' home, it was agreed that he would be on the point for emergencies.

Watching Dr. McDonald begin to talk, Alberto knew that Dr. McDonald was bringing bad news. No matter what Dr. McDonald said to them, Alberto thought, "I am not giving up on my son."

Dr. McDonald looked at both of them directly. He was wearing reading glasses and peered over them as he looked at the Morales'. In his left hand, he was holding a clipboard that contained part of Javier's medical chart. When he began to speak he would alternatively look down at the chart then down at the Morales'.

Nurses and other hospital staff were also nearby. All of them were eavesdropping on the conversation between Dr. McDonald and the Morales'. Everyone working in the hospital knew Javier. Everyone knew his case.

Javier had spent two months at El Paso General, only to be discharged the previous month. He had become the most popular patient in the hospital. They all were pulling for the determined little boy and his spunky father who believed everything would be alright. Though it was never conveyed as such by the staff, few believed that the boy would live.

Dr. McDonald had ushered the Morales' several yards away from the emergency room waiting area, where he huddled with them near a restroom door. Since it was near midnight, the emergency room staff was dealing with the usual drama and trauma of the night. One gunshot, two stabbings, a couple of chest pain patients, four auto crash victims, and so on.

All of those matters seemed to be put on hold as staff grew quiet trying to hear what Dr. McDonald was saying to the Morales'.

"Mr. and Mrs. Morales," he began, "how many other children do you have?"

Upon hearing this question, Fatima, who was holding the family rosary beads, cocked her head to the side and had a quizzical expression on her face. She had no idea why he was asking such a question. Often, because she and her husband were from Mexico and her English was bad, she felt self-conscious about asking for clarification during conversations with Americans. She always felt as though she was missing some background information that everyone else readily knew and understood.

Alberto, on the other hand, felt he knew exactly where the doctor was headed. His face stiffened and his jaw grew tight. Since these mannerisms occurred rarely for Alberto, when seen by those around him, they stood out even more.

Alberto was standing with the aid of crutches. He had been dealing with his own health maladies which led to him having his right leg amputated the previous year. Sometimes, in the evening, he grew tired standing on his crutches, particularly since he stood on them most of the day while working as a construction site welder. His co-workers were amazed at how good he was at his job, even with the crutches.

Alberto leaned closer to the doctor.

"Why do you ask us this question, doctor?"

"Mr. Morales, I was just wondering how many children you had at home other than Javier. How many?"

Unlike Alberto, Fatima felt the need to be responsive.

"We have three other children, Mr. Doctor," she said. "Javier has an older brother, a younger sister and a younger brother."

"That is nice. Thank you, Mrs. Morales. The reason why I ask that question is because I think it is good that you have other children.

They need both of you. As much as I hate to tell you this, it is clear to me that Javier is not going to make it. In my opinion, the best thing for you folks to do is to go home and take care of your other children and let us make sure that Javier leaves us in a peaceful state."

Fatima finally understood the import and impact of the doctor's original question. She burst out in tears, crossed herself, and whispered the name of the virgin Mary.

Alberto reacted much differently.

He placed both crutches against the wall and stood as straight as he could on his one leg. All five feet, four inches of him.

He then looked up at the well-regarded doctor and said, "Sir, I do not want you to touch my son ever again."

Born in Ahumada, Mexico, a small village town sixty miles from the U.S. border, Alberto Morales always believed in God, family, hard work, and education. Although he only went as far as the seventh grade, he saw education as the key to a better life and a better world. While a boy, he had to leave school because he had to work. Everyone in the village worked. Even the children. If you did not work, you did not eat.

But Alberto wanted a better life for his children. As soon as his bride, Fatima told him that she was pregnant with their first son, Ernesto, Alberto began talking about moving to the United States. Fatima had little education herself, but generally followed her husband's lead on such matters. She was, however, nervous about living in the United States. Fatima liked the simple life.

Three years after Ernesto was born, Fatima gave birth to Javier. Two years later Maria. A year after Maria's birth, Daniel was born. After each birth, Alberto would proclaim that each of his children would go to an American college and have a better life. Fatima would patiently smile and wonder when the big move would actually take place.

In the meantime, Alberto had to work while planning for his move. He was becoming a master welder and had a work visa to work on jobs in the states, usually in Texas. He was making contacts and learning from co-workers who had immigrated to the states with their families. By the time Javier was eight, Alberto was ready to move his family to the United States.

Although Alberto had applied for U.S. citizenship and was waiting for that process to unfold, he still had a foreign resident work visa, which allowed him to live in the states.

To his children, moving to the states was a mixed blessing. Through-out their lives, they had heard their father talk glowingly about the educational opportunities in the United States. Each wanted to go to college and all like school. Javier especially liked science and was eager to learn more about science-related topics.

But there also existed a demonstrable reticence toward moving to the United States among the Morales' children. Even though some Americans assume that every foreigner is hankering to relocate to the states, many are comfortable in their country and view, with suspicion, day-to-day American life. Fatima harbored some of those feelings and the Morales' children were quite happy living in their quaint Mexican village.

Alberto was insistent, however, that his children had to be educated in the United States.

As plans were being made for the move, Alberto, as part of the requirement for a physical associated with his construction job, was diagnosed with cancer. Initially, the cancer was found in the right ankle area. Alberto had treatment in both the United States and Mexico, with the primary care coming from a hospital group located in Houston. Shortly after the diagnosis, the treating doctor told Alberto that his leg had to be amputated just above the ankle.

At the time, Alberto had just moved his family to the El Paso area. Since he would miss work for several weeks, he knew he could not afford to keep them in the states during his recuperation period. As a result, the family ended up spending the next eighteen months shuttling between El Paso and Ahumada.

This reality was especially troublesome for the Morales' children. They would end up going to school in the states for a few weeks and then go to school back in Mexico for a few weeks. Javier recalls feeling "trapped between two worlds." At his Mexican school they would call him a gringo; at his American school, he was derisively called a Mexican.

What made matters worse was that Alberto did not receive quality health care during the treatment of his cancer. After part of his lower leg was amputated, he was not placed on chemotherapy. Within months, the cancer had spread to his knee. The doctors then amputated his right leg just above the knee. Still no follow-up chemo. Several months after the second amputation, Alberto was told that the cancer had spread to his lungs. Through it all, Alberto found ways to stay employed by working on construction jobs as a welder. In addition, when told that the cancer was in his lungs, Alberto decided that his family had to stay in El Paso full time. If something were to happen to him, he wanted to make sure that his wife and children were completely settled in the states.

One obvious roadblock was the U.S. citizenship application process. The Mexican–U.S. border immigration issue is one of the most volatile issues in America. It was not easy to gain U.S. citizenship. Alberto could not afford a lawyer, so had to rely on the bureaucrats that he interacted with in the U.S. Customs Office. After each visit, he left with his head spinning.

In spite of his health challenges and the frustrations associated with trying to gain U.S. citizenship, Alberto was a happy and contented man. He had a devoted wife, who he loved dearly, wonderful children, and a good job requiring the skills that he possessed. Both Alberto and Fatima were deeply religious. Like many Hispanic families, they were devout Catholics. The family went to church together every Sunday and Fatima regularly did her rosaries. Alberto believed in God's power and his will.

As the cancer began to ravage Alberto's body, his faith remained strong, but his cheerful, happy manner was tested. His new doctors were talking about removing part of his lung. Over time, three-fourths of his lungs would eventually be removed. At that point, he was already having a hard time breathing and standing on one leg with crutches trying to work construction was taking its toll. Alberto found joy in sitting at home after work with his children having them share their stories about what they were learning in school. Their American schools. That part was most satisfying to Alberto. He pushed his children to study and work hard. Even though he did not read English, he found creative ways to "check" their homework. He was confident that each was doing well. Now that they were in America, he was confident that they could go to college. The citizenship issue had not been worked out, but Alberto had been told that movement on that front was imminent. Things were falling into place. He never said as much to Fatima, but even she knew that Alberto was ready to die.

As Alberto grappled with his aggressive cancer, Javier was settling into his new school in El Paso. Although he missed his friends in Mexico, he liked his new school a lot. Javier made friends pretty easily and liked sports. He was good at baseball, basketball, and swimming. He also was good in the classroom. Not naturally brilliant, Javier had to work hard. Work hard he did. He got that trait from his father. Javier always did his homework and did well in all of his classes. In the evening, while his father was going over his homework with him, Javier would sometimes talk to his father about his future. Unlike his older brother, Ernesto, who was dead set on being an accountant, Javier was not sure what he wanted to do when he finished college. His father always told him not to worry about the future. "Your future will reveal itself, Javier," Alberto used to say. "Concentrate on what you are doing today. Work hard so that you will be prepared for tomorrow." Accepting his father's advice, Javier plowed on day by day, making sure he worked harder than anyone else.

By now eleven and in the sixth grade, Javier enjoyed playing tag with his younger sister and brother as they walked home from school. Indeed tag, hot potato, and other makeshift chase games were a family staple among the Morales' family. In Mexico, where Javier had tens of cousins, they would run and chase each other well into the evening. Fatima used to yell for them and scold them about their dinner getting cold as they chased each other in the dirt fields around Ahumada. Javier, Maria, and Daniel continued these chase games nearly every evening on their way home from school. Since Javier was the oldest, he was, by far the fastest and could run them down easily.

One day, after school, while chasing his sister, he felt tired all of a sudden and could not catch his breath. This had never happened to Javier before, so he just sat down on the curb to rest. Meanwhile, Maria and Daniel had run all the way home, celebrating the fact that they beat their brother, who could not keep up. Nearly thirty minutes later, Javier stumbled into the front door, clearly struggling.

"What is wrong, Javier?" asked his mother.

"I don't know, mama. I just felt tired all of a sudden."

"You run too much, boy! You need to get your rest."

Thinking his mother was probably right (again!), Javier went to bed and fell asleep. Though it was only 4:00 p.m., Javier slept until the next morning.

When he awoke, he felt better, but was still light headed. Javier got dressed, ate some cereal, and walked to school. By the time he walked into his first class, he was sweating profusely. Something is wrong with me, he thought.

While in math class, two periods later, Javier noticed the whole room beginning to spin around him. He felt sick to his stomach and passed out. When he came to, he was in the nurse's office. The school nurse asked if he was ok. Javier said he was fine, whereupon he then vomited. As the nurse tried to help him get to the bathroom, Javier felt exhausted. "I can't walk there," he said. "It's only ten feet away," the surprised nurse said. "But, it's too far for me to walk," Javier insisted. With that, the nurse called an ambulance. Alberto and Fatima soon met Javier at El Paso General Hospital.

It took many days of tests and more tests, but, in the end, the diagnosis could not be more precise. Javier had primary pulmonary hypertension and heart disease. The cause was more than likely genetic. Javier's heart and his lungs were deteriorating at an alarming rate. In order to live, the boy needed both a heart and lung transplant. And he needed them quickly.

No parent is prepared to receive that kind of news about their child. Alberto and Fatima were devastated. They had no idea what to do or how to proceed. Because of his own experience, Alberto did not trust doctors. Now, he was hearing a group of doctors tell him that his eleven-year-old son might die because his organs were failing him. How could that be? Heart disease and lung problems are for old people.

The doctors at El Paso General recommended that the Morales' see a young Houston surgeon who had performed several organ transplant surgeries. Since Javier would have a hard time traveling to Houston, the doctor would have to come examine him in El Paso. Alberto was told that the Houston doctor, William C. E. Roberts, was very busy and may not be able to take Javier's case.

Now convinced that Dr. Roberts was the only man who could save his son, Alberto left the hospital, dropped his wife at home, and drove ten hours to Houston to meet Dr. Roberts.

Dr. Roberts was, indeed, a busy man. He was in high demand because of his growing experience performing delicate organ trans-plant surgeries. He had an amazing rate of success with his surgeries. More than anything, he was a good and decent man. He knew what it was like to struggle, having grown up in public housing in Springfield, Ohio. Fortunately, he maintained his sense of compassion even as he was achieving professional success. That being said, Dr. Roberts had learned how to say no. He just could not take on every case. Unbeknownst to the doctor, Alberto was driving to Houston to meet him. At the same time, Dr. Roberts was telling his colleagues in El Paso that he was not sure that he could help the little boy they had called him to discuss.

But just as Dr. Roger McDonald would find out later, Dr. William C. E. Roberts was no match for Alberto Morales.

Alberto tracked the doctor down in the surgery unit of the Methodist Hospital of Houston. After being pointed in the doctor's direction, Alberto hobbled to him and stuck out his worn down welder's hand.

"Dr. Roberts. Good evening. My name is Alberto Morales. I come to you from El Paso Texas. El Paso doctors tell me that my eleven year old son will die if you don't help save him. They say that you are the only one to save him. They not smart enough. Will you help save my son or let him die."

Dr. Roberts, who had been going over a patient's chart with a nurse, looked at the nurse then back at Alberto. "Excuse me, sir. What is your son's name?"

"My son's name is Javier Morales."

"El Paso just called me about your son this evening. They said you were at the hospital earlier in the day and had just received the diagnosis. You drove all the way here to find me that quickly?"

"If you don't help my son, he will die. Will you help my son?"

By now, everyone within earshot was listening to their conversation. Nurses, doctors, patients. To say that Dr. Roberts was being put on the spot would be putting it mildly.

Dr. Roberts squeezed his forehead with his right thumb and forefinger and blinked his eyes. Alberto only looked into the doctor's eyes, oblivious to everyone else in the area.

"I will help your son, Mr. Morales."

"Thank you very much, sir." With that, Alberto turned around, walked out of the hospital, got into his old Ford pickup truck and drove back to El Paso.

Just days before, Alberto had resolved himself to the fact of his own mortality. Once he learned of his son's illness, Alberto's own maladies were not important. He only cared about his son. Within days, Dr. Roberts had visited Javier in the hospital and assembled his team. El Paso General had never handled anything this significant. Dr. Roberts made sure that Dr. McDonald was his local leader on Javier's case.

Javier was confused by all that was going on around him. When he was told about his illness, he really did not know how to react. Funny thing was that he never really got scared, just tired. Real tired. In no time, it was clear that his energy level was nonexistent. He had gone from a kid who spent most of his nonschool time running around to someone who struggled to walk five feet. The hospital got Javier a wheelchair and set him up with a regular schedule for therapy. Strange as it sounds, physical therapy is important for those suffering from conditions like Javier. Provided that a transplant does take place, the patient needs to have as much strength as possible to withstand the trauma associated with the surgery. Javier was so tired that he could hardly lift his arms, but the hospital staff continued to push him.

Javier struck up an unusual love–hate relationship with one particular male nurse named Bruce. Bruce always pushed Javier to the limits. For that, Javier hated Bruce. He hated to see him walk into the room. When Bruce appeared, pain and fatigue followed, according to Javier. Soon, however, Javier began to appreciate Bruce's efforts. Schoolmates sent homework and notes to Javier and Bruce would help him with his homework. Theirs became a friendship founded in the midst of a very trying and stressful set of circumstances. It was indeed very special.

Javier spent over two months in the hospital. It took that long to finalize the diagnosis, secure the right medical team, and regulate the proper medication for the boy. The entire hospital staff was pulling for Javier and Dr. Roberts was working his organ donor sources to get Javier on the list as soon as possible.

Life-threatening illnesses create a host of emotions, a plethora of ups and downs. The emotional roller coaster associated with the good news, bad news days are often unbearable, always unpredictable. For Javier and his father Alberto, a certain settling in had occurred. Now over the shock, both were steeling themselves for the fight ahead. Alberto continued to encourage Javier and the rest of the Morales' family, while Javier was a walking testament to the perfect patient profile. The boy was simply amazing. Totally focused on the present, Javier never showed signs of discouragement. Once he accepted Bruce's prodding, Javier took what came his way as even tempered as possible. He exhibited no signs of self-pity and continued to engage in made-up games with his siblings when they visited. He struggled to do his homework, but he always did it. He also talked about going to college. He lived in the present, but still planned for his future. Javier was definitely Alberto Morales' son.

Still, the unpredictability of bad news will always pack a punch. Each Morales family member felt as though they had been punched when Dr. Roberts sat them down to update them about the donor list issue. Javier's medical team was comfortable with his medication and he was going to be released from the hospital in a few days. He was very excited and talked his doctors into letting him go back to school. In the meantime, it had been expected that he would be on the donor list and just wait for the call.

The entire nuclear family of Alberto Morales was in the room, as was several relatives from Mexico. Both Fatima and Alberto had several brothers and sisters, all with multiple children. At any given time, the entire visitors' waiting room at El Paso General could be filled with Javier's relatives during his stay there. Bruce told Dr. Roberts that he counted forty-two relatives one day, most of whom were from Mexico.

Alberto could tell by Dr. Roberts' expression that the news was not good.

He also did not like the fact that Dr. McDonald was accompanying Dr. Roberts.

"Folks, let me get right to it," Dr. Roberts began. Our government will not let me put Javier on the donor list because he is not a U.S. citizen. I have been instructed to tell you that even if a donor were found, you would have to pay for it. I also have been instructed to tell you that if you came up with the baseline cost of the surgery, which is 250,000 dollars, then I can put you on the secondary list for paying visiting foreign nationals. That list does not move as quickly as the list for U.S. citizens, but your chances would still be good to find a match. "I am sorry that I have to tell you this." Dr. Roberts then hung his head.

The Morales' family was dumbfounded. As was always the case, the language barrier led to a questionable understanding of the instructions and counsel they had been receiving from Javier's doctors. Language issues aside, however, the impact of Dr. Robert's message was unmistakable. Either come up with 250,000 dollars or no transplant. In other words, they were going to let Javier die.

Fatima began to cry, as did many others in the room. Maria, Javier's only sister fell onto the bed, grabbing her brother's legs. She was crying loudly. Bruce, Javier's nurse, was standing at the door, wiping away tears. Dr. McDonald stood stoically, hands crossed behind his back.

Alberto, who would not, could not cry, spoke first. "Dr. Roberts, please put Javier on the other list. We will raise the money."

At first, everyone looked at Alberto like he was crazy. For some in the room, Alberto included, it takes ten or more years to even make 250,000 dollars. Alberto's declaration seemed, well, almost insolent.

The more everyone stared at Alberto, the more they fed off of his determination. Even Dr. Roberts began to think that there was still hope. "Alright, Mr. Morales," he said. "I will do that. I don't know if or when the call will come, but if it does, you must have the two hundred fifty thousand dollars."

Dr. McDonald said nothing, but stood with a skeptical look on his face.

When the doctors cleared the room, Alberto maintained his defiance. "It is just money. We can raise it. God is on our side."

Javier remembers calmly thinking that he was going to die. He also recalls looking at his father, oddly wondering for a moment how Alberto was doing with his cancer treatments. Alberto's condition had not been discussed in weeks, yet everyone knew he was still in dire straits. To Fatima, Alberto made it clear. "I will not die," he said, "while my son is sick."

In less than two weeks from the hospital meeting with Dr. Roberts, Javier went back to school for the first time in three months. By then, Alberto, Fatima, and several school parents put out the word about the Javier Morales fundraising drive. When Javier got out of his father's truck and into his wheelchair, on that first day, the reception he received was overwhelming. Hundreds of students, parents, faculty, staff, community residents, and relatives burst into cheers and applause. Javier was not prepared for it. He honestly was thinking about the experiment he would get to perform in his science class that he had been working on. Seeing and hearing all those people react the way they did made him numb. He just did not know what to do.

His older brother Ernesto guided the wheelchair to the school's front door, while Alberto hobbled with his crutches behind them. Fatima was holding Alberto's shoulder, as she had grown accustomed to do now that he used crutches to walk. Javier was breathing hard through the oxygen canister attached to the wheelchair. He felt like a basketball star running from the locker room to the court at the start of a big game. As they got closer to the door, it felt like they were in a receiving line. They were engulfed by pats on the back, hugs, kisses, smiles. Javier's tragic illness had become a cause. And a cause to fight for.

The school principal had a microphone and talked about the fundraising effort. "We need all of El Paso to take on this cause!" he bellowed.

El Paso responded. In two months, this poor community had raised over 120,000 dollars. The money came from everywhere. Traditional school bake sales, car washes, yard sales, radio telethons, special dances, bingo night, senior bowling events, church offerings, and on and on. On the other side of the border, Javier's relatives took up the cause as well. In numerous villages within a one hundred mile radius from the U.S. border, collections were taken to support Javier. Keep in mind that the median income in El Paso is approximately 29,000 dollars per year. In Mexico, it is far less.

While the fundraising efforts were progressing nicely, Alberto was also making headway on the immigration issue. Through a co-worker at a construction site, he found a young, aggressive, Berkeley Law grad to take on his case. The lawyer was a Latina and she represented the Morales' family as if they were her only client. Within five months of the infamous hospital meeting with Dr. Roberts, Alberto received his U.S. citizenship. Since Javier and his siblings were minors, they too became U.S. citizens. Now, Javier could be moved to the primary organ donor list, which is given priority status.

The family's joy and renewed hope was tempered by Javier's declining health. After a few weeks, school became too much. Then, the wear and tear associated with the medication and resulting coughing spells threatened to stymie all of their efforts.

By the time Mr. Morales told Dr. McDonald to never touch his son, many had given up hope. While Dr. McDonald may have lacked a soft touch, his assessment was not far off base. The coughing was still a problem and Javier grew weaker and weaker.

It was also evident that Alberto's health was declining. He had not shared with his family his own doctor's prognosis that his time on earth was coming to an end. Alberto maintained that he would see his son through his illness. His grit was helping him keep his promise, but the cancer often beat him down.

On the night when he had his words with Dr. McDonald, Alberto told his wife to keep praying for Javier. "My dear Fatima, God's powers and blessings are stronger than the doctors. Our son will be alright, if we believe." They had left the hospital that night after talking with Dr. Roberts by phone. Once he was "disrespected" by Alberto, Dr. McDonald called Dr. Roberts, who was in Houston. While the two doctors were talking, Bruce informed them that Javier's condition had stabilized; that the violent coughing had stopped.

Fatima crossed herself and hugged her husband. Alberto only glared at Dr. McDonald. The Morales' went to see their son and then went home.

Ups and downs, highs and lows. It went that way for another eight months before the ultimate breakthrough. Javier was not expected to be able to wait those additional eight months, but he did. The coughing spells began to subside and his body was getting used to the medication.

During that time period, Javier and Alberto, both suffering from life-threatening conditions seem to fortify each other. Each was keeping the other alive. Even today, Javier says he would not have made it but for the positive energy he received from his father.

The call came at 7:00 p.m. on a Thursday night. Javier, his parents, and all of his siblings were at home. Dr. Roberts made the call himself. Fatima had answered the telephone.

"Good evening, Mrs. Morales. This is Dr. Roberts. I have good news. We have a donor match for Javier. I am taking a helicopter to El Paso General. Please get there with your son as soon as possible. Congratulations."

Fatima did not know how to respond. She stammered a few thank you's, sí's, and ok's, but basically, she was in shock.

Alberto, without knowing any of the words spoken by Dr. Roberts knew it was a good news call. He was grinning from ear to ear. Ernesto was pumping his fist. Maria, as is her tendency, was crying tears of joy. Javier, who had been preparing himself for death, kept giving high fives to his baby brother, Daniel. Now twelve, Javier got a lump in his throat about what lay ahead, but he was ready.

At the hospital, the entire El Paso General celebrated, albeit briefly. They were all pulling for Javier and the word of the donor match spread like wildfire throughout the building. Bruce had repeatedly told his superiors that he wanted to be the attending nurse, even if he happened to be off duty at the time of the call. He made the other nurses promise to switch shifts with him, if necessary. Sure enough, Bruce was home with his young family when his supervisor called him. He kissed his wife, hugged his five-year-old, and rushed to the hospital.

The Morales' Mexican relatives passed the word as soon as Alberto called one of his brothers in Ahumada. Fourteen relatives drove anywhere from one to three hours from Mexico to sit and wait at the hospital during the surgery.

Word also quickly reached Javier's school and church community. His priest and his principal arrived at the emergency room. About 200 community members gathered outside the hospital with candles and bibles. The group was not sad, their spirits were high. Everyone was cautiously optimistic.

Javier recalls having to take more and more pills in order to get ready for the surgery. He also had to make sure that his bowels were completely empty. Bruce and other prepping nurses kept chatting with him as he went through the preparations.

Finally, Dr. Roberts came into the prepping room where Javier was waiting with his parents. The doctor had his cap and gown on and was ready to work. He greeted Javier with a huge smile. Looking back, he recalls thinking that it was the first time that he and seen his doctor really smile. That smile calmed Javier more than anything else during the presurgery preparations.

"Javier, are your ready, my man?" Dr. Roberts was clearly in a good mood.

"Yes, sir," Javier replied. "I am so ready!"

"Well, let's do it."

Fatima and Alberto kissed their son and watched him being wheeled into the operating room.

Ten hours later, Dr. Roberts walked into the waiting room where nearly thirty Morales' relatives were waiting. Once again, his smile said it all.

"Javier did well and is in recovery. The surgery was a success. We have to wait to see how his body reacts, but as of now, he is doing better than we expected. You folks have one tough kid."

The place erupted. Hearing the screams of joy from the waiting area led hospital staff to whoop it up as well. Soon, the over 500 people with candles and bibles outside of the hospital began to yell, clap, and cry. It was a sight to behold. Ernesto said later that the celebration reminded him of New Year's Eve.

Alberto and Fatima had been sitting in the waiting area with their family holding hands like high-school sweethearts. They loved each other completely. When Dr. Roberts finished speaking they looked at each other and Alberto cupped his wife's face with his hands and kissed her. Real good. When they finished, a blushing Fatima got up and began to hug their other relatives.

Days later, as Javier was getting his strength, he learned that he had received the heart and lungs of a nine-year-old boy. Javier never knew how the boy died, but was told that the boy had been active in sports. Upon being given that information, Javier prayed for the boy's soul.

One year later, Javier was doing just fine. He had almost fully recovered and his life was back to normal. He could run, jump, and even play chase games with his brothers and sister. He also was doing well in school. One by-product of his illness was that it solidified his career plans. While in the hospital, Javier became fascinated and enamored with the work of the hospital radiologists. Javier talked with them incessantly about x-rays and the process of how they work. Once they saw how interested he was in x-rays, several radiologists would bring him assorted films of other patients and explain how they should be read. Javier was now determined to be a radiologist.

During one of Javier's follow-up appointments at the hospital, Alberto asked the hospital receptionist to page Dr. McDonald. Both Javier and Fatima looked at Alberto curiously when they heard him make the paging request. After a few minutes, Dr. McDonald appeared at the reception station. Alberto hobbled over to the doctor on his crutches, turned to point at Javier and said, "Look at my son, doctor. Now you see why I would never give up on my son. You look at him."

Being sheepish does not come easy to Dr. Roger McDonald. But sheepish he was that day. With his head slightly down, the doctor responded. "Yes, I do understand, Mr. Morales. I am very happy for you and your family. I truly am."

The two men then shook hands and the Morales' family left the hospital.

Two months later, lying in bed one night with his bride, Alberto turned to Fatima, smiled at her and said, "My love, I can die now."

That night, quietly, peacefully, Alberto Morales did just that.

Javier graduated from high school, has attended two years of community college and after graduation will enroll in a radiology program. He is more determined than ever to be a practicing radiologist. He is in excellent health.

Each of Javier's siblings has done well in school. Ernesto made it to college, as has Maria. Daniel is also expected to attend college. Alberto would be proud of them all.

Fatima, while still looking after her children, continues to pray and attend church regularly. She deeply misses her husband, thinking about him each and every day.

Maria

To Principal Lance Burton, it was an ironically humorous sight. Sitting on the couch in his office were two seventh-grade girls who were brought to him because they had been fighting. The humor was in the visual. The two girls, Audrey Bowes and Maria Ortega, were, respectively, the biggest and smallest kids in Lakewood Junior High School in Lakewood, Colorado. Twelve-year-old Audrey was a full five feet, ten inches tall. She was a heavier than average size girl with big bones and a sturdy frame. Her flock of red hair, pale skin, and green eyes suggested that you did not want to mess with Audrey Bowes. In contrast, Maria Ortega, who was also twelve was barely four feet, seven inches and tipped the scale at around ninety pounds. Maria had an angelic face which was handicapped by the permanent scowl she wore on it. Her body frame, however, was small in every respect. If Las Vegas bookies looked at the two of them and were asked to place odds on a fight between them, all of the good money would be placed on Audrey. Indeed, that was the irony. Audrey's face was battered and blue, with a swollen red left eye growing blacker by the minute. Maria did not have a scratch on her face. The littlest kid in school had just put a major whipping on the biggest kid in the school.

Though the visual was humorous, Principal Burton was not surprised by the result. Nor was he surprised that Maria Ortega had found her way to his office. Maria was the toughest kid in his school and the leader of the school's biggest gang. She was a true tiny terror. Principal Burton was well aware of Maria's reputation and her anti-social behavior. He knew that sooner or later he was going to have to deal with Maria Ortega. Eyeing the two students in his office, but paying more attention to Maria, he knew that now was the time to address the Maria Ortega problem. Maria had her arms folded defiantly, totally fearless. She looked rather comfortable sitting on the principal's couch with her baggy blue jeans and dirty green tee shirt. As Principal Burton sat behind his desk and silently looked back and forth at both

115

girls, Maria decided to up the ante in the game of intimidation. She unfolded her arms, leaned forward, looked directly at Principal Burton, and audibly sneered. Audrey, who had already been beaten badly enough, quickly bent her head down to make sure that the principal did not associate her with Maria's obvious insolence. Principal Burton returned Maria's stare, but said nothing. To himself he thought, "This is one helluva tough kid."

Maria was the youngest of three children born to Reyes and Angie Ortega, both Colorado natives of Mexican descent. Reyes was a decent, hardworking man, who ran his own flooring business. Angie worked in a local hospital, where she was a respected clerk. Maria's older brother, Reyes Jr. is five years older than Maria, while her sister Elizabeth is four years older. From the time of her birth, Maria was known as the little girl with the big heart. She worked valiantly to play the same games as her siblings, though they were much older and bigger than Maria. Her father loved Maria's spunkiness and continuously lavished praise on his youngest child.

Although Maria adored her father, in many ways, she was just like her mother. Most notably, they both were little ladies with big hearts. Maria grew to be four feet, eight inches, nearly the exact same height as her mother and her grandmother. All three also had spitfire personalities, full of sass and pride. Soon after Reyes married Angie, he realized that it did not take much to set his wife off. He learned the art of listening to her rants while tuning her out at the same time.

Early in their young lives, Maria and her siblings were enveloped in a nurturing environment led by two hardworking parents. That all changed when Maria was five years old. One night, she was awakened by her parents arguing. This was not unusual. Angie and Reyes argued often. This night was different. While wiping the sleep from her eyes, young Maria walked into her parents' bedroom and saw her father packing a suitcase, while Angie stood over him yelling and screaming. When Reyes saw his favorite child, he managed a weak smile, gently picked her up, gave her a kiss on the forehead, and put her back to bed. Maria, however would not stay in bed. When her father left her bedroom to resume his packing, young Maria got out of her bed, grabbed her small Barbie suitcase and began to put some of clothes in it. As she was sniffling and packing, she also resolved to live with her father instead of her mother.

When Reyes was finished packing, he started to load his belongings into his car, while Angie stood on the porch with her arms folded glaring at him the whole time. It was raining hard that night and Reyes' clothes were soaked. As Reyes loaded the last suitcase in his car, five-year-old Maria ran out of the house in her pajamas dragging her packed Barbie suitcase behind her. She had not zipped it up all of the way, so various dresses, underwear, and other clothes were falling out of the suitcase as she ran after her father. Upon seeing Maria, Angie just rolled her eyes and crossed her arms even tighter.

By then, Reyes was in his car, looking at his daughter running toward him. He was sobbing uncontrollably. Maria ran up to her father's car and yanked at the car door handle on the driver's side.

"Daddy, I want to live with you! Please take me with you. I packed my clothes too, Daddy. Please let me go with you. Please, daddy!" Maria was crying and was also soaking wet because of the rain.

Reyes would not open the car door. He did roll down the window and pulled Maria close to him.

"You stay with your momma, Maria. Daddy will see you. You need to stay with your mother and with Reyes Jr. and Elizabeth. Daddy will always love you."

Maria kept screaming for her father to take her with him. Reyes finally pushed her back away from the car and drove off, wiping tears from his eyes as he maneuvered down the street. Maria stood crying in the driveway, oblivious to the rain. Angie eventually gathered Maria as well as the assorted clothes that littered the area and took her back into the house.

Within months, Angie and Reyes were divorced. Later, Maria came to understand that both of her parents were having multiple affairs with other people. In fact, young Maria was familiar with one of the men Angie was seeing. Angie would take Maria with her to his home during the early evening while Reyes was still at work. The rupture in Maria's parents' marriage came when Angie caught Reyes with another woman. Angie, ignoring her own infidelities, cried over the betrayal and demanded that Reyes move out. He did so the night that the couple's arguing woke up Maria.

After her father moved out, life was completely different for the Ortega children. Angie began a string of relationships with different men who she allowed to move into the house. Unlike Reyes, many of these men were violent and unsuitable to be around children. One boyfriend, Miguel, was particularly unstable. He regularly beat Angie, sometimes badly. Once, he locked the door to the bedroom while he was beating Angie. As Maria, Reyes Jr. and Elizabeth took turns watching through the door keyhole, Miguel pointed a gun at Angie and pressed it against her right temple. Maria will never forget the look of helpless horror on her mother's face. Upon seeing the gun, each child began screaming and Reyes Jr. tried to call the police. Miguel then unlocked the door, pulled the phone cord out of the wall, and began beating the kids. Later, he made the kids stand in front of him while he sat at the kitchen table. He then took two forks and stabbed himself repeatedly in the chest with the forks, yelling the whole time. He then got lemonade out of the refrigerator and poured it all over the chest wounds. Throughout, Miguel had a wide-eyed look on his face.

Angie finally developed the common sense to kick Miguel out of the house. The damage was done, however, in many ways. Years later, Elizabeth confided to Maria that Miguel had sexually abused Elizabeth. As is often the case, Angie never knew.

Soon after Miguel left, Angie started seeing Ricardo, who was ten years her junior. Ricardo moved in, but he, too, was ill-equipped to deal with and help raise three children. He was barely in his twenties. Violent by nature, he employed the form of discipline to which he was accustomed. The kind of discipline that comes from a belt. He would beat the kids with a belt for almost any mistake or act of mischief, no matter how benign. Maria ended up with belt whelp marks on her body for things like not making up her bed or not putting the empty cereal bowl in the sink. Angie began to intercede on all of her children's behalf when it became clear that Ricardo was enjoying using his belt on the kids more than he should. Once, Angie had Maria hide in the bottom cabinet of a credenza located in the living room while Roberto stormed around the house with belt in hand, looking to beat Maria. Following this incident, Maria heard Angie talking to Reyes Jr. and Elizabeth about "the right place for you children to live." On the eve of starting first grade, Maria and her siblings moved in with their grandmother, who lived just north of Lakewood.

During this nearly two-year period following Reyes and Angie's divorce, Reyes was involved with his own drama. He fell in love with and quickly married a younger woman, who professed her undying love for him as well. Soon after the marriage, his new wife, Clara, complained whenever his kids came around. Before long, Reyes had been browbeaten to the point where he stopped picking up his own children for weekend visits. Little did he know that his kids longed for those visits because of all of the unsteadiness associated with their mother and her various boyfriends. Reyes had no idea that his children were being terrorized by an assortment of random men. The kids were afraid to tell him and he was caught up into his new life. For the next several years, Reyes was not involved in his own children's lives. He was preoccupied with trying to please Clara. Years later, the light bulb finally clicked on for Reyes when he found evidence showing that Clara only married him to get her green card. Prideful and feeling foolish, he woke up from his years long slumber and divorced her.

As Principal Burton watched Maria flex her tiny yet powerful muscles at him, he thought about the girl's file which he had reviewed the previous week. Burton was not aware of all of the abuse that Maria and her siblings had faced following their parents' divorce, but he knew something was not right. His review of Maria's school record presented a girl with a huge chip on her shoulder. A girl who was angry at the world. He could feel her anger and hate as she stared at him in his office.

Principal Burton's review of Maria's files followed a special meeting that he had with several of the teachers in his school. These teachers wanted to talk with him about the school's biggest menace: Maria Ortega. At the time, it was mid-November. Maria had just entered Lakewood in September. Nonetheless, her presence and attitude had been like a cancer in the school. She was the unquestionable leader of a group of kids, all of Hispanic origin, that continuously wrecked havoc on the rest of the school community. Each day, kids were being attacked and mercilessly beaten by those associated with Maria. Many times, the attacks were for little or no reason. If a kid outside of Maria's group would cast a funny look at a gang member or accidentally bumped into one of the members, chances are that student would be jumped on by day's end. During recess and after school, it was not uncommon to see ten to fifteen gang members pummeling another student just enough to send the needed message of intimidation, just before scattering away from the scene in separate directions. By the time Maria had her fight with Audrey, Maria's gang had grown to between forty and fifty kids, a sizable number in a school with a population of 300.

In October, Principal Burton thought he had stemmed the impact of the gang's reach by issuing a rule that no more than four students could congregate together at any time on school premises. Under the new rule, the teachers could keep better track of and handle the small groups of kids, making harder for the large attacks to take place. For a time, it appeared as the "group of four rule" would work. Maria and her gang, however, worked around that rule. Ingenuous as it sounds, Maria developed a form of signals and sign language that served to inform other gang members of students targeted for beatings, as well as the time and place for the beatings. Once the information got out among the other gang members, as many as five to ten groups of four students would end up being at the same place at the same time, all of whom would take part in beating the hapless victim. Immediately thereafter, all would disband and leave the scene, but with changed compositions within the various groups of four students. This elaborate and reliable approach made it difficult for the school administration to accurately identify the gang members involved in the individual beatings.

Maria utilized the same signal system in each of her classes, causing confusion and disruption every class period. In a moment of exasperation, one frustrated young teacher pulled an old six-foot-high, eight-foot-long screen—similar to what is used in screen windows and doors—and told Maria to sit in the back of the class behind the screen. Maria was then effectively separated from the rest of her class. The teacher told her colleagues she was finally able to do some teaching with Maria shielded from everyone else.

At the special "what do we do about Maria meeting," Principal Burton promised the teachers that he would expand on the isolation approach used by the young teacher. Burton suggested employing an individualized isolation strategy designed solely for Maria. Similar screens would be set up in all of her classrooms and she would be separated from all of the other students throughout the day. A couple of counselors would greet her in the morning and various faculty would escort her around the school throughout the day. Principal Burton promised to employ this new technique the next time he received a complaint about Maria. Everyone in the room knew that such a complaint would take place sooner as opposed to later. One teacher, however, who happened to be a close ally of Principal Burton, took exception with her friend's suggested approach. Isabel Garcia pointed out that the isolation strategy had never been done before and was not recognized in the school district's discipline guidelines. Under the rules, she reminded everyone, a student is first placed in in-school suspension status and then out-of-school suspension status. There was no recognition of any such isolation punishment as an acceptable form of student discipline. Ms. Garcia knew the rules well.

She ran the in-school discipline program and, as such, knew Maria as well. Tall and athletic, with curly blonde hair, Ms. Garcia eagerly embraced her role as the stop gap between a student being kicked out of school and given another chance. She was so positive by nature that it sometimes drove her colleagues crazy. According to Ms. Garcia, a teacher should never give up on a child, no matter what. "They can all be redeemed," she regularly said. Though she was white, Ms. Garcia's husband was Hispanic. More than anything, Ms. Garcia's energy, enthusiasm, and positive attitude made her one of Principal Burton's favorite teachers. She was the perfect choice to run the in-school suspension program.

As designed by Ms. Garcia, students who have violated school rules were placed in her care where they would sit in a classroom with other such students and Ms. Garcia would ride hard on them for the rest of the day. Other teachers loved to dump their problem kids in Ms. Garcia's lap. Principal Burton placed limits on how many times a teacher could send a student to Ms. Garcia, but suffice it to say, all of Maria's teachers had sent her to Ms. Garcia on many occasions. During one of those times that Maria was in Ms. Garcia's in-school suspension classroom, Maria was so disrupting and mean-spirited that she brought Ms. Garcia to tears. The word traveled around the school that positive Ms. Garcia had been brought to tears by the tiny terror.

At the special teacher meeting, one of her colleagues felt compelled to remind Ms. Garcia who they were discussing. "Isabel, we know you love these kids, but we are talking about the demon. That's who made you cry. That little girl is evil. I wish there was a way to get her out of our school. We never had gangs before. That one bad apple has spoiled our whole bunch." Some of the other teachers began to clap.

"Right is right," Ms. Garcia responded. "Even Maria can turn her life around." Upon hearing that, many in the room burst out into audible laughter.

"Yeah, right!" the teacher replied. "You probably will be visiting her in prison." More laughter.

"That's enough," bellowed Principal Burton. "We are going to try my approach." Looking at Ms. Garcia, he said, "I know it isn't in the rules, Isabel and I know it hasn't been done before, but we have got to take a different tack with this girl."

"I hope it doesn't backfire, Lance," Ms. Garcia said. "You may end up giving her more power."

Principal Burton was thinking about his meeting with the teachers while Audrey and Maria were sitting in his office. He finally spoke.

"Audrey, go home. Put some ice on that eye. Come see me tomorrow."

Audrey looked up with her good eye, managed a smile, rolled that good eye at Maria and hurried toward the door.

Maria refolded her arms, waiting to receive her punishment. She was hoping for out-of-school suspension. If so, she would break into the old Forrester home off of Colfax and go foraging in the attic. Just something to do. When she was not in school, Maria and her gang would, on occasion vandalize homes and old buildings. They rarely took anything of value, but usually trashed the place.

"Maria," Principal Burton began, I am going to try something different with you." Maria looked at him curiously.

"We are putting you in isolation." He then described the isolation strategy he had discussed with some of his teachers. He looked closely at Maria to gauge her reaction.

Maria showed no response whatsoever. "Fine with me," she said. To herself, she was thinking, "They can try whatever they want, but if someone deserves a beating, they are still going to get it."

Why was Maria Ortega so angry? How did this twelve-year-old, who was not even close to five feet, become the most feared presence in the history of her school? Was she, as one teacher suggested, a demon? The devil incarnate?

From Maria's perspective, the answers to those questions are not complicated or hard to comprehend. In truth, in the wake of all that she experienced while very young, Maria built a defensive wall around herself that became impenetrable. Over time, that defensive wall took on an aggressive, offensive posture that mushroomed out of control. She took the sports metaphor, "the best defense is a good offense" to a whole new level.

Back when Maria and her siblings went to live with their grandmother, she was introduced to a new community and a new culture. The Denver metropolitan area is a culturally rich and diverse community known for its tolerance and liberalism. Nearly 30 percent of Denver is Hispanic. Lakewood, a suburb just ten miles west of Denver is 15 percent Hispanic. The economic gulf in Lakewood is vast. In the city, there exists a nice well-to-do enclave. But there also is a very poor, crime-ridden part of the town that has all of the negative elements found in larger cities. Like many other cities, the quality and racial mix of Lakewood neighborhoods change almost block by block. As you drive around, you quickly notice the change from a clean, upbeat neighborhood to a community with a beaten down ghetto look.

Maria's parents lived in a small bungalow in one of the border communities bridging stable and nonstable neighborhoods. The neighborhood was ethnically diverse, with the minority population of the schools about 20 percent. Maria's grandmother, however, lived in an upscale, predominantly white neighborhood. When Maria entered first grade at the neighborhood school near her grandmother's house, she was the only Hispanic or, for that matter, ethnic minority in her class. Plus, she was, by far, the smallest child in the class. It did not take long for her to get picked on by classmates. What's worse, even at that tender age, she felt looked down on by her teacher and the white adults in the school building. One weekend, while she was visiting her mother, she complained about the school and how she was being treated. Her mother grabbed her by both arms, got within inches of her face and said, "Maria, don't you ever let anyone push you around. Nobody! People are going to try to take advantage of you and you can never let them do that. You better get them, before they get you."

It was the first time that Angie had ever offered any advice to her daughter. Unfortunately, Maria internalized Angie's counsel and, over time, to it to the extreme. Buoyed by her mother's advice, starting in second grade, Maria would fight back at the drop of a hat. If another kid called her a spic or some other derogatory word, Maria was ready to fight. And, she was always angry. Maria was angry with her father, angry with her mother, angry with her mother's assorted boyfriends, angry at her teachers, angry with her fellow students. She honestly felt that no one had her back and, at seven years old, that she was all alone.

All of that anger affected her most directly in school. Though clearly smart, Maria never applied herself, nor did she want to. No adult in her sphere took interest in her schooling. Because she was so volatile, teachers avoided her. They were happy to promote her to the next grade so she could be someone else's problem. As a result, she just drifted and barely learned.

When it was time for Maria to attend seventh grade, she and her siblings had moved back with their mother in the old neighborhood. Roberto was long gone and Angie was a little more selective in picking her boyfriends. Most significantly, she had learned to not let anyone move in after just a handful of dates. She promised her children that they would not have to deal with anymore crazy men.

Lakewood Junior High School was located not far from Maria's family home. The school had a diverse mixture of students and also had a handful of tough kids. Knowing that she could be viewed as an easy target because of her size, Maria vowed to herself to set the tone early. She needed all of her schoolmates to respect her from day one. Unlike her entry into elementary school, Maria was determined to control her environment by any means. To her way of thinking, control meant power. She would not let anyone take that away from her.

Interestingly, Maria never intended to start a gang. In fact, she really did not have any friends and was not looking for any. She just wanted to make sure she was placed in a deferential status while at school.

Taking that approach, Maria was in a fight during her first week at Lakewood. As would become a pattern, some kid looked at her in a way Maria did not like and Maria went berserk. She dived at the much bigger girl's legs, flipped her over and started to hit her repeatedly in the face. The ferocity of her attack stunned everyone in the cafeteria. Maria was carted off to the principal's office.

Within a few days, Maria beat up another kid. Then another. And another. All the while, she would sit in her classes with a hard look on her face and sarcastically comment on each of her teacher's "stupid" statements.

At the time, Lakewood Junior High School had a small gang problem. Most of the kids in gangs were affiliated with the well-known gangs that actively recruited in Elementary and Middle Schools. Gangs such as the Bloods, Crypts, and MS-13. Maria eschewed such gang life, largely because she was a loner. But, as she started to make a name for herself, she began to attract a crowd of followers. Every misfit, outcast, or wannabe in the school wanted to be around this tiny terror who pummeled other kids with reckless efficiency. These kids felt power just by being in Maria's presence. Within the first month of school, Maria had done nothing to recruit or persuade other students to hang out with her, yet she had a contingent of fifteen to twenty peers who followed her around the building, waiting for her to erupt so they could cheer her on.

Maria soon enjoyed the additional power associated with having a fighting entourage at your beck and call. She started to tell certain followers to let her know if they heard anyone say anything bad about their fledgling group. If such a report was made, Maria would then personally attack the student who disparaged her. Then, Maria would start beating up kids who had beefs with one of her followers. This bought a tremendous amount of loyalty within her group. In no time, Maria had a contingent of up to fifty boys and girls who would do practically whatever she wanted and physically attack whoever she targeted.

In fairness, one thing that set Maria's from the older kids' gangs was weapons. Though they never talked about it directly, it was understood that they not use guns, knives, or other weapons. It was as if they all believed that there was greater power in beating someone down with your fists or feet. "You control them forever if you punish them with your hands," Maria would say.

Because of her size, Maria developed an aggressive, focused fighting style well suited for her speed and intensity. In the beginning of a fight, she would either lunge at the victim's neck or legs, hurling her entire body at them. She would then start swinging, making every punch count. No matter how many times people saw her in action, with each new fight, she continued to marvel because of her sheer nonstop movement and intensity. Her attacking style was reminiscent of those film clips of sharks destroying their prey. Like the sharks' victims, those fighting Maria did not stand a chance.

Today, Maria does not try to rationalize her actions of the past. She simply points out that she was so angry and so tired of people looking down on her, that fighting gave her the control and power she thought she needed to survive. She never even considered another way. Looking back, Maria realizes that much of her anger came from her relationship with her parents. While in middle school, Maria had little or no contact with her father. She was hurt deeply by that hole in her life. Moreover, having moved back with her mother, Maria began to be subjected to the verbal abuse and cutting remarks that her mom would hurl her way. At first, Maria could not understand why her mother was so hostile to her. However, she now realizes that her parents' divorce led to nearly irreparable tension between Maria and her mother. In truth, Maria blamed her mother for her father leaving the family, while Angie's feelings were hurt by Maria taking her father's side. Because of this tension, Maria preferred the isolation treatment at her school to being at home under the continual badgering of her mother.

After being told by Principal Burton that she was going to be in isolation, Maria tried to get adjusted to having a school staff member with her every minute that she was on school premises. In the morning, the Deputy Principal would greet her at the bus stop and escort her into the building. From there, the gym teacher would accompany her to her first two classes. And so on. Each of these adults would also wait outside of the restroom for Maria. Then they would sit with her at lunch. After a few weeks, Isabel Garcia's warning to Principal Burton became prescient. The principal's plan had backfired and unwittingly made Maria more powerful in the eyes of her peers. Think about it. Here was a tiny seventh-grade girl being treated like a mass murderer or the President of the United States, depending on your perspective. Maria Ortega had attained rock star status at Lakewood Junior High School.

Celebrity status aside, the isolation actually forced Maria to do something she really had not done much before while in school. Namely, look at her books. Though she tried to hide her interest, Maria began to listen to some of her teachers' lectures and, since she was sitting in the back of each classroom behind a screen, she also opened up a few of her books.

As part of the isolation, Maria was required to spend time in Ms. Garcia's in-house suspension room during part of each day. Ms. Garcia noticed the subtle change in Maria. In particular, the teacher knew that Maria had a keen interest in science and biology. Ms. Garcia had observed Maria looking at her science book on a couple of occasions, only to close the book when it was thought that the teacher was looking at her. Ms. Garcia also noted that Maria's science book was always with her, even on days when she did not have to go to science class. Ms. Garcia believed that signs of a breakthrough were unfolding.

For the rest of the second semester, Maria continued to slowly show more interest in certain books. More importantly, she began to trust Ms. Garcia more and more. Though she did not open up completely to Ms. Garcia, it was clear that a relationship was forming between the two. Still, the tiny terror had not gone away. Maria would still get into fights, though sometimes the fights were broken up by Ms. Garcia. It was a funny sight witnessing Ms. Garcia wade through a crowd of students only to snatch Maria off of another student and carry her away attached to the side of Ms. Garcia's hip. On some of those occasions, Maria was still swinging while being pulled away from the area. When the school year ended, Maria was still angry, but was also developing a relationship with a caring adult; something she had never had in the past.

During the summer, things were getting worse for Maria in her home life. Angie was becoming more aggressive and mean spirited when yelling at Maria. She would alternatively call her daughter a slut and a future welfare queen. In addition, Maria's older brother, Reyes Jr. was developing a serious drug habit. More fragile than his baby sister, Reyes Jr. had internalized his angst over his parents' divorce and the periodic clashes with his mother's various boyfriends. He began to find solace in relying on the crack cocaine pipe.

To Maria, her whole world seemed to be falling in on her. She also was beginning to realize that she could not beat EVERYONE up. She was fighting all the time and while the fights created a natural adrenaline rush, she was secretly asking herself, "What's the point?" People were still looking down on her, particularly her teachers. All the fighting really was not making people like her more. Fear her? Yes. But even that was a double-edged sword. Now that she had a reputation, she felt she had to prove something with every fight. Plus, she knew that some kids would start to test her just to build their status.

As the-then thirteen-year-old began eighth grade, she was feeling increasingly overwhelmed by her problems and her life. One day, early in the semester, Maria decided that she would just stop fighting. She figured she would give it a try. Sure enough, all of that changed when a ninth grader got in her face in the cafeteria during lunch. Soon, she was back in the principal's office.

Maria felt she was trapped. Almost like being in quicksand. And there was nothing that she could do to get out of it. Maria began to get strong urges to talk with someone. But who? Not her mother. Or father. Or even her sister, Elizabeth. She and Elizabeth were close, but Elizabeth had her hands full with a young child to care for. Elizabeth had a baby at fourteen years of age and at seventeen was living with her baby's father and expecting her second child.

Maria also did not feel comfortable telling Ms. Garcia her innermost thoughts. Her confusion and sense of hopelessness was consuming her. It all came to a bizarre head one cool fall night.

Maria was home alone with her mother, who had been disparaging Maria all night. Earlier in the day, Maria had been in a fight in which she beat the kid up pretty bad. In her room with the door closed, Maria actually felt a sense of guilt about the fight that took place earlier. She also thought about her father and how much she missed him. "Would things be different if he was in my life?" she wondered to herself.

Finally, Maria pulled out a pill bottle full of Ibuprofen pills. She had been contemplating suicide for some time. Now, she believed, was the time. She swallowed half the pills in the bottle and lay down on her bed. Shortly thereafter, her brother Reyes Jr. came home, innocently opened the door to his baby sister's bedroom and saw Maria slumped over, with the pill bottle in her hand. Though still conscious, she was clearly groggy.

Reyes Jr. yelled for his mother, who ran up the stairs, came into Maria's room, observed the scene and said, "What is this? Now, you are going to kill yourself?"

Maria said in response, "It shouldn't matter to you. You don't love me anyway!"

Angie then said something that Maria believed validated the attempted suicide.

"There you go, still thinking about yourself! I'm still going to have to pay for the funeral expenses. It is going to cost money to bury you."

Reyes Jr. was aghast. "Mom! You can't mean that."

Maria, feeling sick after having ingested all of those pills, said, "Just bury me in the backyard. I don't care." With that, she fell back hard onto the bed.

Angie snorted and walked out of the room. She never called for an ambulance.

Reyes Jr. tried to keep his sister awake. Before long, Maria began throwing up. She did so for most of the night.

The next day, bright and early, Maria went to school. There was no need to stay home. Early in the school day, Ms. Garcia saw Maria in the hall and noticed that she did not look right. She was pale and ashen looking. She grabbed Maria, took her to an empty classroom and asked her what was wrong. Maria then completely spilled her guts to Ms. Garcia about the events of the previous night. Ms. Garcia then called an ambulance and, right in front of Maria, called Angie and promptly cursed her out. It was the first time that Maria felt that someone was actually fighting for her. She felt, strangely, loved for the first time.

At the hospital, the doctors said that since she survived the night, she would be fine. They too, could not believe that the child's mother did not seek medical attention for her daughter.

That day was a turning point for Maria. It marked the start of a new journey. For some reason, she felt motivated to change knowing that someone really believed in her. A cloud was being lifted off of her. But there was much work to do.

For the rest of Maria's junior high-school years, Isabel Garcia became the mother that Maria always wanted. That being said, the transition from gang member to productive student was bumpy at best. Every time that Ms. Garcia thought that she had turned the corner with Maria, the young student would do something to disappoint and go back to her ways. During Maria's eighth and ninth grade years, Ms. Garcia smartly picked her spots and did not push Maria. Maria never felt pressured or lectured to by Ms. Garcia. Ms. Garcia also introduced Maria to information and topics that she intuitively knew Maria would embrace. For instance, Ms. Garcia slowly began to talk with Maria about her spirituality and even took her to church a few times. That growing awareness really helped Maria understand her place in society and the world.

Academically, Ms. Garcia seized on Maria's interest in biology by exposing her to all of the careers that flow from a biology degree in college. Maria was amazed to learn that most doctors and dentists have biology degrees. As Ms. Garcia continued to talk with Maria about college and careers, Maria began to privately think about going to college. It was such a foreign notion to her and her family that she was afraid to even share it with anyone. Tough a fighter as she was, Maria's inner self-confidence was extremely low. Step by step, her confidence level and world view were beginning to change.

In addition to Ms. Garcia, another teacher had a profound effect on Maria's transformation. Jody Yates was a young, soft-spoken white teacher who was originally from St. Paul, Minnesota. Ms. Yates was of Swedish descent and she taught math to ninth graders. Ms. Yates never yelled, but her easy manner commanded the total respect and attention of her students. Plus, she made math so much fun. Maria was enthralled by Ms. Yates, almost embarrassingly so. Several weeks into Ms. Yates class, Maria began to realize that she was actually good in math. No longer sitting behind a screen in the back of classrooms, Maria happily sat in the front row of Ms. Yates' class. Maria longed so much for contact with Ms. Yates that she even would get homework wrong on purpose so she could talk with Ms. Yates after class and hear the teacher explain how to fix the mistake.

With Ms. Garcia and Ms. Yates becoming newfound positive influences to her, Maria seriously contemplated what she wanted to do with her life. Her ultimate career goal was oddly shaped while sitting in Ms. Yates math class.

The seats in Ms. Yates classroom were shaped in a semicircle, with about six rows of seats and fifteen seats in each row. As a result, the student sitting on the end of the first row would automatically be facing the student sitting at the other end of the same row. When Maria started to occupy the seat at one end of the first row in Ms. Yates' class, she could not help but notice the girl sitting in the seat directly in front of her at the other end of her row. That girl was petite and naturally attractive, except for a cleft lip. Maria never knew the girl's name, but noticed how the girl always kept her head down and used various methods of trying to hide that which could not be hidden. It bothered Maria. It was a shame that such a pretty girl has to hide her face. "Can't doctors fix that?" Maria constantly thought to herself. For the first time in her life, Maria felt total compassion and empathy for another human being. Someone who she did not even know.

Secretly, Maria started researching cleft lips on the internet. She learned that both doctors and dentists can help in reshaping the faces of people born with such a condition. As Maria began to learn more about dentists' role in such treatments, she became intoxicated with the photos of various dentists work. She then looked at more photographs relating to dentistry and the orthodontic profession. Late one Saturday night, after having spent several hours at a neighborhood library researching dentistry, Maria proclaimed to herself, "I am going to be a dentist!" While she made that vow, she also thought it wise not to tell anyone about her new goal.

Maria's transformation was nearly complete by the time she entered the tenth grade at Samuel Chase High school in Lakewood. As fate would have it, both Principal Burton and Ms. Garcia also transferred to Chase High at the same time Maria did. Burton was the new school principal, while Ms. Garcia taught and also was running a new intervention program designed to help troubled students. Though she kept it to herself, Maria was ecstatic about Ms. Garcia and Principal Burton joining her at her new school.

At Chase, Maria was setting the stage for a terrific high-school experience. She enrolled in dance, joined the Key Club, got involved in volunteer work through the PAL Club, which offered mentoring support to other students and nearby community members. Maria even tried out for the cheerleading team. Although her violent past was known, it did not overwhelm her because she was in a new school environment and many of her old Lakewood gang had either dropped out or gone to other schools. Maria still, however, had to occasionally address her notorious reputation. In fact, Maria's last fight happened solely because of her reputation.

As the word got out to the school community that Maria had made the cheerleading team, many girls did not like it. One girl, Tasha Smith, who did not make the team, was part of an emerging gang which included other tough girls. They all knew about Maria's past and could not believe that she had "gone soft." They also knew that if they beat her up, their respective reputations would grow immeasurably. They were waiting for the right time to corner the former tiny terror.

As soon as the cheerleading results were posted, Tasha gathered four of her friends and plotted on where and how they could attack Maria. Knowing that Maria had dance class in the gym, they decided to wait for her in the hallway between the gym and the girls' locker room. Later that day, as Maria was walking from dance class to the girls' locker, Tasha and her friends jumped in front of her, blocking her path.

"So, you a cheerleader, now, huh, Ms. Maria?" Tasha said.

Maria knew what was happening. Her instant thought was, "Can I ever escape my old life?" She felt like Clint Eastwood's character in the movie, Unforgiven. But like that character, she also was prepared for the worse and would respond in kind.

"Tasha, don't do this. You need to get over yourself. You need to move on."

"Oh, you gonna tell us what to do!"

On hearing that, Maria knew that the inevitable was upon her. There was no turning back. All of those old predatory instincts returned. She was more than ready for the challenge of taking on five bigger and stronger girls.

Like a good gunfighter, Maria had already sized up the situation and had developed a plan of attack. Since Tasha was the leader, with the most courage, she had obviously got the other girls involved. Maria would take Tasha out first. Hard. Then she would go after the biggest girl to her far left. If it all worked out, the other three would be tentative, scared, and then back away.

"Did you hear what I said? You trying to tell us what to do, b___?" Tasha yelled.

Maria sprung into action. She leapt like Superman with arms fully extended and locked her hands around Tasha's neck, thereby knocking her backwards onto the ground. She then wildly, accurately, and furiously punched Tasha's face repeatedly, not giving the girl time to strike even one blow in response. As the other girls tried to run to their friend's aid, Maria then did a somersault, flipped over backwards and kicked out the legs of the big girl, knocking her to the ground. In no time, Maria was then kicking and stomping the girl's face, which quickly caused her nose to bleed. While the big girl tended to her nose, Maria turned her attention back to Tasha, who was beginning to get up. Maria jumped on her, straddled her like a horse and went back to pummeling Tasha's face.

By now, as Maria predicted, the three other girls paused, not sure if they wanted to get into the fracas. As one of them started to step forward, a couple of the boys' basketball coaches arrived on the scene and broke the fight up. If that was to be Maria's final fight, she certainly made sure that it was memorable. As Maria was being led to Principal Burton's office by one of the coaches, a stunned, semiconscious Tasha was barking at one of the girls who did not help. "Where were you? Why didn't you have my back? I told you she could fight!"

As a result of the fight, Principal Burton had no choice but to suspend Maria from school for three days and kick her off of the cheerleading team. Maria accepted the punishment and insisted to Ms. Garcia that she was not going back to her old life. In fact, she became more determined to do the right thing. Needless to say, however, news of the fight spread like wildfire around the school. Instead of trading in on Maria's reputation for themselves, they allowed it to grow even larger, making Maria look invincible.

Following the celebrated fight, Maria got back on track. Maria worked very hard in all of her classes, having learned that the same ferocity that she had applied to fisticuffs could also help her get good grades. Additionally, Maria became an exceptional school citizen and community volunteer. Totally different from the loner student of the past, Maria helped other students with their homework, provided teaching assistant services to several teachers, and reached out to younger students who were trying to find their way. During lunch, Maria would look for the kid who was sitting alone and would go sit with that student. By her senior year, Maria was the most popular student in the entire school.

Maria eventually made it back onto the cheerleading team and by the time she graduated, she had a record of success virtually unmatched by her fellow graduates. Maria was Vice President of her senior class, President of the Key Club, a member of the cheerleading and dance teams, and she received the award for the biggest GPA turnaround among her classmates. She ended up with an honor roll GPA of nearly 3.4 out of 4.0. Plus, she won all the major "queen" crowns including Homecoming, Parade, Dance, and Prom. Because she had so dominated the queen crowns, Principal Burton issued a rule that one person could not win all of the crowns in the same year. As he announced the new rule, even he had to chuckle at his recollection of his need to change the rules at Lakewood Junior High School so he could place Maria in escorted isolation status.

Maria also fell in love. Throughout most of her high-school years, Maria avoided dating, largely because of the dysfunctional relationships that she had witnessed. During her senior year, however, she started seeing Jamal Awad, a childhood friend from her neighborhood. Jamal was part African American, part Filipino, and came from a very stable, drama-free family. Jamal was a young sergeant in the Air Force and was working on his engineering degree. He was a good guy and he was good for Maria. He continued to praise Maria for all that she had accomplished and he encouraged her to go further with her education. Like Principal Burton, Ms. Garcia, Ms Yates, and the entire Ortega family, Jamal was very pleased when Maria was accepted into Colorado State University. By then they all knew that she would be a biology major, especially since she was going to be a dentist.

At graduation, class Vice President Maria Ortega had a speaking role in the ceremony. When Principal Burton introduced her, the entire audience went crazy. While Maria was receiving her standing ovation, Principal Burton looked in the direction of the seated faculty, caught Ms. Garcia's eye and mouthed the words, "Thank you." Ms Garcia was beaming broadly and nodded back to her principal.

Four years later, Maria and Jamal were in a local WalMart, browsing down the aisles. The couple was getting an apartment together and they needed to buy an assortment of items for their new place. While Maria was looking at picture frames, Jamal decided he was going to get a tool box in the hardware section. They agreed to meet at the check out in fifteen minutes. After grabbing a couple of frames and placing them in the shopping cart, Maria looked up and saw a tall, big woman with two young kids pushing another shopping cart down the aisle heading in her direction. The woman looked familiar, but Maria just could not remember who she was. As the woman got ten feet from Maria's cart, she noticed Maria for the first time and their eyes met. Both seemed to recognize each other at the same moment.

"Audrey Bowes!"

"Maria Ortega!"

They both hugged. A funny sight since Maria's head was still level with Audrey's chest.

"How are you, Audrey? It has been a long time."

"I am fine, Maria. I am very happy. I am married and here are my kids." Audrey then formally introduced Maria to her two little girls, who were ages four and three.

The two caught up for a couple of minutes and then they both stopped talking. A few seconds of awkward silence followed.

Maria broke the silence.

"Audrey, I owe you an apology for fighting you and being mean to you when we were in junior high school. I had a lot of anger in me and was a different person back then. I want you to know that I am sorry."

Audrey smiled, looked at Maria and said, "I know you are, Maria. I also know how well you have done; how you have turned your life around. I am really proud of you. It takes a lot of guts to do what you did."

The two old classmates hugged again. Thinking that the conversation was over, Maria began to push her shopping cart past Audrey's and was about to say goodbye when Audrey held up her hand.

"Maria, there is something that I think that you should know."

Slightly confused, Maria said, "Ok. What is it, Audrey?"

Audrey's eyes started to well up with tears.

"Maria, I know that you are not the same person, but when we had that fight, you really damaged my eye. I can't see out of it well and the vision is blurred. The doctors think they can fix it, but (she then pointed to her children) my husband and I can't afford the surgery. I am not bitter. I just think you should know that."

On hearing this, Maria's eyes began to tear up as well. Maria had been so proud of her transformation that she often treats her past life like it did not exist. But it did exist. On occasion, one of her former schoolmates will walk up to her and tell her how much they feared her; that they were scared to be in the same room with her and so on. But hearing Audrey talk about the permanent damage to her eye reawakened Maria to the fact that one's actions bear consequences. And, we cannot run from those consequences.

"I am so glad you told me, Audrey. Yes, I am different. But I can't be allowed to forget the pain that I have caused for you and many others. Can you please forgive me?"

Maria wanted to fall on her knees and cry, but she just stood looking at Audrey.

Audrey simply smiled and said, "Maria, you have been forgiven a long time ago. I was serious when I said that I am proud of you. I really am."

They hugged again, only to be joined by Audrey's two girls, who wanted to be in on the action. As they laughingly were separating from each other, Jamal walked up and said hello.

After being introduced, the three chatted for a few more minutes before Audrey began to push the cart down the aisle, saying that she had to go find her husband. As Jamal and Maria were waving their goodbyes to Audrey and her girls, Audrey looked at Jamal and said with a wink, "Jamal, you be sure to take care of my girl. She is one hell of a fighter!"

Maria is finishing up college, works full time as a dental assistant and will graduate with a degree in biology. She plans on attending dental school thereafter and wants to do missionary work in poverty-stricken communities. She is still with Jamal and they are very happy.

After having been divorced for over ten years, Angie and Reyes got back together and remarried. They are doing very well. Maria and her mother have a much better relationship and are able to communicate more than they ever could in the past.

Elizabeth is married with two children. She is a Fulbright scholar, college graduate, and Licensed Practical Nurse. She and Maria remain close.

Reyes Jr. got into gangs and drugs and spent a brief time in jail. He is trying to put his life back together.

Isabel Garcia still teaches and continues to put children on the right path. She and Maria talk regularly and are very close.

Dr. Lance Burton is still active in education and is now superintendent of a school district. He says that Maria Ortega is the biggest success story that he has seen in all of his years in education.

Donald

"I don't care what you say," Mrs. Jones said to the police Captain, "we don't see any police patrolling in our community. I can sit on my porch for hours and not see one squad car. It is obvious that the pO-lice," she emphasized, "don't care nothin about us!" The room began to erupt in a smattering of applause and cries of "Amen," "That's right!" and "You tell 'em, Mrs. Jones!" But Mrs. Jones did not need any encouragement. She was just getting warmed up.

"We all see them boys hustling those drugs. I know you must see them. They puttin' poison in our community. Since ya'll don't want to do your jobs, why don't you tell the Mayor to put more money in recreation programs so that these boys have something else to do other than fall prey to them no good hustlers. We need more young men like Donald. Stand up, Donald!" Mrs. Jones bellowed. At that moment, a tall, hulking dark-skinned young man, with a striking resemblance to Oscar-winning actor Forest Whitaker, dutifully rose from his seat. The audience of approximately twenty-five people, most of whom were senior citizens began to clap. Other than the two young police officers, who were at the meeting with their precinct Captain, Donald was the only person in the room under forty years of age.

The people in the room were attending the March meeting of the Far Westside Civic Association which was held the first Tuesday of every month in the cafeteria of Frederick Douglas High School located in the Kinloch section of St. Louis, Missouri. Kinloch is universally known as one of the roughest neighborhoods in the country. Among urban neighborhoods, it ranks near the top in crime, poverty, drug and alcohol abuse, homelessness, and teenage pregnancy. The drug trade is the biggest industry in Kinloch and Far Westside Civic Association President Ruth Jones has been fighting drug dealers and the police who let them peddle their wares for years. With each tirade, she alternatively blasts the boys on the corner while at the same time clamoring for more activities that would keep them off the streets.

Donald Sims was always the example she used when she wanted to point to a "good kid."

Donald was a student at Douglas High. He was a senior scheduled to graduate in three months. Donald was repeating his senior year. His problem, however, was not one of academic deficiency. Quite simply, Donald had no support at home.

Donald attended nearly every Far Westside Civic Association meeting. He was the first to show up and the last to leave. He had not missed a meeting since early last fall. Mrs. Jones loved Donald, even though she hardly knew him. She was just glad that a young person would take the time and make the effort to come to her meetings every month.

With Donald now standing, Mrs. Jones continued with her speech. "Captain, we are not here for ourselves," she stated. "We are here for young men like Donald. That boy is our future. Now, you need to clean up our streets so more of our young-ins, like Donald, can come to our meetings!" Fully satisfied, Mrs. Jones sat down and let the Captain finish his report. He basically agreed with Mrs. Jones about more recreation for the kids, but blamed the city's budget for his inability to provide regular patrols. Donald, now back in his seat, listened intently and occasionally nodded his head to show that he was paying attention. In truth, he could not wait for the meeting to end. After every meeting, the attendees are treated to light snacks and punch. To Donald, this was a luxury, something he looked forward to each month. He was hungry and could not wait to eat.

Little did Donald know that he was not the only person from the Douglas High School community attending the meeting. Or at least monitoring the meeting. Samuel Klein, one of Donald's teachers, was watching the meeting from the far corner of the cafeteria, virtually out of site from nearly everyone in the room. Mr. Klein was, in fact, hiding from Donald. He did not want Donald to see him, because he was waiting to see where Donald was going when the meeting was over.

Mr. Klein was worried about Donald. He liked Donald a lot, but knew that Donald had major issues at home. As the two of them got to know each other, Mr. Klein found out more and more details about Donald's dysfunctional home life. Donald told Mr. Klein about his tempestuous relationship with his mother, Doris, who is an alcoholic, a mean alcoholic who does unthinkable things when she is drunk. His mother always referred to Donald as her problem child when compared to her other son, Donald's older brother. The truth is that Donald was not a problem child, but rather, his mother was a mean, difficult woman who harbored ill will toward Donald largely because he is the spitting image of his father. In short, Donald never had a chance with her.

Donald told Mr. Klein about his father, who he never really knew, but who shows up every now and then to see who in the house has some money to "loan" him. That amounted to a visit once a year or so.

Against this backdrop, Donald pretty much raised himself. He and his older brother, Tommy, had a good relationship, but Tommy was eight years older and long gone during the rough times. When his mother got mad at Donald, she would kick him out of the house, often for no reason. She berated him and abused him, physically and verbally. She constantly told him that he would not amount to anything; that he was going to be a nobody just like his father. So she offered Donald no support, no encouragement, no love.

But despite his background and his mother's negative influence, Donald had two things going for him that no one could take from him: he was smart and he was determined. Donald was by far one of the smarter students in his class. His grades did not reflect his aptitude, but there was no question that he was naturally smart.

Mr. Klein saw how smart Donald was the previous year, Donald's first senior year. Mr. Klein teaches English grammar and AP English to seniors at Douglas High. He has been doing so for twenty-five years. And his students love him. To say that Mr. Klein is legendary at Douglas is an understatement. He joined the staff at the school right after getting his masters in English at Yale. Since then, he taught thousands of students and witnessed firsthand the decline of the neighborhood. From white to black, from middle class to poor, Mr. Klein has seen it all. Amazingly, he possesses that rare likable trait that endears him to everyone. Part of that attraction is his appearance. Tall, with long blond hair and soft blue eyes, Mr. Klein presents as the least threatening person you could ever meet. Born and raised in North Carolina, he has a slight southern drawl, but not the accent that conjures up images of racist southerners. When one hears Mr. Klein speak, you assume that he grew up in a family that was sympathetic to the civil rights movement. Which is exactly right. Mr. Klein's father, Samuel Klein Sr. did volunteer legal work for the NAACP in Durham, North Carolina.

The main reason why Mr. Klein is so beloved at Douglas is because he cares so much for the kids. His whole life centers around his students. Girlfriends have come and gone for that very reason. His last fiancé bluntly told him. "Sam, I refuse to marry Douglas High School, but it seems you won't have it any other way!" Over the years, Mr. Klein has done what good, committed teachers do every day in this country. He gives his own money: to students, to get classroom supplies, to pay for class trips, to pay for meals, to pay for clothes, to pay rent, to pay for college applications, whatever it takes to help a child that he feels he can help. But Mr. Klein also does more. As the neighborhood changed and the students became more poor, Mr. Klein noticed an increase in homelessness among his students. It was not unusual for him to have two to three students in a class coping with day-to-day living issues. Some were living in shelters, some in between relatives, a few on the streets. Mr. Klein became very resourceful in finding ways to help these students who did not know where they may sleep from one day to the next. He knew the rules and requirements for all of the local shelters, he knew where and how to access the area food banks and he knew the local young Alderman, Antonio Hubbard, who he would call when he really needed a big "ask."

Mr. Klein also had a bedroom at his apartment ready, when needed, for crisis situations. Mr. Klein has lived in the same three-bedroom apartment for over ten years. His place is located less than four miles from Douglas and several years ago, as the neighborhood changes became more evident, he set up one of his bedrooms as a guest room of sorts for students in need. He has his own internal system of do's and don'ts associated with staying at his place. No drugs, no sex, and doing homework is a requirement. He also limits individual stays to two weeks, usually more than enough time for him to maneuver around the system to find a more permanent solution. He also had to establish a rule limiting repeat visits. He developed this rule when he discovered that a student, who became attached to Mr. Klein, fabricated his homelessness so he could live at Mr. Klein's place. The boy did have challenges when he and his mother were evicted, but she found a new place rather quickly. After three days with Mr. Klein, the boy decided he would prefer to live with him than his own mother. Hence, Mr. Klein does not allow repeats.

Interestingly, Mr. Klein has noticed that the growing student homelessness problem is bigger among boys than girls. He does not know why that is the case, but it makes it a lot easier for him because he does not allow female students to stay at his place, for obvious reasons.

As Mrs. Jones was wrapping up the Far Westside meeting, Mr. Klein was eyeing Donald from across the room. Something is up with Donald, Mr. Klein thought. He wondered whether his mother had kicked Donald out again. He hoped the kid was alright.

Donald stayed with Mr. Klein for ten days the previous year, Donald's first senior year. Their friendship was etched in stone after that visit. At the time, Donald was a student in Mr. Klein's senior English class. Of all the students that Mr. Klein has met, none was quite like Donald. The kid had been through so much. But he continued to persevere. Candidly, Mr. Klein did not know another child who had faced the cruelty that Donald had endured in his young life. Mr. Klein will never forget that night, when Donald poured out his heart and soul, telling Mr. Klein things that no one knew. Donald had been staying at Mr. Klein's apartment for about a week when the floodgates opened. Mr. Klein was unprepared for all that he heard that night. Halfway through the conversation, at about 3:00 a.m., Mr. Klein told Donald he had to go to the bathroom. He did that so he could sit on the stool and cry. How could anyone be so mean and vicious to an innocent child?

In sum, Donald's mother had abused him consistently since his father moved out when Donald was six. For years, she would wake him up in the middle of the night and beat him. For no reason. During the day, she would constantly berate him. She said he was a ghetto child, just like his father, who would never amount to anything. She always referred to him as no good. She refused to cook for him, preparing just enough for her and Tommy. When Tommy started to share his food with Donald, she would beat them both. As Tommy got older and intervened more during Doris' beatings of Donald, she began to strategically pick on Donald when Tommy was not around.

Occasionally, Doris would have men in the apartment. They would drink, have sex, and pass out. By then, Tommy was practically living with a friend. He could not wait to move out when he was eighteen. Donald, on the other hand, was left to fend for himself. When Doris had company, Donald used to lock his door. He started locking his door after getting a beaten by his mother and a boyfriend one night. They just came into his bedroom in a drunken stupor and beat him with two belts.

Then the worse thing happened. One night, Donald fell asleep, forgetting to lock his bedroom door. His mother had one of her boyfriends over that night. Both were drinking, both passed out. In the middle of the night, however, the man came into Donald's bedroom while he was asleep and sexually assaulted him. Donald was nine years old.

From that moment on, Donald became totally insular. Always a bit of a loner, Donald became the kid in class who talked with nobody and hung by himself. Back then, he was slight in his size. So he was picked on a lot. There were days when he would be beaten up by classmates only to go home to be beaten by Doris.

In spite of it all, Donald had something in him that transcended all that he had to endure. This trait is what attracted Mr. Klein to him even as Donald shared his story that night. More than bitterness, Donald conveyed a determination to succeed beyond what was expected by anybody. That night, Mr. Klein told Donald that he was smart and had the ability to go to college. Donald response was to look at Mr. Klein like he had seen a ghost. In Donald's world, no one in his family had graduated from high school. Tommy dropped out in the twelfth grade, but was good with his hands and worked with a home improvement company. Plus, the years of verbal abuse by Doris left countless confidence scars on Donald. His goal was simple: graduate from high school and join the army. Although Mr. Klein continued to urge Donald to consider college, he vowed that night to do everything in his power to help him reach his goal of graduating from high school.

Mr. Klein knew that Donald had deep-rooted psychological challenges. No one could go through what Donald has and be unscathed. Mr. Klein could tell that he needed counseling, but he did not push the issue that night. It was the first time that Donald had ever opened up like that with anyone. Mr. Klein would keep gaining Donald's confidence and, at the right time, get him to a counselor.

The Far Westside meeting was now officially over. Mr. Klein smiled to himself as he saw Donald make a beeline to the food. The senior citizens were fawning all over him. One stout lady grabbed his hand and took him to another tall, thin woman who was "fixing" everyone's plate. With a big grin, she gave Donald an extra helping of everything. These old ladies loved the fact that a teenager was a regular at their meetings. Donald was eating it all up, literally and figuratively. He was clearly enjoying himself.

Watching Donald eat made Mr. Klein feel hungry. "That boy sure can eat," Mr. Klein thought. He then chuckled to himself as he recalled the time he took Donald to his first fancy restaurant, Ruth's Chris Steakhouse. Mr. Klein and another teacher took Donald there to celebrate the "A" grade he had received in both of their classes. Donald confessed that he had never been to a restaurant where he had a waitress wait on him. Donald literally "destroyed" the steak and lobster he had ordered. He was having the time of his life. When he finished, he went to the restroom. After he was gone for over ten minutes, Mr. Klein became concerned, so he went to look for Donald. As he was walking toward the restroom, he saw Donald standing in front of the fireplace located near the bar with a big grin on his face. "What's wrong, Donald?" Mr. Klein asked. "I thought you got lost." "Nothing, Mr. Klein," Donald replied. "This is great. I have never seen a fireplace before and the bartender says they burn it all the time." He was eighteen at the time.

As Donald waited for the stout lady to get him one final glass of lemonade, Mr. Klein hoped that whatever he finds out that night will not leave him depressed. He cared about Donald and knew that the kid had been hurt a lot. Recently, Donald had been more secretive, less forthcoming. He did not think that Donald was into drugs, but something was not right. Every time Mr. Klein tried to engage Donald about his mother or his living situation, Donald would avoid the conversation and move on. As Mr. Klein became more observant, he noticed that Donald was always at the school. Not only did he come to every Far Westside meeting, he would show up at band practice, even though he was not in the band. Mr. Klein also saw Donald at all the girls' basketball practices, though that could be because Donald had been dating Teisha Smalls, one of the stars on Douglas' girl's basketball team. Still, Mr. Klein fretted over what was happening at home with Donald and his mother. As a result, he decided that he would do what any good nosey snoop would do. He was going to follow Donald home.

By now, Donald had hugged everyone in the meeting, including the police Captain and the two young cops. He was waving his goodbyes and was walking out of the north door to the cafeteria headed toward his locker. Mr. Klein, hiding at the south door, emerged from behind the pillar where he had been standing and passed his way through the cafeteria, extending greetings to the community folks who were cleaning up from their meeting.

Donald's locker was just past the cafeteria entrance, about thirty feet past the door. Mr. Klein watched as Donald opened his locker and carefully placed several books and notebooks into his backpack. He then closed his locker and started to walk down the hall. Surprisingly, when he reached the end of the hall, Donald made a left instead of a right, which would have taken him toward the exit doors. Mr. Klein quietly followed behind Donald and watched him walk down the hall and then go up the stairwell leading to the second floor of the building.

"Where is he going?" Mr. Klein thought.

Mr. Klein hurried down the hall, stopping at the base of the stairwell so he could peer up the stairs. He could hear Donald's lumbering frame overhead on the next floor. Mr. Klein ran up the stairs and, upon entering the second floor hallway, looked both to his left and right, but did not see a thing.

Just then, he heard a commotion coming from the boiler room, the entrance of which was located about fifteen feet to the left further down the hall. Mr. Klein bolted down the hall and quietly opened the door to the boiler room. The room was nearly pitch black, but he could make out Donald's frame at the top of a ladder in the back of the room. The boiler room was full of boiler equipment, heaters, and tanks, some of which extended as high as eight feet. The walking space was very narrow inside the room and Mr. Klein would have never seen Donald on the ladder if he had not entered the room at the very moment that Donald was on the top rung.

Mr. Klein maneuvered to the back of the room toward the base of the ladder. Above him, he heard a bit of clanging and shuffling. "What the heck is this kid, doing?" Mr. Klein thought to himself.

Mr. Klein then grabbed hold of the ladder and began to climb it. Just as he was approaching the top rung, it became eerily quiet. Mr. Klein wondered if Donald had realized that he was being followed. Suddenly, Mr. Klein noticed that he was dripping wet with sweat. "I am getting too old for this stuff," he thought.

Taking a deep breath, Mr. Klein reached for the ladder's top rung and climbed over the bar upon which the ladder was resting. Looking around, Mr. Klein recognized that he was in a storage attic near the school's roof. There were boxes, shelves, and debris everywhere. Looking to his left, in between two floor and ceiling shelves, he noticed that a light was on. Mr. Klein crept toward where the first shelf was located. He had to carefully walk around randomly placed boxes and paper.

When he reached the shelf, he poked his head around the end of it and saw a school desk with a lamp on it. He also saw a old cot just past the desk with a crusty pillow on it. Hangars with a few clothes were hanging from pipes coming down from the ceiling. Books, notebooks, binders, and various stacks of papers were positioned near the desk and the cot. Sitting on a chair, stationed right by the desk was Donald, with his AP English book open. He was doing his homework. Donald Sims was living in his high school.

There comes a time when every good teacher questions what they do and how they do it. This was one of those times. Of all the things that Mr. Klein expected to see, he did not expect to see what he saw. One of his students was living in his high school. Donald's initial reaction was defensive. "What are you doing here, Mr. Klein?" he asked. Mr. Klein merely folded his arms, cocked his head to the side, raised his left eyebrow and said nothing. Donald responded by doing what any other kid would do under the circumstances. He began to cry.

Mr. Klein realized that this was not the time for lectures. He simply briefly and gently hugged Donald and said, "Let's go to my place so you can get a good night's sleep. We will work this out in the morning." So much for the no repeaters rule. Donald and Mr. Klein ambled down the ladder and through the building. They then got into Mr. Klein's car and went to his apartment.

Once at Mr. Klein's place, he prepared some hot chocolate for Donald, one of his favorite drinks and they sat at the dining room. Mr. Klein sat prepared to receive the second spilling of the guts session with Donald, fully hoping that this session will not be as hard for him to receive as the first. To begin, Donald shared information that Mr. Klein already knew. He was aware of the fact that during Donald's first senior year, he and his mother had a major run in. It happened in November, right after Thanksgiving. Donald was, by then seventeen and fully developed. In fact, Donald had grown from a scrawny kid to a large human being: six feet, four inches and over 240 pounds. Donald played on the high school football team as an offensive guard and he was no longer picked on by classmates. Nobody messed with Donald Sims. Always a bit of a gentle giant, Donald would still react violently if pushed into a corner or if someone got in his face, particularly if they tried to approach him by surprise. Donald did not like people sneaking up on him or crowding his space. One would guess that years of being awakened in the middle of the night to be beaten would have that affect on you.

In fact, the first time Mr. Klein saw Donald was during Donald's junior year while Mr. Klein was monitoring the parking lot during lunch time. Apparently, Donald and another boy were having a disagreement near some parked cars. The boy was also on the football team and he was just about the same size as Donald.

Donald rarely, if ever raised his voice, but the other kid was yelling the whole time. Finally, Donald turned to walk away, saying, "Man, just leave it alone." The boy then ran toward Donald getting within inches of Donald's face. Before, Mr. Klein could say or do anything, Donald picked the boy up, like the wrestlers do on TV and hurled him over two cars. After landing on the third car, the boy staggered to his feet, muttered something about Donald being crazy, and stumbled back into the school. That was Mr. Klein's introduction to Donald Sims.

Due to his size, Doris limited the middle of the night surprise beatings. She continued to verbally chastise him, but the physical abuse died down. On one night, however, Doris came home plastered by alcohol. Donald was sleep when she came in, but she began to pitch a fit about the dishes not being washed. She burst into Donald's room with a butcher knife in her hand, screaming and hollering the entire time. Donald placed his arms near his face to shield himself from her violent, swinging arms. In doing so, Donald sustained several cuts on both forearms. He was finally able to wrestle the knife away from his mother and push her to the floor.

One of the neighbors in a nearby apartment heard the noise and they called the police. As soon as the police began banging on the door, Doris begged Donald not to tell them that she had cut him with the knife. She literally dropped on her knees while pleading for him to cover for her. Donald calmly answered the door, explained to the police exactly what had happened and showed them the cuts on his arms. Doris glared at him hatefully as she was being handcuffed by the police.

Since Donald was seventeen at the time, the Missouri department of Child and Family Services needed to find a place for him to live. Donald resisted foster care. He had heard so many horror stories about kids being abused in that system and, aware of his own history had planned to stick it out with his mother until he could graduate and get in the service. It was decided that Donald could live with his brother Tommy and his girlfriend, who stayed in the suburbs about fifteen miles from St. Louis. Since Tommy's girlfriend was initially resistant, Donald offered to pay part of the rent. He then started to work at a KFC near Tommy's residence and had to drop out of school.

Donald was so naïve that he did not understand the notion of transferring credits or moving to a new school. He mistakenly believed that if he did not graduate from Douglas, he would have to practically start over. So he dropped out. After several months, however, he grew weary of his mother reminding him that she was right about him: that he would never graduate from high school and that he was no good like his father. Therefore, he decided to swallow a little pride and move back home so he could finish his senior year. He also agreed to pay his mother the rent he had been paying Tommy.

Mr. Klein was aware of these facts, but he let Donald keep talking. It was evident that the kid needed to get it all out. The butcher knife incident occurred approximately six weeks after Donald stayed at Mr. Klein's apartment the first time. That stay was generated by Doris' spontaneous insistence that Donald leave the house. Apparently, she was "sick and tired of looking at his face." Donald gladly obliged her request because he was sick and tired of being berated while he was trying to do homework, so he called Mr. Klein. Mr. Klein distinctly remembers getting that midnight call from Donald. As a practice, Mr. Klein writes his home telephone number on the blackboard on the first day of every new class. He tells his students to call him if they face a crisis. That offering has led to late-night visits to jails, hospitals, and shelters, as well as other assorted venues in St. Louis. One of the more surprising and noteworthy calls came from a female student who was all alone, but about to deliver a baby. Mr. Klein picked the girl up, but they did not make it to the hospital in time. Mr. Klein delivered the baby. Proudly, he is now Samuel Klein Jabari Simmons' godfather.

After that week with Mr. Klein, Donald made up with his mother and moved back home. Little did Mr. Klein know that less than two months later, Donald's mother would attack him with a butcher knife, forcing him to drop out of school. Strangely, Donald never sought advice from Mr. Klein about his schooling options when it was decided that he would move in with Tommy. Accustomed to shrinking within his shell, Donald burrowed himself deep into a shell after being attacked by his mother. Fortunately, he found his way back in school, another testament to the willpower and determination that Donald uniquely possessed.

Mr. Klein pressed Donald about what had happened to lead him to move out. Donald then related that in order to pay his mother the rent, he had begun to work at McDonald's which was located halfway between his mother's apartment and Douglas High. By then, Donald was dating Teisha. One Saturday, in early December, Teisha picked Donald up from work in her car so they could go to the movies.

Donald needed to stop by home to change out of his work uniform. As soon as they walked in, Doris began to taunt them both. "Ain't you that basketball star I've seen on TV?" she said to Teisha. "Why you wasting your time with my son? You know he ain't no good." Donald was furious. He had always shielded his friends, what few he had, from his mother. Now, he was totally embarrassed. He grabbed his clothes, took Teisha's hand, and the two of them walked out of the door toward her car. Donald changed in the car and they had a great time at the movies, never once mentioning the episode with his mother.

For Donald, the incident was the last straw. He just could not take it anymore. But, he remained determined to graduate from high school and join the army. He fervently believed as long as he stayed focus, he would reach his goal. That being said, he could no longer live with his mother.

After Teisha dropped him off in front of his mother's that evening, Donald walked in the apartment to get some of his things. Fortunately, his mother was not at home. He put his books in his backpack, loaded a few clothes into a duffel bag and left. The problem was that he had no place to go. He was well aware of Mr. Klein's no repeaters rule and Donald had lived his life in a way that did not allow many people to get close to him. He decided to go to Douglas High, sleep in the boys' locker room for the rest of the weekend until he could decide on a permanent solution. Donald knew how to sneak into the school and once inside, he decided to explore every nook and cranny he could find. That was the night he discovered the attic located in the boiler room.

After a few nights, Donald realized that the sleeping above the boiler room may work for longer than he first suspected. He soon picked up on the schedules, the comings and goings of every one on the staff. He knew the maintenance and janitorial crew were fundamentally lazy. They never went up the ladder to the attic to clean and when it was time to store something they tossed it over the bar and let it stay where it landed.

Donald also developed his own daily schedule, which ended up being fairly productive. He was up everyday at 5:00 a.m. and would go to the boys' locker room for his daily shower. The custodial staff was supposed to clock in by 6:30 a.m., but Donald soon discovered that the four of them rarely clocked in before 7:00 a.m.

Donald still worked at McDonald's, but only on Monday, Wednesday, and Saturday. On work nights, he would head back to the school, do his homework, and fall asleep exhausted. On Tuesdays, he attended the various events and meetings at the school. This ranged from Mrs. Jones' Far Westside civic association meeting to band practice and the chess club meeting. On Thursday, he sat in on the girls' basketball practice. He really like to watch Teisha play. They still dated somewhat, but she did not know he was living at the school.

On Sunday, Donald would attend service all day at Mount Sinai Baptist Church. Like the civic association members, the church ladies doted on him incessantly. Donald loved the attention. He especially loved the sumptuous repast which they prepared after the last service. That Sunday church dinner represented his best meal of the week.

By living in the school, Donald also picked up on the juicy clandestine stuff. He knew where the kids hid and did drugs, something he did not know before taking up residence in the school attic. One night, he also heard two young teachers sneak into the boiler room to make out. He enjoyed sharing that information with Mr. Klein almost as much as he enjoyed watching them from the attic.

While listening to Donald, Mr. Klein kept thinking that something was wrong with this picture. How could a student, one of his students, live in his high school for three months and nobody know it? Mr. Klein stood up and looked evenly at Donald. "Donald, he said, you are an amazing young man. Don't you ever believe that you are no good. You are one of the best people I know. Now, why don't you get a good night sleep. I will reach out to Alderman Hubbard tomorrow and we will work this thing out. And don't worry, you will graduate and make it to the service." Donald had a huge smile on his face as he walked to Mr. Klein's guest bedroom. He felt like a load had been lifted off of his shoulders. That night, he slept like a baby.

Alderman Antonio "Tony" Hubbard was a rising star in St. Louis political circles. He was tall, articulate, and decent looking, with a winning smile. And he cared. That was the problem. Alderman Hubbard ran for office to make a difference in a big way. He wanted to be a major player in crafting solutions to those problems that ail urban communities. But his constituents live in one of the toughest communities in the nation. They did not need esoteric help. They needed real help now. In many ways, Alderman Hubbard was overwhelmed by the depth and the breadth of the need. He and his staff worked hard to rise above the level of crisis solvers, but, in many ways, that was the thing they did best everyday.

Rodney Jenkins was Alderman Hubbard's right-hand man and Director of his Constituent Services Office. Jenkins was the man to get things done. He would make sure that the pothole got filled, the roof got repaired at the recreation center, and that the police showed up, at least most of the time. Truth be told, the recent crime wave in St. Louis had put almost every other issue on the back burner. Like Mrs. Jones at the Far Westside civic association, Alderman Hubbard had been all over the police about visibility and neighborhood patrols. It had become the number one priority of his office. In fact, the Alderman was on the phone with the St. Louis Chief of Police when Jenkins walked into his office, motioning for the Alderman to cover the phone.

"What's up, Rodney?" Alderman Hubbard whispered.

"I've got Sam Klein, the teacher at Douglas High on the phone. He wants you to come to the school right away to show you something. He says he can't talk about it, you need to see it," Jenkins said.

"I'm talking to the chief," the Alderman replied.

"Boss, I think you need to go see what Klein wants you to see."

That was all that Alderman Hubbard needed to hear.

"O.K.," he said, "But, you are riding shotgun."

Mr. Klein was waiting for them as they arrived at the school and pulled into the parking lot. "Hi, Sam," the Alderman said, "this better be good."

"Mr. Alderman, you just needed to see it for yourself. Just follow me."

Mr. Klein then led the Alderman and Jenkins down the hall, up to the second floor, into the boiler room, up the ladder, around the shelves, and showed him Donald Sims' living place. After explaining the circumstances, the Alderman asked how long had Donald been living in that space. Once he heard Mr. Klein say three months, the Alderman's eyes rolled toward the ceiling.

"Don't worry, Sam. We will get the kid situated. Can I meet him?"

Mr. Klein then led the Alderman and Jenkins down the stairs to the school cafeteria, where Donald was sitting at a table, with a book in his hand.

Upon seeing Donald, the Alderman exclaimed, "Hey, I know you. Aren't you the kid who attends Mrs. Jones' civic association meetings?"

Eventually, Jenkins was able to get Donald in his own place, but not without some finessing. Under Missouri law, one must be under eighteen to gain access to the children's shelters. Through an unexplained quirk, one had to be twenty-one to gain access to the adult shelters. Therefore, if you were between eighteen and twenty-one and homeless, you had no where to go. Jenkins leaned on some federal government contacts and obtained for Donald an emergency section eight housing voucher. Within a couple of weeks, Donald had his own place.

Mr. Klein, true to form, made sure that Donald had all the essentials that he needed to outfit his new place. A school counselor gave Donald dishes and cookware. Another teacher gave him a television set and some old clothes. Mr. Klein bought Donald new sheets for his bed. It truly was a new beginning.

By the time May rolled around, Donald was ready to graduate and join the Army over the summer. To celebrate Donald's accomplishment, Mr. Klein enlisted a friend who owned a boat docked on the Mississippi River and invited Donald to join him for a boat ride. Donald was blown away by the sight of the boat and by being on a boat traveling down a river. He had never seen a boat before, so this was a real treat. Watching the joy on Donald's face reminded Mr. Klein of the expression Donald had upon seeing his first fireplace in Ruth's Chris Steakhouse. This kid certainly relished simple pleasures.

While on the boat, Mr. Klein did want to talk with Donald about graduation and his future. Mr. Klein knew that Donald was smart enough to go to college and wanted to take another stab at that issue. Mr. Klein had found out that Donald would be a Cum Laude graduate, so he was sure that he could get him into college somewhere. Plus, Mr. Klein was deeply concerned about Donald's ability to survive military life. It was apparent that Donald did not like folks in his face and Mr. Klein could envision Donald picking up his commanding officer and throwing him across the room.

As they discussed college and the army, it was painfully obvious that Donald's mind was made up. No matter what Mr. Klein said, Donald did not see himself as college material. He also did not have a clue as to how he could pay for it. College was such an unrealistic notion to Donald that the conversation was a nonstarter.

Donald was equally stubborn about the military. He continued to view military service as his ticket out of poverty. He could see the world, learn a skill and, eventually be left alone. Mr. Klein still shakes his head at the thought of that discussion.

Finally, Mr. Klein broached the subject of graduation tickets with Donald. Each graduate had two tickets that they could use to invite whoever they choose to attend the graduation. Previously, when they discussed this topic, Donald said that he wanted to invite his mother and his brother, Tommy. The more Mr. Klein thought about it, the more it bothered him that his mother would get an invitation. As far as Mr. Klein was concerned, this woman did everything in her power to nearly destroy a good kid. She did not deserve to witness his moment of success.

Mr. Klein shared his thoughts on the topic with Donald. Donald listened patiently and nodded his head, just as he would when listening to speakers at Mrs. Jones' civic association meetings. When Mr. Klein was finished, Donald stood, put his hand on his teacher's shoulder and said, "Mr. Klein, you mean more to me than anyone in the world. You believed in me and helped me when I couldn't always help myself. But I need to have my mother at my graduation. For my entire life, she has been telling me that I would never finish school and that I would never amount to anything. I want her to see me do what she never thought that I could do. I want her to be forced to brag and tell people that I am her son."

Mr. Klein could only nod his head slowly in response.

For the seniors at the Frederick Douglas High School graduation that year, the weather was as glorious and sunny as could be. The pomp and circumstance was at a fever pitch. Smiles, back slaps, and random picture taking was everywhere. People were happy.

When the school principal called Donald Sims name, he also included Cum Laude after it. Sitting with the other teachers, Mr. Klein wanted to cry, but kept it together. Donald pranced on the stage, grabbed his diploma, turned to the audience, and bowed a simple, elegant bow. He then slowly walked off the stage, fully satisfied with his accomplishment.

After the ceremony, Mr. Klein was chatting with some students when he saw, out of the corner of his eye, Donald walking toward him. He was holding Teisha's hand. Teisha had also graduated and had received a scholarship to play basketball at the University of Missouri. Walking on the other side of Teisha was a slight, older woman, who was obviously Donald's mother, Doris. Tommy was walking just behind Doris.

At first, Mr. Klein did not know how to react. Inside, he wanted to go to her, yell at her, and curse her for the things she did to her son.

But he saw how happy Donald was and remembered how mature he sounded that day on the boat. Boy, had he grown. This was not a petty kid. He had a big heart and had made his point. As hard as it was, Mr. Klein was not going to rain on Donald's parade.

Donald made the introductions, smiling the whole time. Mr. Klein shook everyone's hand and gave Donald a big bear hug. As they ended their embrace, one of Donald's football teammates walked by, gave Donald a high five, and started to introduce Donald, Teisha, and Tommy to his family. Doris walked closer to Mr. Klein and said, "I have heard a lot about you from my son. Thank you for looking out for him."

Hearing that, Mr. Klein could not contain himself. He sarcastically said in response, "Well, I have heard about you too, Mrs. Sims. A lot of what I have heard wasn't good. But, I am glad you are here on Donald's special day."

Looking her squarely in her eyes, Mr. Klein could see the meanness that he had heard so much about. Not breaking the stare, Doris said, "Sir, there are always two sides to every story. As a teacher, I would think that you would know that."

By then, Mr. Klein had gathered himself. He was done. There would be no more fighting or snippy word games. He simply said, "As I said, Mrs. Sims, I am really glad that you were here for Donald on his special day."

Picking up on the new vibe, Doris backed down as well, nodded, and began to walk away. She then caught herself, turned back around, and walked even closer to Mr. Klein. "I do have one question, sir?"

"Sure," Mr. Klein said, "What is it?"

Looking around, Doris lowered her voice and said almost conspiratorially, "What does Cum Laude mean?"

Mr. Klein could not believe it. This is better than even Donald expected, he thought. Trying hard to contain his glee, Mr. Klein leaned forward and said, "Cum laude is a special designation for graduates who have the highest grade point average. Mrs. Sims, your son was one of the smartest boys in the entire school."

Doris' eyes got as big as saucers. Clearly, you could have knocked her over with a feather. She looked at Mr. Klein, then aggressively turned to look at Donald, who was still reveling about things with his friends. She was in total shock.

Mr. Klein was ecstatic. Serves her right, he thought to himself.

Finally, Donald refocused on Mr. Klein, gave him a wink and, with family in tow, walked away. Doris kept looking up at her son in amazement.

Donald enlisted in the Army and was stationed in Georgia. At first, he did well, but Mr. Klein's fears were realized when Donald threw a fellow soldier into a wall. From all accounts, the soldier had been picking on Donald for some time. Realizing that Donald had psychological deficits due to his background, the Army discharged him and let him come back home. Donald is still a loner, but works everyday and is self-sufficient. He also still periodically sends his mother money. More than anything, he remains proud of graduating from high school against all odds.

Mr. Klein retired from teaching after over thirty years on the job. He has tried to stay in touch with Donald, but admits that Donald's tendency to be alone creates a challenge for their friendship. If Mr. Klein could change anything, he would have preferred to have met Donald during his freshman year. Had that occurred, Mr. Klein is convinced that he could have gotten Donald the counseling he needed and also talked him into considering college. While he has met hundreds of students with a myriad of challenges, Mr. Klein believes that Donald is one of the most resilient and fascinating people he has ever met.

Cristina

"Why did it have to be a man?" Cristina thought while crossing her legs and then tapping her foot. She was sitting in one of those gray metal folding chairs that line the walls of many community centers. In fact, the room in which Cristina was sitting was a refurbished community center, now redesigned as a community health building containing various health-related offices. Fourteen-year-old Cristina walked by the building everyday on her way to the bus stop to and from her new school. Once the construction was completed, she was intrigued by the sign on the window announcing free psychological counseling. After all that she had been through, she knew that she needed to talk to a professional. "I might as well do it now," she thought when she first walked into the door a week earlier. "Especially, if it's free."

What she did not really think about, however, was whether the counselor would be a man or a woman. She did not even ask when she made the appointment. She just told the lady that she needed to see a counselor. The lady told her that Cristina would be seeing Dr. Lewis. Cristina did not know that Dr. Lewis was a man. Not until she was sitting on that metal chair in the waiting area when a man came through the door and asked the lady if Martin was still seeing patients. The receptionist said in response that "Dr. Lewis has one more patient," nodding in Cristina's direction. The man looked quickly at Cristina and walked back out the door. Martin is a man's name, Cristina thought.

"How can I talk to a man about all of this?" Cristina thought. "How can I trust him?" As she pondered these questions, Cristina also wondered how much she should tell Dr. Lewis. She was just coming to grips with the fact that she needed help. But, she had not met a man who she could trust. Not one. To the contrary, nearly every man that had come into her life hurt her. Badly. Cristina did not trust men at all.

Just then, the receptionist called her name, interrupting Cristina's thoughts. She followed the lady down the hall to a small windowless office with a desk, a small couch, and two chairs. Cristina sat in one of the chairs. A tall, good-looking man in his late thirties flashed a wide smile, shook Cristina's hand, and sat in the other chair. "Hello, young lady, I am Dr. Martin Lewis. How can I help you?"

The doctor's manner put Cristina at ease. She began to tell her story. After a few minutes, however, she noticed that the doctor's eyes would occasionally shift to glance at her legs. Then they would focus on her chest area. He would then lock in on her eyes with his, conveying a subtle, yet unmistakable "come hither" look.

Cristina knew that look all too well. This cannot be happening, Cristina thought. Is he not a doctor? Finally, she stopped talking and announced that she needed to get home. Cristina bolted out the door, even after the doctor called after her. Over the next several days, Dr. Lewis called her mother's apartment, looking for Cristina. She avoided him for a time, then finally spoke with him over the phone. He asked her out. She hung up the phone, thinking to herself, "I guess I have to work my problems out by myself. I sure can't count on any man to help me. They all are the same."

Cristina was originally from Puerto Rico, as were both of her parents, Luis and Flora Hernandez. Cristina's parents had what could best be described as a volatile relationship. Luis beat Flora regularly. Sometimes Flora fought back, most of the time she did not. But Flora loved Luis passionately. She always held out hope that he would "come around."

Luis also had a drinking problem. When Cristina was very young, she remembers hating the very sight of a whiskey bottle. Her father would get drunk, beat her mother, and pass out. Flora would then curse at and break all of the whiskey bottles. Young Cristina would help. For years, Cristina believed that alcohol was the root of all evil.

Cristina was the oldest of three children. Three years behind her was Moises, two years behind him was baby Luca. Both parents had family living in the U.S. mainland, mainly in New York, New Jersey, and Washington, DC. Luis, a career construction laborer, would periodically leave the family, disappearing for weeks at a time, without a word. Flora would then get a call in which Luis would lay out an elaborate story about a new construction project in Puerto Rico or in the States that he had been working on and how he was a new man. He would then either come home or send for his family. Things would be good for a short period of time before the drinking and beatings would begin. Then he would leave. The cycle was repeated many times during Cristina's early years.

When Cristina was eleven, Flora declared that she had had enough. She was resolved to have a better life and stop the madness. She had a first cousin, Vanesa, in DC, who said that she could get Flora a job at, of all places, the liquor distillery where Vanesa worked. Flora packed up her kids and moved quickly.

At a young age, it was evident that Cristina had all of the spice and beauty associated with Puerto Rican stereotypes. With her long black hair, flawless features, and confident gait, she drew double takes from men and women alike, even when she was four years old. "You should put your daughter in the movies," passersby would say to Flora on the street. "What a beautiful little girl," others would say. As she grew older, Cristina's womanly shape also developed quickly. When the family moved to Washington, DC, she looked older than her eleven years.

Cristina was also a fighter. Having dealt with an irresponsible father and wounded mother, Cristina assumed the role of family protector. Comfortably situated as the oldest child, her protector role was needed at school in Puerto Rico, to look after her brother, Moises. Moises was sickly and weak as a child. While Cristina's spirit was more like her father's, Moises adopted many of his mother's docile tendencies. He was picked on and beaten up as soon as he started school. That meant that big sister, Cristina, had to pay someone back at their school every week.

Although Cristina was smart, while in Puerto Rico, she never had the luxury of enjoying school. Most days, she came to school worried about her mother and wondering when she would next see her father, hoping against hope that he would change his ways. That stress was multiplied when her brother started school. She often would sit in her class worrying about whether Moises was surviving in his own classroom. All in all, young Cristina was happy to be moving to the United States.

Vanesa lived in a four-story row house located in the Columbia Heights section of Washington, DC, a neighborhood that was developing an significant Latino population. Interestingly, most of the Hispanic immigrants in DC came from El Salvador and other parts of Central and South America. Unlike New York, DC did not have a large Puerto Rican population. But being in a neighborhood where Spanish was commonly spoken, even at the McDonald's and in the supermarkets, made the Hernandez' transition to the states a lot more tolerable.

Like others in that community, Vanesa regularly had relatives pass through her house for extended periods of time. Vanesa had three children who lived with her, along with her sister, Teresa and her two children. With Flora and her three children, that Columbia Heights property would house three women and their eight children. As is usually the case, the understanding was that the accommodations were temporary. Teresa had been living with Vanesa for seven months and was hoping to get her own place within the next year. But it could take longer. Upon seeing the situation, Flora knew that she also needed to be vigilant in finding her own place.

Cristina was excited about her new school. The class was bilingual and within weeks she was thriving. For the first time in her life, Cristina was in a position to enjoy school. She liked her teachers and early on knew that she could compete. Fortunately, Moises was also doing well. He found his own niche with a group of students in his class and Cristina did not worry about him during every minute of the school day. Knowing that her mother was settling in, that her brothers were safe and that she had no need to wait for her father, Cristina walked to school every day with a smile on her face. The first three months in America were the best of her life.

Vanesa had two younger brothers who also lived in DC. Ramon was in his early thirties and married to Consuela. They had two young children. Jose was in his late twenties and was married to Rosa. They were expecting their first child. On Sunday's, after church, Vanesa would host a big dinner in which Ramon and Jose would bring their families as well as other friends. On any given Sunday, as many as fifteen to twenty people could pass through the house.

During one of these Sunday dinner gatherings, Cristina happened to also be washing clothes in the basement of the house. As folks were eating, drinking, laughing, and watching the Washington Redskins football game on television, Cristina was running up and down the stairs shifting clothes from the washer to the dryer and then folding them. Happy that she was almost finished, Cristina was placing the last load in the dryer when she heard a sound behind her. She turned around and saw Ramon standing over her.

Ramon was about five feet, ten inches tall and slightly built. He fancied himself as a ladies man and always wore an open collar shirt with a couple of gold chains hanging around his neck. He had deep dark eyes and kept his wavy hair slicked back.

When Cristina turned around, Ramon was fingering one of his gold chains and eyeballing the girl in a suggestive and seductive way.

"Cristina, Cristina, Cristina," he said leeringly. "You are such a pretty young thang. You got a boyfriend?"

"I don't like boys, Uncle Ramon," Cristina said, feeling instantly uncomfortable.

The basement was dark, damp, and unfinished. Beams greeted those who walked down the stairs. At the bottom of the stairs, you had to make a hard right past the hot water heater to get to the washer and dryer. A single ceiling light hung near the appliances. To turn it on or off, one had to pull the long string extending from the light fixture. Ramon stopped fingering his gold chain, moved to his left and, with his right hand, started to play with the string. He looked at the string, then up at the light, then back at Cristina.

"My pretty little Cristina," he said, "I think that you need a boyfriend. Don't you?"

Now beyond scared, Cristina lowered her head and tried to run past him to the stairs. Ramon grabbed her, covered her mouth, and whispered in her ear, "It's either you or that cute baby brother of yours!"

Tears were streaming down Cristina's cheeks. She still squirmed and tried to get away, but to no avail. He was finished in five minutes.

Years later, Cristina reflected on how easy it is for one person to ruin the life of another or to set them on the road toward self-destruction. "How do you get off of that road?" she still asks. Does one ever really get off of that road?

For Cristina, the journey was just beginning. Numb for days, then weeks after being raped by her uncle, Cristina did not know how to respond. First, she wondered what she had done to bring this to herself. She had been told her whole life that she was beautiful and attractive. Maybe she drew too much attention to herself. Or walked a certain way. Or looked a certain way. Maybe it was all her fault.

She felt like she could not tell her mother. Would she believe her? Would anyone? Her mother did not have any money. If Cristina said something about Vanesa's brother, she might not believe it and may kick them all out. Her mother had no where else to go. Ramon had also threatened her about Moises. She could not let that happen. She did not know what to do.

Then, it happened again. And again. Anytime, Ramon was around, he would try to corner Cristina. He would learn everyone's schedule, take off from work and be waiting for Cristina as she got home from school. He would grab her, take her in the basement and rape her again.

Each time, Ramon would tell Cristina that if she screamed or told anyone, he would do the same thing to her brother, then kill her.

A couple of times, Ramon waited for Cristina outside of school. He would pull the car in front of her as she began her walk home and make her get in it. He would then pull into an alley and molest her.

Cristina would try to outfox him. Whenever he was around, she would cling to her mother, never leaving her side. If her mother went to the bathroom, Cristina would go with her and wait outside the door. Her mother never quite caught on, but used to ask Cristina why she was so clingy. Cristina would merely talk about how much she loved her mother and was proud of how she was making a new life for them.

Cristina also would arrange for several schoolmates to walk home with her. She announced to her friends that they could study at her house. Vanesa and Flora marveled at how many friends Cristina was making and they were happy that Cristina was hosting study sessions. Cristina was able to survive a few weeks through these diversions.

Suddenly, school was different for Cristina. She no longer looked forward to school. She was always worried about what was waiting for her when she got home. "I hope my mother isn't late coming home from work today," she would think to herself in the middle of class. She could not concentrate on her homework. She was always scared. This was no longer the happiest period in her life.

One Sunday, while all the family members were gathered, she saw Ramon eyeing her while whispering to his brother Jose. They were smiling, nodding, and slapping hands together in a knowing way. Jose blew Cristina a kiss. Later, Cristina was in the kitchen doing the dishes with most of the family members only fifteen feet away in the living room watching television. Jose came into the kitchen, looked around to make sure that no one else was paying attention to him and whispered in Cristina's ear.

"Meet me in the basement, beautiful one."

In response, Cristina let out a loud, long bloodcurdling scream. In her mind, she had had enough. This was not going to continue, she vowed to herself. Though still just eleven years old, that fighting, spicy spirit was coming back.

Everyone in the house ran to the kitchen and looked at the two of them in the kitchen. Jose's wife, Rosa had her hands on her hips and was staring at her husband. "What did you do to her, Jose?" she said.

"I didn't do nuttin," he stammered. Ramon was standing in the back, away from everyone else, with a look of fear in his face.

For once, Cristina had the upper hand and she knew it. Looking directly at Ramon, she said, "I just saw a mouse! You all know I am scared of mice."

Not satisfied, Rosa said that it was probably time for them to go home. Jose sheepishly followed his wife out of the kitchen and they soon left. Everyone else left as well. Later, Flora asked Cristina about what "really happened in the kitchen." Cristina stuck with her story, but the abuse was over. Her uncle had been raping her repeatedly for nearly a year, but never after that day.

Within a couple weeks of that incident, Flora and Vanesa had an impromptu birthday party for Cristina's twelfth birthday. It was really a double celebration. Flora had found her own place, so the Hernandez family would be leaving Vanesa's house. To celebrate Cristina's birthday, Ramon's wife Consuela, had bought Cristina several nice dresses. Consuela always treated Cristina good. It made Cristina feel all the more guilty about what had happened between her and Ramon. At least it was all over.

For Cristina, who already had issues with her own father's actions, having been abused by her uncle, left her to distrust all men. It also sapped the drive and zeal for life out of the once optimistic girl. By the time Cristina and her family moved into their new apartment, her self-esteem had plummeted and she just did not care about school or anything else. Still a beautiful girl, she felt like she was the ugliest girl in her school, having been wracked with guilt over being abused.

When she was older, Cristina came to understand that all women face sexual abuse or harassment of some kind. Oftentimes, such abuse occurs in families. More likely than not, the abuse is suppressed and, like Cristina's situation, never adequately addressed. At the time, however, as a twelve-year-old girl, Cristina felt painfully alone, just like millions of women around the globe are left to fend for themselves and work through the myriad of emotions and consequences resulting from having been abused.

One immediate consequence was that Cristina's spicy side took on a mean persona, especially with boys. She began to get into fights at her school, something that she had not done since moving to the States. She started to curse like a wayward sailor and was suspended from school for the first time because she cursed out a male teacher who was monitoring the playground. The teacher was merely trying to get Cristina to stop playing kickball and come in from recess. Overreacting, Cristina hurled a string of expletives at the teacher, causing all the kids nearby to look at her with astonishment. Sitting in the principal's office, Cristina admitted to herself that the teacher looked a little bit like her uncle Ramon. He never knew what hit him.

What made matters worse was the reemergence of her father. Just a few weeks from Cristina's thirteenth birthday, Luis appeared on the family's doorstep, ready to be welcomed back into the fold. By then, however, Flora had the strength to resist his advances. They never reconciled as a couple.

It took a while for Luis to believe that he could not win his wife back. He had moved to the Washington area and was working on several downtown construction projects. Since Flora would not let him move back in, he found an apartment in the Shaw neighborhood, near Howard University.

Cristina hated her father. In her mind, she naturally blamed him for all that had happened to both her and her mother. Not only was she abused, but the family was still very poor. In many ways, being poor in the States is worse than being poor in Puerto Rico. Flora was struggling daily to get by and there was nowhere to turn for additional support. It galled Cristina to see her father smiling and trying to woo her mother after all of this time.

In truth, Cristina was more hurt than she was angry. Like most little girls, she loved her father and needed her daddy, something Luis could never be. When Luis appeared on their doorstep, Cristina actually shared the feelings of her mother: anger, sadness, joy, excitement, and relief. Strangely, she still longed for his love and his approval.

Although he was a scoundrel, Luis' intuitions were sharp. He soon realized that his daughter had assumed the role of leader in the family. He initially tried to win Flora back by courting Cristina with kindness. When this did not work, he tried to bring Cristina down, at least in Flora's eyes. Luis would come by the apartment two or three times a week, ostensibly to check in on Moises or Luca and ask about school. Cristina always greeted her father with disdain, often leaving the room when he came by, sometimes loudly slamming the door behind her. Through conversations with Flora, Luis learned of Cristina's problems at school and began to weigh in on the matter.

"You know what the problem is, Flora," he would say. "Look at her. She wants to be a woman; she is not interested in being in school. Watch, one of these knuckleheads will be sniffing around her real soon! You just mark my words."

In reality, Cristina was so hostile to boys that getting involved with them was the last thing on her mind. There was one boy, however, who Cristina viewed as a friend. Gabriel Boler was a year older than Cristina and attended the middle school in which she had just enrolled. His mother was from El Salvador and his father was an African American from DC. Gabriel was a good, nice kid. Frankly, that is the only way that he could have been Cristina's friend. He put up with all of her crap.

Cristina treated Gabriel badly, but he kept taking it. He would carry her books as they walked to the bus stop as she was cursing him out the whole time. He never raised his voice with her and was totally deferential to her. Other schoolmates could tell that Gabriel was in love with Cristina and would tease him about how he let her treat him. He would just smile and let them talk. As far as Gabriel was concerned, Cristina was the sun, moon, and stars. He would take whatever she dished his way.

After a while, Gabriel would drop by Flora's apartment to pick Cristina up so they could go to school or attend school events together. Though not officially dating (Cristina would have none of that), the two teens were spending a lot of time with each other. One day, Gabriel dropped by while Luis was visiting. Luis looked Gabriel up and down and scowled at him. Gabriel, feeling uncomfortable told Cristina that he would see her at school because he had left something at his house. The frightened boy hurried out of the door.

Cristina was livid. She jumped right in on Luis. "You have no fu--- right to treat any of my friends like that. None whatsoever. It's too late for you to act like the caring father. Why don't you just let us be?"

Not to be outdone, and recognizing that offense was always better than defense, Luis went in another direction.

"Don't try it, miss thang. Your father knows what is going on. I see your body. I see how you walk. You are just covering up what you and that boy are doing. Don't you be bringing no babies in here. Your mama can't handle another mouth to feed."

Flora, who had been watching the entire scene, just hung her head.

Cristina was stunned. She alone knew what she had gone through. She alone harbored that which her father could not give. Now, her father was calling her a whore. She did not know how to react. She looked at her mother and her lowered head. "And my mother won't defend me?" she thought, in horror.

Cristina began to cry. It would be a long time before she would cry again, but she cried that day. Then she responded in the self-destructive way that many do when they are deeply hurt. Without saying a word, she walked out of the door, and went to the corner not far from her apartment where the drug boys hung out. Cristina then talked one of the boys into going into a liquor store to purchase some whiskey for her. The boy got for her the same kind of whiskey that her father used to drink in Puerto Rico. When the drug runner showed her the bottle, it brought back memories of Cristina and her mother breaking similar bottles while her father was in a drunken stupor.

Cristina then walked to Gabriel's house and asked him to take a walk with her. She led him to an isolated section of Rock Creek Park. Cristina then initiated two things that she had never initiated before, drinking and sex. She was crying the whole time.

Gabriel really did not know what was going on or, for that matter, what he was doing. He was but a bit player in the drama that had engulfed young Cristina's world. When they finished, Gabriel gently tried to help Cristina get dressed. She slapped his hand away. "Don't you ever fu--- touch me again."

As the two of them walked home, Gabriel began to cry. They did not say a word to each other all the way back.

They had awkward sex three or four more times over the subsequent few weeks. Soon, Cristina found out that she was pregnant. She was thirteen years old and in the eighth grade. By now, Cristina had no desire to be in school. As fate would have it, the middle school that she and Gabriel attended was one of the worst in the city. Very little learning was taking place in the school. Once it was discovered by school leaders and classmates that Cristina was pregnant, there were no horrified gasps or looks of shock. She was viewed as another statistic in a school full of statistics. It was largely assumed that Cristina would eventually drop out and many in the school secretly hoped that she would.

Cristina was doing all that she could to prove the prognosticators right. Of the 180 days of school in her eighth grade year, Cristina was marked present in her homeroom on only thirty-three days. She regularly would cut school and hang out with her friends. Sometimes she would include Gabriel, sometimes not. When she found out she was pregnant, she cursed him out and "put him on ice" for a while. Being the nice guy that he was, he hung in there and eventually, she treated him much better as the pregnancy advanced.

Flora was devastated. Not knowing her daughter's history of abuse, she had no idea where things went wrong. Luis made matters worse by being in the "I told you so" mindset; that he knew Cristina was sexually active. That approach did not help him with Flora. She began to blame him for all of Cristina's travails, claiming that things were fine before Luis came back into their lives.

Cristina finished eighth grade, turned fourteen, had her baby, a beautiful son named Eduardo, and resolved to find a way to get a job as a truck driver. Why a truck driver? In Puerto Rico, she was always fascinated by trucks. She played with miniature trucks and once, her father let her sit behind the wheel of an eighteen wheeler. What power, she thought!

Since education was not emphasized in her family, Cristina was conditioned to think about getting some kind of job right after high school, if not sooner. Most of her relatives did not have a high-school degree, so Cristina never viewed college as a realistic option.

Still, as she references even today, Cristina has always had that little voice inside her head that will not go away. Call it conscious, reason, or providence, but Cristina's little voice constantly whispers to her the right way to go, the right path to take. Sometimes, she heeds the voice immediately, sometimes she does not. Eventually, however, Cristina listens to that voice.

While she was changing her new baby's diapers, preparing for another year at her bad school, biding enough time to get her driver's license so she could fulfill her dream of driving a truck, Cristina kept getting flashbacks. Flashbacks that she could not shake. Cristina kept thinking about those first three months in the United States, before the abuse, before the drama. She remembered how much she liked school, how much she enjoyed learning new things. Cristina also recalled how good she was in school. She distinctly remembered one of her teachers commenting on an A she received on a math test. "You keep performing like this young lady, and college math will be a breeze for you."

It was the first time in her life that anyone had associated Cristina with the prospect of going to college.

That simple statement from that one teacher kept gnawing at Cristina as she cared for her newborn. Was it possible for her to get more out of her life, in spite of all that she had been through? Her little voice kept telling her that it was.

The voice grew louder one day as Cristina was visiting the health clinic for one of her postpartum checkups. On the coffee table in the sitting area, there were pamphlets advertising a new charter high school that would be opening in the fall. The new school would have a focus on math, science, and community empowerment. Cristina began reading the pamphlet and could not believe it when she read that the school would be providing day care for students with young children. Her little voice screamed.

After several calls and a school visit, Cristina enrolled in the Columbia Heights Community Charter School. With little Eduardo ensconced in day care nearby, Cristina was hoping to commit to school and see where it would lead her.

Needless to say, Cristina had a lot of emotional baggage to address. Her relationship with Gabriel was growing more and more strained, largely because Cristina continued to take all of her anger on the young man who had become her unwitting foil. Though she wanted to do the right thing, she just did not have the tools to do so, in light of the damage she had suffered. By the time she started at Community, her shattered confidence led her to retreat when times got tough. For instance, early in the new semester, Eduardo got sick, making it difficult for Cristina to keep up with her homework in one of her classes. Afraid that she would be embarrassed in class for being unprepared and uneasy about honestly confiding in her teacher, Cristina started to cut that class. Then another. The old pattern was starting. Plus, Cristina's living situation did not make things any easier for her. Both she and her baby were sleeping on the basement floor of the house her mother was renting. They could not afford a bed. Cristina was having a harder and harder time getting a good night sleep. Her back always hurt and the baby kept her up a good portion of the night. She was having a difficult time juggling everything.

Then she got a call from the clinic informing her that her pap smear was irregular, so she needed to come to the clinic right after school the next day. In school the next day, Cristina worried and worried about possibly having cancer. By lunch time, her anxiety was so intense that she knew she could not sit through any of her afternoon classes. She was a walking jumble of nerves. She considered leaving school right then, going to the clinic and picking up Eduardo at the end of the day.

That is when Vice Principal Bryan Stewart entered her life. Mr. Stewart was one of the cofounders of the Columbia Heights Community Charter School. Along with the other founder Glen Berman, they were intent on creating an environment designed to meeting kids where they were as opposed to forcing them to fit into an already existing system. Stewart and Berman realized the daunting challenges facing the neighborhood where they were starting their school. Crime, poverty, and teenage pregnancy were all commonplace. Once their charter was approved, the two aggressively recruited students who were left out and viewed as hopeless. They left school brochures in shelters, health clinics, and other unusual locations throughout the community. Their mission was simple. They wanted to offer a vision and hope for kids who had neither.

All Mr. Stewart knew about Cristina was that she was extremely attractive, clearly unsure of herself, and a teenage mother. No one knew her whole story.

Cristina walked by Mr. Stewart as she was headed for the school's exit, just after lunch.

Mr. Stewart said to Cristina, "Cristina, is everything alright? What's wrong?"

Cristina looked up at the tall, bald-headed African American educator, whose face showed nothing but genuine concern. Even at her tender age, Cristina was only used to ogling eyes from men. The look on his face made her even more emotional. Tears welled up in her eyes. She did not cry, but the sadness was evident.

Mr. Stewart did not know all that was troubling this young girl, but he knew enough to know that she felt all alone. He also knew that he had to be careful. Her whole demeanor exuded a hands off air. He decided to take a chance.

"Cristina, is it ok for me to give you a hug?"

Upon hearing this question, Cristina instinctively recoiled. But the look on Mr. Stewart's face was unlike any she had seen on any man in her life. He really did not want anything from her. Her little voice was telling her that. With her arms crossed and her head lowered, she just nodded a yes. Mr. Stewart then wrapped his arms around the girl, who, in turn felt enveloped by his warmth and compassion. He started the hug, but she would not stop it. Later, Cristina would recount that it was the first time in her life that she felt comforted, like someone really cared about her. If Mr. Stewart had asked her to jump off a building at that moment, she would have done so. Cristina was so needy and so emotionally neglected that a simple genuine, caring hug transformed her into compliant and eager to please little girl.

Having had to tear away from the girl, Mr. Stewart led Cristina back to his office. For the next several hours, she poured out her soul to the Vice Principal. They talked for so long that Mr. Stewart took it upon himself to call Flora to have her pick up Eduardo from the school's day care. Defiant and independent, Cristina rarely asked her mother to help with her baby. Mr. Stewart instinctively knew that he needed to let Cristina get it all out. He allowed her free reign to speak as long as she wanted.

Mr. Stewart was a seasoned educator. Formerly, he worked in one of the toughest high schools in southeast DC. But even he had to cringe during parts of Cristina's story. Though he remained silent, he wanted to punch out Ramon and he had heard of Dr. Martin Lewis. He was going to find a way to go after that creep.

When he did speak, Mr. Stewart assured Cristina that none of what had happened to her was her fault. He told her that she was smart, engaging, and had the ability to make her future whatever she wanted it to be. On that day, he also became the second person in Cristina's life to tell her she was college material. "It is all up to you, Cristina," he repeatedly said.

Mr. Stewart also told her not to worry about the pap smear. As they neared the end of their conversation, he called the clinic. All of the clinic staff knew him well. He found out that they wanted to give her another test, but there was no need for alarm.

That day represented an important step forward in Cristina's life. For the first time, she believed she had had a conversation with someone who truly was looking out for her interests. Mr. Stewart gave Cristina a reason to believe in herself. He knew, however, that her reclamation would not be complete with one heartfelt conversation. Throughout the course of the next two years leading up to her senior year, Mr. Stewart was Cristina's mentor, coach, psychologist, friend, sounding board, and father. When stressed, Cristina would retreat, tend to cut class, and go into a shell. On those occasions, Mr. Stewart would cajole her and prod her into going to class. Knowing when she was in those moods, Mr. Stewart would stop by her mother's apartment on his way to school to make sure she was ready for school. Mr. Stewart would talk with Flora and encourage her to support Cristina's need for school, walk up to Cristina's bedroom, and wake her up.

Mr. Stewart also became very close to Cristina's brother, Moises. Like Cristina, Mr. Stewart saw potential in Moises and began to invest time in his development. The entrance of Mr. Stewart into both Cristina and Moises' made a huge positive difference.

Cristina's sassiness was always with her. As a result, when she felt pushed into a corner, she lashed back, often in a mean spirited way. Mr. Stewart mediated several disputes between Cristina and fellow classmates. In doing so, he did not cut her a break. If she was wrong, he punished her. The hallmark of his approach was fairness. Through it all, Mr. Stewart never approached Cristina in a romantic way. Nor did he look at her suggestively. He had introduced Cristina and Flora to his wife, who would sometimes join him during his visits to the Hernandez home. Not surprisingly, Cristina began to see Mr. Stewart as the father that she never had.

Mr. Stewart tried to get Cristina to go to counseling, but after her experience with Martin Lewis, she believed that she could do better on her own. Mr. Stewart tried to fill in the gaps, but knew that she needed real professional help. He hoped that she would come around in time. Where Mr. Stewart had the biggest impact was with Cristina's self-esteem. He kept telling her how smart she was and how she had too much talent and brain power to waste. On the day she told him that she longed to be a truck driver, he simply shrugged his shoulders and said, "Why don't you learn the trucking business after college and eventually start your own trucking company?" It seemed to Cristina after every conversation with Mr. Stewart, she was looking at things differently with a new perspective.

By her senior year, Cristina's grades were strong enough to be admitted to college. She needed to do well on her SAT exam. Cristina blew the test away. Her SAT scores were high enough, along with her grades for her to garner several college scholarships. Mr. Stewart was proud, but not surprised. More than anyone, he had always believed that she had what it takes to be successful in school.

Flora did not quite know how to take it. She had never thought about college as a realistic goal for any of her children. Once Cristina had Eduardo, she was expected to get a job and drop out of school. She completely underestimated her daughter's determination. Cristina had worked part time as a cashier at a local drug store and also, in effect ran the Hernandez household. Moises remained a challenge. He just could not seem to find his way. He began to fall in with the wrong crowd and in high school developed a drug addiction to heroin and alcohol. Cristina used to fetch him from the streets away from the drug boys with Eduardo in tow. Cristina felt guilty about Moises, believing that she could have saved him if she had paid more attention to his challenges rather than her own.

Cristina did have high hopes for Luca. He was very smart and she spent a lot of time with him going over his homework. Luca was also good with Eduardo, which was a big help to Cristina.

Though she had several out-of-state college offers, Cristina knew she had to go to college in the DC area. She could not disrupt Eduardo's life, nor could she leave her mother and her brothers to fend for themselves. Cristina decided to accept the scholarship offer from George Mason University, which was located in northern Virginia, just across the Potomac River. She would major in Urban Development.

As excited as Cristina was about going to college, she still was dealing with her demons. She continued to have issues with men. She had convinced herself that Mr. Stewart was truly one of a kind. She trusted no other man. She had long since broken up with Gabriel, though she saw him regularly because of Eduardo. Always a trooper, Gabriel did what he could as a young father to support Eduardo. He visited often and his parents regularly gave money to Cristina.

Soon after starting at George Mason, Cristina began a series of brief relationships in which she treated the men as badly as she treated Gabriel. All of the men had the same or similar shortfalls as her father and other men in her family. As much as she knew they were not right for her, she continued to be drawn to them.

Though she never told anyone, she was also intimidated by college. Without Mr. Stewart around every day to encourage her, Cristina easily succumbed to pity and self-doubt. She consistently had a hard time believing in herself. She started to find other releases. Ignoring that little voice, she began to hang out with the party girls at her college. That crew, along with her poor male choice of the month helped Cristina pull herself further and further away from the day-to-day responsibilities associated with being in college. At the end of her sophomore year, Cristina was passing, but her grades were not high enough to keep her scholarship. If she was going to finish college, she was going to have to pay for it herself.

That fall, Christina decided to go to school part time and find a job so she could help support the family. Problem was she was having a hard time finding a job. By winter, she had to go on welfare in order to make ends meet. That little voice in her head was working overtime by then and Cristina was finally ready to listen.

The pivotal moment came when she was standing in the line waiting outside of the welfare office to pick up her check. The line stretched around the entire block and it took about forty minutes to get inside the building. While standing in that line, in the freezing cold, Cristina was shivering and shaking.

She looked up and down the street and in the faces of all the beaten down citizens with no place to go and no prospect for work. Just before entering the building, Cristina said to herself, "I am better than this." And, for the first time in her life, she believed that she was. It was a watershed moment for Cristina Hernandez.

She picked up her check, walked to the bus stop, and caught the bus home. The next day, she called Mr. Stewart.

"Mr. Stewart, I messed up and I need your help."

"But are you ready, Cristina?" he said. "Are you really ready?"

"I think so. But what I do know is that I am better than what I am doing now. That has to be a start, right, Mr. Stewart?"

"Yes, it is, Cristina. It definitely is a start. Tell you what, come to the school tomorrow. I have a job for you."

Cristina felt relief at first, then thought of another question.

"Mr. Stewart, have you been waiting for this call?"

"More than you know, young lady. More than you know."

Starting that next day, Cristina worked as a secretary at her former high school. She finished George Mason where she received her bachelor's degree, then a master's degree. She eventually worked her way up to become Dean of Admissions and Development Director at the Columbia Heights Community Charter School. She has worked at the school for over fifteen years. For her, the best thing about her job is the private interaction she has with young girls facing challenges similar to the ones she faced. When needed, she candidly shares her story with students grappling with their own issues.

Cristina's mother continues to live with her, but has stopped working because of an assortment of health issues. Cristina's father Luis still struggles with his alcoholism and remains nomadic by nature.

Moises died of a heroin overdose when he was nineteen. Luca graduated from college. Cristina's son, Eduardo is now in college.

Mr. Stewart started his own all boys academy, which caters to boys from challenged neighborhoods. He and Cristina continue to be close.

Ramon became a police officer, but was fired when he was convicted of sexually assaulting his wife's twelve-year-old niece. He spent a few years in jail. Cristina still sees him from time to time at family gatherings, but never speaks directly to him. She has never told anyone in her family about the abuse.

Patrick

Patrick Mykanyiri was inordinately rambunctious, even for a four-year-old. The young Rwandan native would never sit still. It just was not in his nature to do so. Patrick's parents, Bernard and Francine, would smile, throw up their hands, and rely on Patrick's big sister Grace to get her little brother in line. Grace needed each of the six years of seniority between her and Patrick to rein him in. From the moment he woke up in the morning, Patrick would run around the house, explore the land in and around the family home located near the Rwandan West Province city of Kibuye, and slow down just enough to grab a bite to eat, which also took place while he was on the run.

It helped that Patrick was surrounded by a loving family who nurtured him and tolerated his restless spirit. Patrick's father, Bernard, was a practicing gynecologist and his mother, Francine, was a civil servant working for the Rwandan government. During his young life, Patrick and his ten-year-old sister, Grace, were as happy as any two siblings could be in a nation as poor and poverty stricken as Rwanda. While their parents worked, Patrick and Grace went to school for part of the day, then were under the watchful eye of relatives who lived nearby. New to preschool, Patrick had already distinguished himself with his teacher. She had called out his name at least ten times more than any other student, usually followed by "...get back in your seat!"

At the time, 1994, Rwanda was in a state of flux. The Republic of Rwanda is a small landlocked country located in east-central Africa bordered by Uganda, Burundi, the Congo, and Tanzania. Rwanda is a poor, farming nation with 90 percent of the population living off of the food they grow on small family farms. For centuries, conflicts in Rwanda existed between two ethnic groups of settlers, the Hutus and the Tutsi. Over time, the tension between the two groups literally divided the country. The majority of the country's people were Hutu, but the Tutsi represented the ruling class and controlled the country politically. As had occurred in many African countries, the natural ethnic tensions between the Hutus and Tutsis were exacerbated by the European colonizers, who began to arrive in the country in the 1880s. The Europeans instilled the notion that the Tutsi were a superior race, which fermented the Hutu–Tutsi conflict.

In the 1960s, 1970s, and 1980s, periodic clashes of violence occurred between Hutu rebels and the ruling Tutsi government. By the 1990s, the Hutu rebels gained momentum by the emergence of two separate Hutu militia forces and a Hutu power group known as the Akazu. By the beginning of 1994, however, the situation was becoming more stable due to a peace agreement between the two factions and due to the leadership of a dynamic, peace-toting leader, Rwandan President Juvenal Habayarimana.

Dr. Bernard Mykanyiri was a Hutu, while his wife, Francine was a Tutsi. Neither one of the couple bought into the ethnic purity arguments promulgated by either group. The two met, fell in love, married, and wished that their fellow countrymen would focus on Rwanda's decimated economy rather than which group is superior. Bernard was a brilliant thinker. Though he practiced medicine and was quiet by nature, he also had a bit of his son's restless spirit. He had grown weary of the daily patient treatment grind and was more attracted to learning more about the root causes of the illnesses that afflicted his people. He had found out about a epidemiology PhD program in the United States which offered the knowledge and training he could use to help combat some of the many infectious diseases prevalent in Rwanda. The program was being offered by Xavier University in New Orleans, Louisiana. Bernard applied for the program, was accepted, and had been in New Orleans for several months entering into 1994.

The Mykanyiri family missed their patriarch, but each was busy enough with their own day-to-day activities. Francine liked her job, in which she processed applications for government benefits. Grace was very good in school and had a lot of friends who followed her lead. Apparently, the skills she had developed in keeping young Patrick in line were easily transferable to her network of friends. They liked being in her company.

Though Patrick was a handful, he was also a pleasant, sweet kid. And he loved his sister. They would play together for hours in and out of the house. The Mykanyiri home was a small two-bedroom house located on approximately two acres of land. Like nearly every Rwandan, the family grew their own vegetables and fruit. They also had a couple of cattle on their land. As he and Grace played, Patrick loved to find hiding places and would cajole Grace to try and find him. One of his favorite hiding places was underneath an old four feet by four feet shed located eighty feet from the back of their house. Bernard used the shed to store old farm tools and grain for the cattle. Young Patrick found a way to wedge his tiny body into a crawl space inside the shed, so that he could not be seen if someone opened the door to it and looked inside. Once, he lay inside that shed for nearly an hour as Grace scampered around looking for him.

The Mykanyiri's bucolic life came to an abrupt end in April 1994. On April 6, a plane carrying Rwandan President Habayarimana was shot down. Traveling with President Habayarimana was the President of the neighboring country Burundi. The plane had been shot down by the Hutu power group, the Akazu. Suddenly, the fragile peace that Rwandans were beginning to embrace was destroyed. Within hours, Hutu militia moved to take over the country. The assassinated President's administration tried valiantly to hold the country together. President Habayarimana's top military leaders announced that his widow would make a statement the next day and that the ruling government was still in control. The President's widow had armed security with her as she prepared to give her message of peace designed to restore calm.

By the next day, however, the Hutu militia had seized control of the radio and television airwaves. Even worse, before she could give her address, the militia attacked Mrs. Habayarimana's supposedly secure presidential compound, whereupon they killed her as well as every one of the guards protecting her. Rwanda was officially in chaos.

For the next one hundred days, the Hutu militia embarked on an ethnic cleansing murder spree never before seen in the history of mankind. Using vicious machete-wielding tactics, the Hutu sought and killed nearly one million Tutsi throughout the country.

Bernard was leaving one of his Xavier University classes when he saw the news about his country's President's death. He instinctively knew that more trouble lay ahead. Even he, however, could not predict how bad things would get in his homeland.

Within days of the assassination, Hutu hit squads broke into the homes of known Tutsi throughout the country. They would rape the women and kill them and all other family members. No one was spared.

Though it all is a blur to him today, Patrick will never forget what he saw when the Hutu hit squad barged through the front door of his house. He had been playing in the backyard with Grace when he heard the commotion. Grace, exhibiting her usual leadership, ran back into the house to check on her mother and see what was going on. Patrick, not having a clue what was happening, went to his hiding spot in the shed, planning on making Grace look for him when she came back outside.

As he settled into his hiding area, young Patrick heard yells and screams. He had never heard screams before. It scared him.

He then peeked through the shed's wood slats and saw three men drag his mother and sister out of the house and into the backyard. Patrick was horrified, but did not make a sound.

The men were carrying machine guns and three-feet-long machete knives. One at a time, the men each raped his mother and sister, ignoring their screams and protestations. Then, while two of the men held them down on the ground, the third man calmly used his machete to behead them both.

Patrick watched it all. He did not scream. He did not cry. He just stared at the scene, frozen and shocked by the horror.

When they finished, the men began to search around the house and the yard. Soon, the man who had wielded the machete, opened the door to the shed and saw four-year-old Patrick, standing inside, staring out at the bodies on the ground. The man cavalierly grabbed the boy and carried him away.

In New Orleans, Bernard was frantically trying to get information on the plight of his family. He had been trying to get back to his homeland, but the destabilizing situation precluded travel in and out of the country. As the days, then weeks passed, he learned that several family members had been killed and slaughtered. In fact, the genocide raids ultimately led to the deaths of 90 percent of the Tutsi population of the city of Kibuye. Sadly, he then found out that he had lost his wife and his daughter, as well as countless other close relatives. In all the reports that he received, however, there was no mention of Patrick. He continued to hold out hope that his son was alive.

Young Patrick does not remember all that happened during that time. The Hutu hit squad that killed his mother and sister took him to a refugee camp, where they dropped him off and left. No one knows why they did not kill him. Other boys of Patrick's age and younger met the same fate as his mother and sister during the genocide raids.

Still hopeful, Bernard finally made it back into the country and rummaged through refugee camps throughout the West Province. The breakthrough came when a cousin told him that he had heard that a little boy was in one of the camps telling people that his father was in school in the United States. Bernard rushed to that particular camp and miraculously found Patrick. Both were overjoyed. The reunion took place six months after the murder of the rest of the family. Bernard hastily arranged for them to leave the country. As much as he loved his country, he could not wait for things to stabilize at the risk of losing his son. The United States would have to be their new home. Bernard took Patrick to New Orleans.

For the next ten years, Patrick and Bernard carved out the best life that they could in the Crescent City. New Orleans, Louisiana, USA, was markedly different from Kibuye, Rwanda. On arrival, Bernard enrolled Patrick in a well-known, highly regarded catholic school. Bernard knew Patrick was smart, but his son did not know English. It would take time for Patrick to get accustomed to the school and to life in the states. In particular, young Patrick had to become indoctrinated as to the "ways of the south" as it relates to race and class. He and Bernard lived in an apartment building near Xavier University, not far from downtown. Nearly everyone living in the building was low-to-moderate income and African American. Since the school Patrick attended was predominately white, he quickly became assimilated into two different worlds, requiring two different approaches. At school, he acted one way, while at home with his neighborhood friends, he acted another way.

Always smart, Patrick did well in school. He picked up English quickly and soon was one of the better performing students in his class. At home, Patrick began to act more street like to fit in and it just did not work. He would occasionally get teased by other neighborhood boys, who were constantly trying to get him to join them in their mini juvenile delinquent activities.

At the time, Patrick was ten years old. By then, the rambunctious, ever-active Patrick was long gone. That precocious four-year-old was replaced by an emotionally battered and scarred boy who was forced to witness a terrible, unimaginable horror. The new Patrick was extremely quiet, soft spoken, and reserved. Still pleasant and warm, Patrick remained instantly likable. But, he was unmistakably and understandably damaged by all that he had endured. Distant is the best word to describe his aura following the tragedy in Rwanda.

It all affected Bernard dramatically as well. When he first came to the States to study, he was optimistic about being a doctor for his people. He was excited about the future. After bringing Bernard back with him to New Orleans, he finished his PhD program, but had a hard time finding a job. With all that had happened in Rwanda, it was also hard for him to get a license to practice medicine. Through friends, he ended up getting a job working for the state, but losing his wife and daughter sapped his energy for life. Soon, he started to experience serious health problems. He was diagnosed with diabetes, hypertension, and suffered from gout. His whole existence was wrapped around his only son.

The experience at the catholic school and his accompanying success gave Patrick's life meaning. He was acutely aware of the sadness which engulfed his father and he also knew how much Bernard wanted him to have a good life. By the time he was in seventh grade, Patrick became more and more determined to do well in school as an honor to his father. Patrick's appetite for learning became insatiable. He worked harder than all the other kids and then some.

Patrick still had to navigate the treacherous waters involving his neighborhood friends. On one occasion, the mother of one of his neighborhood friends got into an argument with another lady who lived in the same apartment building. Patrick's friend decided that he would gather some of his buddies, break into the lady's apartment and then intimidate her. Patrick was asked to be the lookout. Everything went according to plan, but Patrick did not feel right about the whole thing. The two other boys crawled into the woman's apartment through a window and immediately began to curse and threaten her. They never touched the woman, but they surely put the fear of God in her. Standing outside of the window, Patrick felt horrible. He turned and left. As fate would have it, another neighbor saw the boys and told Bernard about the incident. Bernard really gave Patrick a hard time. "Son," he said. "You know that this is not the way. You are better than that. You must do honor to your family."

Though Bernard did not specifically mention Patrick's mother or sister, the message was clear. Patrick hung out less and less with the neighborhood crowd. As time passed, he grew more comfortable in his own skin, with his own purpose.

By 2005, Patrick was progressing well in school and looking forward to his future. Slight in size but athletic, he was reminiscent of many of the African soccer players you see during the world cup matches. He was good in track, with decent times in the 100 and 200 meters and he learned how to play the guitar. Patrick had also settled in on a career. The fifteen-year-old wanted to be a lawyer. With the grades he was making, he was well on his way.

Late that summer, the journey of life took another tragic turn for Patrick. That turn was called Katrina. Having been in New Orleans for several years, Patrick and Bernard were used to the hurricane warnings. Like many Louisiana natives, they soon fashioned themselves as weather experts. The ultimate storm was never as bad as it had been predicted. Of course, we now know that Hurricane Katrina was different. Very different.

As the time for the storm grew near, Bernard and Patrick followed instructions and hunkered down in the bathtub of their second-story apartment located near Xavier University. Bernard, who was on an assortment of medications, had a well-stacked satchel full of medicine, a radio with batteries, water, and selected snacks. As they nestled in the tub, both joked that they had spent too much time packing because the storm would probably be a dud. In actuality, they did not pack enough.

We all now know how devastating Katrina was to the city of New Orleans. At the time, however, most residents had no idea how bad it would be. The bulk of the storm hit on a Sunday. The next day, Bernard and Patrick looked out their second floor apartment window and saw water everywhere. While that sight was cause for concern, they believed that it would eventually recede. Little did they know that the levees were breaking and the water levels would continue to grow. When this became apparent, both Patrick and Bernard began to panic.

By Tuesday, they were close to running out of water and did not have much food. Patrick went to the first floor and the water was to his neck and it was rising. He could not swim and his father was too weak to swim. Other apartment residents had gone to the roof to wave at the passing helicopters and small planes. Folks in small boats started to navigate up the street. Bernard began to realize that the water could reach the second floor before they would be rescued. Moreover, he figured, they could easily starve to death even before drowning.

Still armed with his radio, Bernard heard New Orleans Mayor Ray Nagin's plea to all residents that they go to the Superdome as soon as possible. Since they were near downtown, the Superdome was only three miles away. Bernard told Patrick that they should walk there. Patrick was not worried about his ability to make the trip, but he was worried about his father. Bernard was not in good health and his stamina was weak. Patrick questioned whether his father could walk three miles under the best of conditions. How could he make such a walk with water up to his neck?

Patrick decided to see if they could find someone else in the building to walk with them. The more support, the better. As he canvassed the building, he happened upon Jacques Chardineaux, one of the few white tenants in the building. Now into day three, many of the other apartment residents were giving Jacques a hard time. It did not help that he always wore his security guard uniform, even after hours. White men in authority were not very popular at that time in New Orleans.

Jacques knew of Bernard's delicate physical state and agreed to walk with the Mykanyiri's to the Superdome. The trek took over three hours. During the walk, the water never was below Patrick's chest. On the way, the three smartly decided to go up to Interstate 10. If they had continued on the city streets, they would have surely drowned.

The scene and the conditions at the Superdome was appalling. The set up was woefully unorganized. Soaking wet, the three apartment dwellers were forced to stand in line to gain entry into the stadium. Folks were being allowed in one person at a time. Thousands were standing in line waiting to get in. By now, Bernard had run out of water and had not been able to take much of his medication. Fortunately, during the wait, someone nearby began to circulate six-liter bottles of Sprite. Bernard was able to take his medicine.

Once inside, Bernard, Patrick, and Jacques each found a seat in the stadium. There they stayed for three more days. There was limited water and the food was inedible. Since he was one of the few whites in "refugee status" in the stadium, Jacques was being subjected to increasing harassment. By Saturday, he had left the area where they had been camping out to find, as he said, "a better hiding place." Bernard and Patrick never saw him again.

On Saturday, the inept officials running the show asked the women and children to stand in one line and the men to stand in another. Though they were never informed of their destination, the women and children were being sent to Houston, while the men were being sent to Dallas. Many of the families separated during this process did not see their family members or know where they were for months.

That day, Bernard and Patrick flew to Dallas, where things were far better organized. The two finally were able to take their first shower in a week and change into fresh clothes. Plus, they had a hot, well-balanced meal. Patrick thought it was the best meal he had ever eaten.

Consider the ironies. By fifteen, Patrick Mykanyiri had been intimately involved in two of the major catastrophes to afflict mankind over the last one hundred years. Incredibly, one occurred in Africa, while the other took place in North America. During and after each event, Patrick inexplicably survived when the odds were against him. More importantly, though emotionally beaten, he kept his sense of self and his sense of purpose. The kid was a survivor beyond all reasonable means of expectation.

While languishing in Dallas, Patrick longed to be back in school. With all that he had been through, getting his education had become his place of refuge. Bernard also knew that he needed to get his son back in school, away from the putrid stench of those growing use to living in shelters. Working through friends, Bernard arranged for Patrick to be flown from Dallas to Boston. It was hoped that Bernard's friends could help get Patrick into Bennett Academy, one of the most exclusive private high schools in the nation. Bernard's friends had key connections and they had laid the groundwork for Patrick to get an interview with the school's headmaster.

As Patrick headed to Boston, Bernard stayed behind in Dallas. It would take him a while to make it up north, but knowing that his son was gone from the area gave him an immediate boost of energy. Bernard did not allow himself to think about his late wife, Francine much. It was too painful. Bernard harbored a lot of guilt over Francine and Grace's deaths. If he had been there, could he have stopped it? Maybe he would have gotten the family out of the country right after the President's assassination. Francine stayed around because she just did not know how fragile things were. Bernard knew. It all ate him up inside.

Now, all Bernard had was Patrick. Bernard was determined to do all he could to make sure that Patrick had a good life. His son had seen too much death, too much sadness. Bernard would do all in his power to make things right for Patrick. Bernard was very pleased that Patrick was on his way to Boston.

Elliott Rollins is the headmaster of Boston's Bennett Academy. Having served in that role for over twenty-five years, much of the school's success and reputation stems largely from Headmaster Rollins' deft touch. Tall, gangly, with a full head of white hair, Mr. Rollins appearance conjures up images of a better-looking Abe Lincoln, in part because he exudes the same calming demeanor that existed in our legendary President. A good measure of Bennett's success lies in the fact that

Mr. Rollins has been true to his commitment to a diverse student body, even in the notoriously segregated Boston community. Bennett's classrooms contain sons and daughters of some of Boston's most elite citizens (including a handful of Kennedy heirs) along with children of color and working-class whites from impoverished backgrounds.

In the midnineties, Mr. Rollins agreed to have Bennett participate in a controversial scholarship program managed by the Boston Scholarship Society (BSS). In effect, the BSS cobbled together public and private funds to provide tuition assistance for low-income students to attend some of the most exclusive private schools in the Boston area. Under the terms of the program, BSS would guarantee at least half of the school's tuition, while the participating schools would gift the remaining amount. Each school had a limit on the number of kids they could accept every year. With over thirty participating schools, by 2005, thousands of low-income students had been able to get a top-notch education that would otherwise be denied to them.

When Mr. Rollins first suggested to his Board that they participate in the program, some offered resistance. "How will this effect the school's esprit de corp," he was asked. "Could this lead to too much diversity or negatively impact on our academic performance?"

Mr. Rollins remained unmoved. He promised his Board that the school would be better for it and the outputs for even the current kids would grow. He was absolutely right. Since being a participant in the BSS program, Bennett's test scores have risen and the school community is more diverse than ever.

Mr. Rollins grew up in Charleston, South Carolina, with Mary Reynolds, a PhD classmate with Bernard at Xavier. Mary Reynolds hailed from a wealthy family in South Carolina, but she also lived in the Boston area. She was a true, committed liberal. On many occasions, Mr. Rollins would get calls from Mary about potential students that she believed would fit in his school. Mr. Rollins loved his childhood friend's heart, but knew better than to commit to admitting a student without going through the necessary steps. That being said, Mr. Rollins was intrigued when Mary related the saga of Patrick and his father.

In spite of his interest in meeting Patrick, Mr. Rollins knew that he could not admit the student during the current school year. Bennett had reached their limit for BSS students and all of the other scholarship sources had been tapped to the limit. Due to his own curiosity and his friendship with Mary, he agreed to meet with Patrick.

When Patrick landed in Boston airport on that mid-September evening, he was struck by the chill in the air. He had never been in a place where the temperature dropped below sixty degrees. He remembers wondering to himself which was worse: walking around for several days in wet clothes or walking down the street in cold weather.

Mary had arranged for Patrick to stay with some of her friends who lived near Cambridge. If things did not work out at Bennett, Mary's friends would try to get Patrick into a catholic school. Mary was also working on a job for Bernard at Boston University. With luck, Patrick and Bernard would be able to get their own apartment and be in a stable situation by November. As far as Mary was concerned, Bernard and Patrick were two people who were entitled to a few breaks.

Patrick met with Mr. Rollins two days after arriving in Boston. Mr. Rollins was instantly struck by Patrick's easy, effortless gait and his calm, laid-back demeanor. When they started to talk, Mr. Rollins was further taken with Patrick's soft-spoken voice. Patrick's speaking voice is more of a whisper than a tonal sound. Mannerly to a fault, he exudes comfort, confidence, and competence. "There is no way," Mr. Rollins thought, "that this kid could have experienced all the things that I have been told he has experienced. He is much too put together than what those experiences would suggest."

The two hit it off immediately. They talked for almost two hours, which was unusual for Patrick. Over time, he had become an obsessive introvert. Sure, he was pleasant, engaging, and responsive among schoolmates, but he really was a loner. For Patrick, it just made sense not to let anyone get too close. He knew better than most that tomorrow is not guaranteed to anyone. Deep down, he did not want to lose anyone else who was close to him.

Following his meeting with Patrick, Mr. Rollins called Mary. "You were right, Mary," he said. "Patrick is the most amazing young man that I have seen in over thirty years of teaching."

"Yes, he is, Elliott. You going to let him in?"

"I don't know, Mary. We are at our limit."

On hearing that and, more significantly, noting the tone in which Elliott was speaking, Mary smiled to herself. "He's going to find a way to let Patrick enroll," she thought.

To Elliott, she said, "Do what you can, my friend. I really appreciate you taking the time to meet him."

Mr. Rollins did work his magic. But it was not easy. The BSS has strict rules about their guidelines. They were under constant scrutiny and criticism from school system administrators and union leaders who had labeled the scholarship students as "voucher kids." The BSS Executive Director told Elliott that Bennett was at their limit and that he could make no exceptions.

"You would change your mind if you met this kid," Elliott exclaimed.

"You are probably right, Elliott. That is why I don't want to meet the kid."

Mr. Rollins, however, was not deterred. Knowing that he could not access BSS funds and that his own scholarship resources were exhausted, he decided to make a plea directly to his Board. He would do something that he had never done before, namely request that Board members commit to raising 30,000 dollars for each of the next three years to fund a separate scholarship for one student.

At the special Board meeting, Mr. Rollins made the most impassioned plea of his career to his Board. They knew Mr. Rollins was passionate about his work and had grown used to him going the extra mile for certain students, but none had ever heard him speak as he did that night. When he finished, the Board President offered to personally raise 10,000 dollars. In a matter of minutes, Patrick's tuition for the next three years had been raised.

True to Mary's wishes, Patrick gained enrollment to Bennett and Bernard was employed at Boston University by November. They also settled into a nice apartment not far from the BU campus.

Patrick fit in well at Bennett. He played guitar in the band and expanded on his previous success in track. He also was a superb student. Mr. Rollins was proud of Patrick's success. He had never told any of his faculty about the full extent of Patrick's background. When he gave that impassioned plea regarding Patrick to the Board, he swore them to secrecy. "We don't want this kid to enter our halls only to be looked at like he is a sideshow," he said. The Board kept their knowledge of Patrick's background to themselves.

Patrick still struggled with the memory of the atrocities he witnessed. For many years, he would wake up from crying nightmares. Bernard would calm him down and put him back to sleep. Nightmares aside, Patrick never would cry when he was awake. Even when he witnessed the death of his mother and his sister, he did not cry. He was in shock, but did not cry. It was almost as if all that he witnessed had a permanent numbing effect on him, one that exists even to this day.

Bernard remains emotionally traumatized by all that has happened. He and his son have a special relationship grounded in a history that only they can fully understand. Interestingly, they do not talk much about Francine or Grace. It is just too hard. In fact, they often do not talk much at all. The two of them can sit for hours in their apartment's living room, with the television on and not say a word between them. Not surprisingly, each is comforted by the other's presence. Words may just spoil it.

One of Bennett's legendary traditions is their Thursday morning worship hour. Every Thursday, all the high-school students, faculty, and staff gather in the auditorium and sit in silent reflection. During that time period, anyone can say what they want or not. Some mornings, several students or faculty members may choose to vent about personal challenges. Other mornings, no one says a word. One morning, during Patrick's junior year, a young white girl from a well-to-do family stood up and spoke for fifteen minutes about her angst over seeing her estranged father the following week. She talked about how angry she was at her father for divorcing her mother. She then launched into a tirade about her sister not respecting her by taking other people's side whenever she was in an argument.

Hearing all of this, for some reason, prompted Patrick to want to speak. He had never stood up and spoken during the morning worship hour in the past. Of course, he was very uncomfortable sharing any of his emotions. While the girl was speaking, Patrick kept thinking of his mother and his sister, Grace. That day happened to be Grace's birthday. As much as he liked the schools that he had attended in the States, every day he was reminded of the big hole in his life by not having his mother and his sister around. He would hear classmates talk about mother's day and then find a way to ease out of the conversation. Friends would talk about their big brothers and big sisters and he would think about Grace. Yes, he was only four when she died, but he vividly remembers Grace. He would love to have his big sister back.

With all of these thoughts swirling in his head, Patrick stood up and began to speak. The whole room fell eerily silent. Folks were stunned that Patrick Mykanyiri had decided to speak during the morning worship hour. "What in the world is he about to say," everyone in the room thought to themselves.

Patrick spoke for less than three minutes. As is his style and preference, his words were brief and to the point.

I am sorry that you are angry at your father and your sister, but, honestly, you are so lucky to have them both around. I wish that I had my mother and my older sister here with me so I could get mad at them. When I was very young, I saw my mom and my sister get raped and beheaded in my native country of Rwanda. I think about them every day. Today is special because it is my sister Grace's birthday. If she were around, what would we talk about? What would we do? How would I relate to her? How would I relate to my mother? Would me and my sister, Grace, hang out today on her special day? I ask these questions of myself all the time and I guess that I always will. More than anything, I wonder why I have been subjected to all that I have seen. I now know that it all is preparing me for my purpose in life. I appreciate everything. I just think that you should appreciate your family, no matter what happens between you. (Patrick then looks around the entire auditorium) You all should appreciate your families. You have no idea what life is like when they are taken from you.

Everyone in the Bennett Academy school auditorium was in tears that morning. Mr. Rollins was standing in the back of the room in disbelief. Tears were streaming down his cheeks.

What made Patrick's words even more powerful was not just the content, but the delivery. Throughout, he maintained the same whisper-like tonal quality. He did not raise his voice at any point while he spoke. To call his morning worship message that day mesmerizing would be a vast understatement. Mr. Rollins believes that it was the single-most powerful set of words that he had ever heard spoken by anyone at anytime, in person or in film. "That moment," Mr. Rollins recalls, "was entirely spiritual. A certain energy descended on each of us in that room while Patrick was speaking. We were witnessing something bigger than ourselves."

After Patrick sat down, the poor girl who started it all was left standing in the center of the room. She too, was balling like a baby. Realizing that she was the only one standing, she sat down. Everyone sat quietly for the remaining few minutes of the period, each managing their own tear flow differently. Some wiped their faces, some sniffled, some, like the headmaster, just let them flow freely. Patrick was still surprised at himself for speaking as he did. One small tear flowed down his left cheek.

That evening, Patrick walked into his apartment with a feeling of calm. He rarely talked about the deaths of his mother and sister and had never done so in front of a group of people. As crazy as it was, he felt oddly relieved.

Bernard was sitting on the living room couch with the television on. He was smiling, looking down at a photograph lying on the coffee table in front of the couch. Patrick had seen the photo before. It was a picture of Bernard lifting four-year-old Patrick in the air the very moment he had found him in that refugee camp. Someone had snapped the picture at the precisely right moment. Both Bernard and Patrick are grinning broadly, joyful beyond words.

Seeing Patrick walk into the room, the normally quiet and stoic Bernard pointed at the photo and said, smiling, "This was the happiest day of my life."

"Mine too, dad," Patrick said, also smiling.

"Today is your sister's birthday."

"I know, dad," Patrick responded. "We honored her at my school today."

Bernard just nodded his head. Patrick then sat on the couch next to his father and the two silently watched television for the rest of the night.

Patrick graduated from Bennett with honors. His academic performance in high school along with his SAT scores helped him obtain an academic scholarship to a prestigious college.

Bernard continues to nurse his diabetes, but is doing well. He is very proud of his son and is confident that he will do well in life.

Elliott Rollins retired as headmaster at the Bennett Academy. He believes that Patrick is the most remarkable student that he had encountered during his thirty-plus years in education.

Mary Reynolds died while Patrick and Bernard stood beside her hospital bed. She had become a surrogate mother to Patrick once he had moved to Boston.

Patrick remains comfortable with his destiny and his purpose.